COSTUME, MAKEUP, AND HAIR

BEHIND
THE SILVER
SCREEN

BEHIND THE SILVER SCREEN

When we take a larger view of a film's "life" from development through exhibition, we find a variety of artists, technicians, and craftspeople in front of and behind the camera. Writers write. Actors, who are costumed and made-up, speak the words and perform the actions described in the script. Art directors and set designers develop the look of the film. The cinematographer decides upon a lighting scheme. Dialogue, sound effects, and music are recorded, mixed, and edited by sound engineers. The images, final sound mix, and special visual effects are assembled by editors to form a final cut. Moviemaking is the product of the efforts of these men and women, yet few film histories focus much on their labor.

Behind the Silver Screen: A Modern History of Filmmaking calls attention to the work of filmmaking. When complete, the series will comprise ten volumes, one each on ten significant tasks in front of or behind the camera, on the set or in the postproduction studio. The goal is to examine closely the various collaborative aspects of film production, one at a time and one per volume, and then to offer a chronology that allows the editors and contributors to explore the changes in each of these endeavors during six eras in film history: the silent screen (1895–1927), classical Hollywood (1928–1946), postwar Hollywood (1947–1967), the Auteur Renaissance (1968–1980), the New Hollywood (1981–1999), and the

Modern Entertainment Marketplace (2000–present). *Behind the Silver Screen: A Modern History of Filmmaking* promises a look at who does what in the making of a movie; it promises a history of filmmaking, not just a history of films.

Jon Lewis, Series Editor

1. ACTING (Claudia Springer and Julie Levinson, eds.)
2. ANIMATION (Scott Curtis, ed.)
3. CINEMATOGRAPHY (Patrick Keating, ed.)
4. COSTUME, MAKEUP, AND HAIR (Adrienne L. McLean, ed.)
5. DIRECTING (Virginia Wright Wexman, ed.)
6. EDITING AND SPECIAL/VISUAL EFFECTS (Charlie Keil and Kristen Whissel, eds.)
7. PRODUCING (Jon Lewis, ed.)
8. SCREENWRITING (Andrew Horton and Julian Hoxter, eds.)
9. ART DIRECTION AND PRODUCTION DESIGN (Lucy Fischer, ed.)
10. SOUND: DIALOGUE, MUSIC, AND EFFECTS (Kathryn Kalinak, ed.)

COSTUME, MAKEUP, AND HAIR

Edited by Adrienne L. McLean

I.B. TAURIS

LONDON · NEW YORK

For Larry, always and forever,
and my parents

Published in 2017 by I.B.Tauris & Co. Ltd
London • New York
www.ibtauris.com

Copyright Editorial Selection © 2017 Adrienne L. McLean
Copyright Individual Chapters © 2017 Prudence Black, Robin Blaetz, James Castonguay,
Karen de Perthuis, Mary Desjardins, Tamar Jeffers McDonald, Adrienne L. McLean,
Drake Stutesman

ISBN: 978 1 78453 755 5 (HB)
ISBN: 978 1 78453 756 2 (PB)
ISBN: 978 1 78672 106 8 (ebook)

A full CIP record for this book is available from the British Library

Printed and bound in the United States of America

CONTENTS

ACKNOWLEDGMENTS

I thank Jon Lewis and Leslie Mitchner for asking me to edit this volume and their help in shaping it into the book you hold in your hands (or are reading on a screen), and of course the contributors for their excellent work, especially those who paid attention to deadlines; you had to wait a long time to see this volume in print, and I appreciate your grace and forbearance. I also send heartfelt gratitude to Ned Comstock of the Cinema Arts Library at the University of Southern California, and the archivists and librarians, in particular Barbara Hall and Libby Wertin, at the Academy of Motion Picture Arts and Sciences library in Beverly Hills—your research expertise was, as always, invaluable. Nor could I have gotten along without the help of the librarians and staff of McDermott Library at the University of Texas at Dallas, or the support of my dean, Dennis Kratz, of the School of Arts and Humanities. Other good friends at UTD, who were a source of advice and support through difficult times, include Michael Wilson, Erin A. Smith, and Deborah Stott. And finally, everybody in this volume is indebted to the wonderful staff of Rutgers University Press, starting with Leslie and her kindness and perspicacity in all things, as well as Marilyn Campbell and Lisa Boyajian; special thanks are also due Eric Schramm for his eagle-eyed and very helpful copyediting.

COSTUME, MAKEUP, AND HAIR

INTRODUCTION   Adrienne L. McLean

In March 1981, the *Los Angeles Times* featured a short piece in the entertainment section under the headline "Academy Snub Miffs Makeup Artists."[1] The topic was the demand for Academy Award recognition by Makeup Artists Local 706; the guild had made the same appeal "many times in the past" but was always "politely ignored." Now, the union was "mad as hell and [wasn't] going to take it anymore." Said Howard Smit, the guild's business representative, "We are the only craft union which isn't recognized in the Awards. . . . We want to know why we're being ostracized."

According to Smit, the Academy of Motion Picture Arts and Sciences always used "the same rebuff" when denying the guild's request: "that there isn't enough to look at each year in terms of special makeup to justify a category on its own." But this time, the guild sent the Academy's board of governors a list of more than four hundred films which "could not have been made without the contributions of the makeup artists," including the classics *Frankenstein* and *Dracula* as well as then-recent films *Raging Bull* and *The Elephant Man*.

Of course, it does not take much reflection to realize that there is almost no commercial film of this century or the last that could have been or could be made "without the contributions of the makeup artists." As one of those artists remarked to the *Los Angeles Times* reporter, "It's not just horror. . . . We do beauty, bald caps, aging, reconstructive work, even temporary facelifts." And while hairstyling is never mentioned in the piece, in fact the full name of Makeup Artists Local 706 was, and remains, the Make-Up Artists and Hair Stylists Guild. Both crafts, then, but for two honorary Oscars for makeup in the 1960s, had been ignored during awards season since the Academy first began handing out statuettes in 1929.[2] But in 1981 the guild finally got what it was asking for; in December an Academy press release announced the addition of an Oscar category for "Best Achievement in Make-Up," effective immediately.[3] Although there still was no mention of hair styling in the description of the new category, hair stylists, in addition to makeup artists, art directors, cinematographers, and "other recognized experts in the field of make-up," would be appointed to the Make-up Award Committee. Not until 2012, when the category was renamed "Makeup and Hairstyling," did any Academy Award explicitly acknowledge both crafts.

From our vantage point, the lack of official recognition of makeup and hair design to the success of Hollywood's films in the past is a bit startling, given the clear contributions of the two crafts to the fantasy, superhero, and period films that have dominated the box office for so many years. But the crafts were important in more basic ways as well; filmmakers in the early silent era quickly learned that makeup and hairdressing were crucial simply to telling coherent stories with actors on film. As costume historian Alicia Annas writes, "The origins of film makeup and hair design have little to do with creating an illusion of history or a beautiful star image so much as preventing severe distortions of performers' faces on the screen and awkward cuts from scene to scene. . . . [The] process of shooting scenes demanded 'continuity'—that actors' faces and hairstyles look exactly the same, even when different bits of a scene were filmed weeks apart."[4]

By the 1910s, as the close-up itself became tied to Hollywood's fortunes through its relationship to creating and maintaining audience identification with actors ("To be a star means to have the right to a close-up," Michaela Krützen declares in her study of Greta Garbo),[5] studio personnel were even more acutely aware of the importance of makeup and hair, "those two most personal aspects of adornment," in Annas's words, to the success of their films.[6] It has become the stuff of Hollywood legend that when actors saw themselves in close-up for the first time they were horrified: "The camera close-up turned dimples into craters, freckles into polka dots, the tiniest blemishes into carbuncles. It made stray hairs stand out like lone trees on a moonscape," Annas writes. Wigs showed their "joins" and looked more like clown caps than hair. Because all film stocks render colors with some degree of distortion—a high degree, in the case of silent-era black-and-white orthochromatic stock, which turned red, even blood vessels under the skin, to black, and blue to white—cinematographers were the first adjudicators of the suitability of makeup, which initially was applied, following the theatrical tradition, by actors themselves. Conversely, Max Factor's son Davis told Academy members in 1928, during the industry's conversion to panchromatic stock, that "we cannot stress the fact too much that make-up is the greatest ally of the cinematographer."[7]

Costuming, too, which initially meant not much more than the clothing a given actor happened to be wearing when he or she arrived on the set, was also crucial to continuity, as well as to creating plausible characterizations in films set in the present, past, or future. Costumes had to be more carefully sewn and trimmed than for the stage; loose or dangling threads, the indentations of undergarments, the artificiality of padding that would appear natural from a great distance all became distracting on the screen. It took some time simply to figure out how to make clothing interesting in the new medium. In designer Howard Greer's words, "When you strip color and sound and the third dimension from a moving object, you have to make up for the loss with dramatic black-and-white contrasts and enriched surfaces."[8] Costumers had to learn which fabrics and trims photographed well, neither "strobing" nor reflecting or absorbing too much light.[9]

Just as vital to the industry as a capitalist enterprise, costuming quickly developed a particular association with fashion that would "please the ladies," as historian Michelle Finamore puts it in her book *Hollywood before Glamour*, which became an "even more intense" focus in the early studio era:

> Advances in the mass production of ready-to-wear clothing, combined with the streamlining of the fashion silhouette, made the latest Parisian styles more accessible than ever. In addition, the number of women attending films continued to rise and many audience members had more disposable income to spend on garments, including working-class women, from their jobs in factories (including clothing factories), department stores, and offices. All of the changes outlined above coincided with the establishment of the film industry's "studio system" and the rise of the credited in-house designer; by 1920, a distinctive style of glamour, now often regarded as epitomizing "classic Hollywood" (or Hollywood in the period 1930–50), was in its embryonic form.[10]

However, despite costuming's importance on all of these levels, costume design as such was also ignored by the Academy until 1949 when, for the first time, Oscars were awarded for both black-and-white and color costume design for films made the previous year (the craft had formerly been considered a "division of the Art Directors Branch").[11] This even though costume designers were among the first craftspeople to be regularly featured in film credits from around 1925, and as the prestige of motion pictures grew they became stars in their own right in studio promotion and publicity.[12] By 1929, Hollywood's costume designers were being exhorted to produce original designs so that the time lag between film production and exhibition did not result in out-of-date fashions; it is well known that this, along with "buy American" campaigns in the contexts of the Great Depression and World War II, especially, helped to make America the locus of significant fashion trends, usurping much of the previous dominance of Europe in the process.

To further complicate historical study of the three areas, in the classical era the studios lumped makeup and hair together as subcategories of costuming.[13] Although by the 1920s most of the studios had separate facilities for costume (usually called "wardrobe") and makeup, with hair design and styling generally budgeted and housed with the latter, the decoration, "improvement," and visual alteration of actors' faces and bodies, from star to lowliest extra, was always thought of as costuming. But alone or separately, costume, makeup, and hair often employed the largest number of people in any studio from the 1920s through the 1950s, while also sharing turf with or—especially after the push to unionization in the late 1930s—defending that turf from other crafts.

Wally Westmore, one of several brothers in a dynasty of studio makeup artists and wigmakers working in Hollywood from the 1920s on (there are still Westmores doing makeup in Hollywood), colorfully explained the situation to the *Saturday Evening Post* in 1956.[14] If you had to "strap down the bosoms of women so they can play young girls," he stated, that was "wardrobe," because it involved a "special corset which does the trick"; but if a star or a starlet "doesn't have enough bosom," that was makeup, because the "larger bosom" would be created out of rubber or foam latex, the purview of the makeup "man." But when "you see a man in a film spit out teeth or a tooth, he started the scene with teeth stowed in his mouth for spitting. Those teeth don't come under the jurisdiction of make-up; they're props. On the other hand, if we show that actor without his lost teeth, that is make-up. We black out the 'missing' teeth with dull black tooth enamel so they won't shine." Makeup was also responsible for the gelatin capsules an actor "bites down on" to simulate blood, which could only come from inside the mouth (no visible cuts), Westmore cautioned, per the Production Code's prohibition against graphic violence. (After the demise of the Code in the 1960s, electrically wired squibs began spurting blood from any part of the body, but they were, as now, the province of "physical" special effects.)[15]

As Westmore's remarks indicate, costume, makeup, and hair were evaluated and managed by the industry in the context of other elements of mise-en-scène (though they would not have called it that), especially acting and staging, props (like "teeth for spitting"), sets, and special effects. Equally important were how they were lit and framed, how they were affected by the technical and chemical (or, now, digital) means of recording them all, and how they were edited into the finished product. Once filmed, the designer's job was done, but this could engender its own insecurities—"because no matter how good a designer you may be," in Edith Head's words, "until you actually see something on the screen you are not sure."[16] And as Westmore had pointed to, in the classical era everything on the screen had to satisfy Code requirements in relation to violence as well as sexuality. Following the rules in the latter category meant inventiveness in the management of women's cleavage and the movement of breasts, careful assessments of the tightness of sweaters and the amount of skin showing in the upper leg area, and the covering of adult belly buttons with *mousseline de soie*. Some genres, such as backstage stories or musicals, allowed certain kinds of more revealing costumes in dance or show numbers, but never in the narrative (color plate 1).

The topic of this volume is thus three separate but interconnected professions, each of them an art form in its own right, that comprise a range of creative and practical activities and processes that center on performers, human or otherwise, and their bodies and faces (when they have them).[17] Like any other film-related craft, they are collaborative but also evolved to be hierarchical, with laborers working under a department head or, now, a lead designer. In the classical era each division employed huge numbers of people whose tasks included everything from research and purchasing or renting, to design and invention, to manufacture and application and styling as well as maintenance (at times, in post-studio or low-budget independent films, one person may have to cover the jobs formerly performed by hosts of people). The fields have ridden waves of technological, industrial, and social change that always engendered innovation, sometimes desperately so; World War II caused "shortages in almost everything the movies use," from the imported hair with which wigs were made to silk and even makeup sponges.[18] The methods and locations of some of the labor in each craft have perforce changed in the digital era—when an algorithm might replace the draping of fabric on a dressmaker's dummy or the aging of a character's face and body, or even composite one actor's face onto another—but all three remain central to the appeal of commercial cinema.[19]

That said, as *concepts* costume, makeup, and hair are easy enough to understand; they *are* "personal," are all around us, every day, which itself likely underpinned the Academy's dismissal of them as professions for so many years. A gown or a shirt may be more lavish in a Hollywood film, but it is still a gown or a shirt. Hair, whether growing from the scalp or as a "beaver" on an actor's face, or supplied in a form of a wig or toupee ("chest toupees" were also available), is hair. And as an Eastman Kodak "color demonstrator" put it in 1942, "There is no great mystery about straight make-up—just get some good cosmetics and practice a little."[20] "Straight" makeup was one of the three codified categories that craftspeople developed and employed in the studio era for descriptive, scheduling, and budgeting purposes. According to Perc Westmore, who headed the makeup and hair department at Warner Bros. from the 1930s through the 1950s, straight makeup should simply look "natural" and "pleasing."[21] Corrective makeup attempted to make every female face as "perfect" as possible, according to what Alicia Annas calls Westmore's "pseudo-scientific" but widely adopted theory—based on a "classical Greek ideal of beauty"—that the "oval shape" was the "most ideal" for faces (there were six other non-oval facial types that necessarily required "correcting," on or off the screen).[22] Corrective makeup also was needed for what Westmore describes as "lesser defects of contour—sunken or protuberant eyes, hollow or too-full cheeks, etc." (color plate 2).[23]

Straight makeup oscillated between responding to and creating images of the normal and natural on and off the screen, manufacturing ideals of beauty that were at once special or innate but also potentialities for all (if you were white) because the ideals relied on products, like Max Factor's Pan-Cake or makeup from the "House of Westmore" and other retail companies, that anyone could purchase and apply. Following industry practice, makeup artists were also assumed to be hair designers, and Max Factor and the Westmore brothers (especially Perc and Wally) offered "expert" advice in newspapers and magazines about personal hygiene, hairdressing, and cosmetics use, and even whether cigarette smoking was good for the face or how to raise young girls to be "ladylike." They also opened their own salons in Los Angeles and other major cities, and manufactured or trademarked products under their own names that stars' images could be used to endorse through studio licensing agreements.

As Mel Archer states in the final paragraph of an article on the makeup artist in Hollywood for the *National Board of Review Magazine* in 1939, "You may have noticed that I have laid great emphasis on similarities between the screen player and the plain citizen. This is because the aim of every good make-up artist should be to make the star look as natural and as normal as the girl in the street. I cannot emphasize enough that our aim is naturalness and individuality, and that the only real difference between the star and her sister is that the former has an expert to handle her make-up and a highly sensitive camera to record the results."[24] There are comparatively few promotional or publicity stories about straight makeup used on male stars, however, nor on "correcting" their faces to suit some imagined perfection of shape or contour. And that *Variety* liked to call makeup artists "lily gilders" suggests that, despite the fact that studio heads of makeup and hairdressing were almost without exception male (as opposed to the prominence of women such as Helena Rubinstein, Elizabeth Arden, and Madam C. J. Walker in the designing and retailing of beauty products off the screen in the first half of the twentieth century), there was still an assumption that straight makeup was for "girls."

In marked contrast to lily gilding, the most labor intensive and spectacular of the three types was character makeup, which was frequently publicized both as a difficult technological achievement and as okay for, and again virtually always nominally created by, men. More than the other two types, it frequently crosses the line into special effects, especially in the digital era (as Anthony Lane puts it in his capsule *New Yorker* review of 2015's *Mad Max: Fury Road*, "Some of the makeup is so drastic that you can barely distinguish between human flesh and the bodywork of cars").[25]

Historically, character makeup is most famously associated with certain actors such as Lon Chaney in the 1920s (the "Man of a Thousand Faces," from the Phantom of the Opera to Quasimodo), extreme aging (Maurice Seiderman transforming the youthful Orson Welles into the elderly Charles Foster Kane in 1941, although he was given no screen credit for doing so),[26] or the creation of monsters (Jack Pierce's and Boris Karloff's iconic Frankenstein's monster in 1931, with Elsa Lanchester's bride added to the mix in 1935, also with no screen credit for makeup or hair in either version, compared to the twenty-plus makeup artists credited with turning Robert De Niro into the monster and Helena Bonham Carter into a short-lived bride in the 1994 adaptation) and historical beings (Paul Muni as Louis Pasteur, uncredited makeup by Clay Campbell and Norbert A. Myles, or as Juarez, makeup by Perc Westmore and hair by uncredited Margaret Donovan; or Bette Davis as Queen Elizabeth in the 1930s and the 1950s, with makeup credited to Perc Westmore in both cases [color plate 3], or Cate Blanchett in 1998, makeup and hair again credited to twenty-plus individuals).[27] It is also, as is well known, the form of makeup most likely to represent and reinforce but also at times to engage and undercut Hollywood's and U.S. culture's racism and ethnic prejudices through the making up of white actors as other races or ethnicities, or the enforced exaggeration of stereotypes when the actors themselves are nonwhite.

According to Perc Westmore, however, character makeup is "really a matter of painting a new personality over one's own features."[28] As a category it is governed always by "the character to be delineated and the basic features of the model or actor" and as such requires more in the way of prosthetics and other three-dimensional "additive" techniques. Chaney is rumored to have taken most of his makeup secrets with him to his grave, but his available materials, many in long use on the stage, included heavy rubber, modeling putty, mortician's wax, collodion or nitrocellulose (both liquid plastics formerly used on photographic plates and with a regrettable tendency to burst into flames as well as irritate the skin), gelatin, cotton, hair (human, animal, or synthetic),[29] and fish skin, in addition to heavy paste makeups and fiberglass or wooden teeth.[30]

In the late 1930s, Jack Dawn, George and Gordon Bau, Maurice Seiderman, the Westmores, and others working in Hollywood developed or improved various forms of flexible and lightweight latex and latex foams that could be molded and layered onto the face and body, where they could then be made up much like skin would be. *The Wizard of Oz* (1939), with makeup credited to Dawn, was one of the first movies to use foam latex "appliances" on a large scale; there were some thirty additional uncredited makeup and hair artists on the film (color plate 4).[31] Dick Smith came to cinema from the hectic world of live television in the late 1950s, where he had begun the practice of layering multiple latex appliances on actors' faces, which looked more natural than single large masks and were more comfortable to wear. Silicone, which is "translucent like real flesh [and] jiggles like flesh," was one of the variety of plastics and resins added to the arsenal of techniques in the early 1990s for producing more explicit and graphically realistic effects, as were subtractive methods made possible by digital erasure and other computer-based technologies.[32] Only with CGI can one convincingly remove parts of an actor's face or body from a projected image, although it is used for the creation of many additive effects as well, up to replacing the face or body of one actor with another's.

Character makeup and hair design, then, across the last century and into this one, were valued as the most spectacular and virtuosic deployments of the two crafts in narrative filmmaking; it is not surprising that the only honorary Oscars given for "outstanding makeup achievement"—to William Tuttle in 1964 for *7 Faces of Dr. Lao* and to John Chambers in 1968 for *Planet of the Apes*—were for transformative character makeup. But otherwise, as again the Academy's general neglect both signifies and possibly helped to produce, the professions were held in low esteem. However famous their "men"—and however large and well funded the departments they ran—they were often needled with subtle and not-so-subtle digs. Wally Westmore received mail addressed to the "Bag and Sag Department, Paramount Studios, Hollywood, California." Besides lily gilders, the press called studio makeup and hair artists "face painters" or "face molders," "thatch designers," "medicine men," and other faintly derisive epithets. *Variety* also referred to them in 1938—under the headline "Makeups' [sic] Prestige Up"—as "the more or less forgotten folks among the film industry's technical divisions" until the increase in the use of Technicolor made "producers makeup-conscious."[33]

Even Jack Pierce, Universal's makeup genius (besides Frankenstein and his bride he designed the Mummy, the Wolf Man, and many others), was fired for being too slow and too old-fashioned in 1945 and was all but forgotten by the 1980s.[34] Similarly, costume designers like Adrian, Travis Banton, Orry-Kelly, Howard Greer, and Irene, who were close to household names in the 1930s and 1940s, had to fight—often unsuccessfully—to retain control over how their designs were used off the screen in retailing franchises ranging "from Saks to Sears, Roebuck," as Sarah Berry puts it in her book *Screen Style*.[35] And as can be said of other crafts, the supporting laborers for all three divisions—from seamstresses to beaders and embroiderers to fabric dyers and cutters, from hair-combers and washers to manicurists to body makeup men and women, from wig ventilators and hair mixers to cobblers, not to mention workroom sweepers, costume cleaners and pressers and menders, and others who performed quotidian tasks on the studio lots—were often condescended to and treated badly.[36] "In the early days of the Hollywood studio system," film scholar Elizabeth Nielsen writes, "the costume department was a favorite place for studio bosses to place 'girlfriends' and inept relatives for whom they could find no other job in the studios. This practice undermined serious union organization and also contributed to the generally low regard in which the costumers were held by their co-workers in other departments. Conditions and wages for the costumers were among the worst in the motion picture industry."[37] They were even worse for makeup "girls" and hairdressers.

It did not help that the studios liked to promulgate the notion that many male stars did not wear makeup at all, or detested being made up when they had to be because of its association with femininity or with "swishy" men. Warner Baxter, reported newspapers in 1937, "was surprised when some children shouted 'sissy' at him. When he next looked at himself in the mirror, he understood why. His hair was disgustingly marcelled for his 'Cisco Kid' characterization."[38] Men were also allowed to wear their own clothes for films set in the present; military wear and other sorts of uniforms were most often rented from sources such as the Western Costume Company, in continuous existence since 1912 and founded initially to correct the image of Native Americans in early films.[39]

In the postwar years, influenced by nonclassical modes such as Italian Neorealism or the French New Wave and upon the enforced breakup of the studio's monopolistic practices and the disruption of its factory system, the formerly "indispensable" departments were the first to disappear, their highly paid designers and supporting laborers set loose to compete as freelancers in an uncertain marketplace. The very glamour value that expensive design provided to the Hollywood studios became actively a liability in "new ugly" film style and the comparatively impoverished environment of the New Hollywood of the 1960s and 1970s.[40] No longer could filmmakers afford a designer who would make clothes only for the stars and another who would take care of the rest of the actors (neither Irene nor Adrian nor most of their cohorts ever designed the costumes for an entire movie). Nor could they afford artist-designers like Irene Sharaff, who *would* handle all the costumes for an entire film but could pick and choose among jobs in couture, theater, and ballet as well as in Hollywood from the 1940s through the 1960s.[41]

Deborah Nadoolman Landis, a practicing film costume designer who has also focused attention on the field by writing or editing a number of important books on the topic in the past ten years, claims that in the post-studio years "fashion and costume design were conflated by industry professionals, fashion publications, and the public alike, lumped together by the untrained eye," the prestige of the costume designer diminished by the assumption that "any given stylist could costume a picture, that it was essentially a shopping job."[42] But even when poorly paid costume designers had to start combing thrift stores or shopping in malls in order to clothe a film's actors, that clothing still had to be chosen with an eye to how its surfaces and textures and colors would register on film in addition to supporting narrative demands and expressing and revealing character.

Skin color is no longer a de facto barrier to stardom, of course, nor do makeup artists spend as much time correcting a face to seem oval when it is not (although they are occupied with fabricating many more tattoos now, because of the ongoing popularity of "tats" across all classes, genders, and occupations). And while hair design still has to be evaluated in the context of maintaining continuity because hair grows (and cannot be uncut), it usually need not be elaborately coiffed (wigs, as in the classical era, are likely to be used in period or fantasy films and are rented from specialty wig houses).[43] Nevertheless, with a vanishingly small number of exceptions "there is no such thing as an uncontrived face [or, one could add, uncontrived hair] in the movies," as James Naremore writes in *Acting in the Cinema*.[44]

In the digital present, there are new internecine battles between computer animators and programmers and the traditional crafts as more and more of what appears on the screen no longer has a connection to a prior physical reality. But there are signs of a resurgence of the importance of costume, makeup, and hair design with regard to the ever-finer-grained digitally animated image, even if the character being designed for is Shrek or Princess Fiona, an Ewok, or a talking mouse, or lives next door to a Monster House.[45]

Spectacular Invisibility

This brief overview underscores a paradoxical but familiar dynamic marking the relationship of costume, makeup, and hair to commercial narrative filmmaking. On the one hand, their departments were large and well funded and headed by "glamour masters" who not only burnished the prestige and maintained the images of Hollywood's stars but were essential to the creation of the story worlds and spectacle that drew audiences into theaters. But on the other hand, they were meant to do all these things through the trope of formal invisibility; as with other crafts, the platonic ideal of Hollywood's "invisible system" suggests that costume, makeup, and hair are, or should be, designed primarily to support the narrative and the actors who embody its characters rather than to loom large or draw attention to themselves on their own. As Barrett Kiesling put it in his 1937 book *Talking Pictures: How They Are Made, How to Appreciate Them*, "If the settings and gowns are really fine, the audience should be entirely unconscious of them. They are part of the background before which our story moves. If any portion of this background becomes obtrusive, something is wrong."[46] Film scholar Jane Gaines reiterates this sentiment; costume "was perceived as a troublesome distraction which could divert the viewer's attention from the story itself."[47]

But clearly stylistic invisibility, real or ideal, was always running up against what might be called nondiegetic visibility, or nontextual visibility, in Hollywood cinema. Deborah Landis contends that "costume designers are invisible. We don't have publicists, we work for hire. . . . We are not mentioned in fashion magazines but we help create the story and the people who inhabit the clothes."[48] These comments refer to the job in today's media culture, but even with that qualification it is not always accurate (Landis is herself quite famous).[49] It is proffered as a truism by many designers (and some scholars, even in this volume) that costume is not the same as fashion; costume, makeup, and hair instead "design the people in the movie," in Landis's words,[50] supporting every other element working toward the compelling and convincing creation of a specific time and place, whether "real" or fantastical, present or past or future. But equally as often, and not necessarily distinct from the above, Hollywood's costume, makeup, and hair were also meant to lure audiences beyond films to the products and fashions that extended the industry's commercial reach, and there is arguably now even more crossover between the fashion and costume worlds. Other crafts can show us a certain car, say, that we might crave because James Bond drives it, or a particular brand of candy that becomes appealing because a cuddly space alien likes it; or they can create a sound track whose music we desire to purchase and download so that we can listen to it whenever we want. Just like these, the crafts of costume, makeup, and hair, no less than the stars they were so crucial in helping to manufacture, were, and remain, almost as potent in their attraction off the screen as on.[51]

Before turning to chapter summaries, I want to make two overarching points about the historiography of costume, makeup, and hair. The first continues the discussion of visibility and invisibility in the classical film; the second considers how the professions interact with notions of film authorship. On the first item, Patrick Keating notes in his volume on cinematography in this series that, even in studio-era Hollywood, the focus on storytelling was never rote, and was frequently accompanied by, or subsumed under, "the value that the system placed on other functions, most notably glamour lighting, which studios insisted cinematographers practice independent of narrative motivation."[52] The same is obviously true of costume, makeup, and hair, which were ostensibly meant to be read in a narrative context but were often so idiosyncratic, fantastic, or impossibly lavish or perfect as to seem independent of it (in some films they were meant to be, as with the fashion shows, often in Technicolor, that dotted Hollywood films from the 1930s on) (color plate 5). But Hollywood's self-professed interest in depicting the natural and the normal in makeup ("just get some good cosmetics and practice a little") created an extra dilemma for period pictures and for films about characters—period or otherwise—who were not meant to be admired.

As Alicia Annas argues, precisely because by the early 1930s "film stars were exerting as much influence off-screen as on," screen and fashion styles "became more interconnected," locking both studios and stars into "a modern makeup image no matter what the period of a film. Anything else ran the risk of alienating the fans."[53] Therefore, "Hollywood moviemakers' use of makeup and wigs in films, both period and non-period, was usually inspired more by commercial considerations than by a concern for history." Although narrative and stylistic coherence and something that read as authenticity were allegedly the goals, "it was economically vital that the star's image was not sacrificed to history. [One] can see a systematic approach to the way they handled makeup and hair, com-bining stars' modern images with illusions of historical accuracy" (Annas calls this "the photogenic formula"). Promotional and publicity discourses surround-ing individual films or produced for fan magazines assumed that hairstyles were designed by makeup artists (such as the Westmores or Max Factor), and there is comparatively little separate discussion of it. But Annas concludes that because "women's film makeup was always modern, their hairstyles had to follow suit to a degree," although there was more flexibility in the use of coiffures to set styles and new fashions. "Hairstyles became the key visual component for merging the female star image and its modern glamor makeup with the historical illusion provided by costumes and settings."

Thus, Annas writes, was Norma Shearer's wig in *Romeo and Juliet* (George Cukor, 1936) "an ingenious blend of 1930s fashion and the styles worn by young *men* in Renaissance Florence" (italics hers).[54] In 1939, however, Margaret Far-rand Thorp reported in her book *America at the Movies* that the hair stylists for *Romeo and Juliet* claimed that the coiffure was "Greek in origin, suggested by the Olympic games," whereas fan magazines wrote that Shearer borrowed it, "with variations, from [popular opera diva] Gladys Swarthout" or that it came from Adrian, MGM's head costume designer, who insisted that the hairstyle was "inspired by an angel head in Fra Angelico's 'Annunciation.'"[55] Whichever version one prefers, all the accounts point to how makeup and hair intersected with the need for all stars to look contemporary independently of narrative con-text, and the fact remained that for "a year or two afterwards," in Thorp's words, "almost every other girl in the country wore her hair smooth on the crown and curling up into a soft fluff below her ears," often topped by Adrian's "Juliet cap" which, "made up of anything from string to pearls, appeared all winter at every party in the country."[56]

On the other hand, if one examines the styling of the male and female leads of the most popular period picture of the classical era, *Gone with the Wind* (1939), some of the hair and makeup styles certainly read to us now as being from the 1930s; see Scarlett O'Hara's/Vivien Leigh's shoulder-length hair held back at the temples in the film's opening scenes, or Rhett Butler's/Clark Gable's slicked-back locks throughout. But they are also quite different than those of *Romeo and Juliet* or many other period films of the decade. The notoriously obsessive producer David Selznick was adamant that the costumes, makeup, and hair be "authentic" rather than "modern glamor makeup," and Frank Westmore reports on his oldest brother Mont's months of "monumental" research into the era before the film was even cast.[57] So it is also clear that Westmore's designs (for which he received no screen credit) were a conscious attempt to be period-appropriate, as can be seen in the other hairstyles the stars wear and the lack of tweezing of the eyebrow lines and the subdued colors in the lip treatments of most of the lead women characters. In such cases, then, even slight alterations in the visual image, such as thicker eyebrows, or simply visible dirt or beads of sweat on a star's face and body, were enough to shift the frame of reference from the present to the past as well as from glamour to authenticity—for which *Gone with the Wind* was indeed praised (color plate 6).[58] Conversely, as was the case with *Romeo and Juliet*, *Gone with the Wind*'s antebellum and postbellum star fashions as well as the makeup and period hair styles inspired numerous, if somewhat incongruous, modern updates and tie-ins.

Thorp employs the term "double influence" in her discussion of the "power of the movies to popularize a style wherever it may have originated":

> No fashion magazine, however skillfully edited, can compete with them when it comes to making it seem imperative to own a particular hat or frock or necklace. Neither adjectives nor photographs nor drawings can make a woman feel about an evening wrap as she feels when she sees it on the shoulders of Irene Dunne or in the arms of William Powell. It is both the glamorous background against which it was originally seen and the, probably unconscious, recollection of what was said to the lady wearing [it] which makes it seem infinitely desirable when it is hanging on a clothes rack in the local dry goods emporium.[59]

What Thorp calls "double influence" we might well call postmodern pastiche, the point being that throughout cinema's history, even when the goal and the methods employed to achieve it were also driven by an interest in authenticity, there were practices of appropriation and adaptation by audiences as well as film-makers. And they were acknowledged as such, and discussed publicly, by cultural critics before the age of television or the Internet.

In her book *Hollywood Catwalk*, Tamar Jeffers McDonald also points to problems created by stars playing "weak, wanton women," as Joan Crawford ("the most copied girl in the world") did in *Rain* and *Letty Lynton* in 1932.[60] Crawford was "charged with initiating the fashion for over-use of lipstick," and in response she (or a staff writer writing in Crawford's name) wrote in *Motion Picture* that it was only a "performance," that she was wearing "character make-up" that "should never have been put to use in private life." But it was, to the consternation of guardians of genteel culture, and so were stars' offscreen fashions, the ordinary clothing they wore in their daily lives, whenever they happened to be caught by the camera.[61] Perhaps the best way, then, to think about most costume, makeup, and hair in commercial cinema is always as a "double influence"—visible as well as invisible, evaluated through its plausibility as a component of a particular narrative but always also in relation to its use-value in spectators' lives and the potentialities for social change as well as pleasure embodied by such use.

The same analytical approach can extend to questions of film authorship and the historical record. As is well known, scholarly convention since the popularization of the auteur theory in the United States in the early 1960s dictates that we identify a film with its director. But of course most reasoned critical assessments of how a given film came to be would have to point to "an emphasis on collaboration," in Patrick Keating's words. It surely would be difficult to imagine a scenario by which costume, makeup, and hair designers provide the controlling artistic visions of any body of film texts, even when theatrical designers, like Natacha Rambova in the silent era or Irene Sharaff in the 1940s and 1950s, designed sets as well as costumes. But as the scholarship on costume, makeup, and hair grows, it cannot help but elucidate the complexity of collaboration itself, and inflect our understanding of even canonical films in new and interesting ways.

For example, Tay Garnett's 1946 black-and-white adaptation of James M. Cain's hardboiled 1934 novel *The Postman Always Rings Twice*, which stars Lana Turner as a somewhat sympathetic femme fatale, is famously known as a "study in white" because Turner wears white in all but two scenes. It was first called a "study in white" by the *New York Times* in 1945; and "according to wardrobe specifications, Miss Turner will be seen in forty-one different costumes—and they all will be white. The film is to be produced by Carey Wilson, to whom the studio and Mr. Breen give credit for overcoming the censorable portions of the story and for the white costuming idea."[62] When Peter Brunette and Gerald Peary interviewed Cain for *Film Comment* in 1976, Cain reported that Harry Ruskin, "the guy who did the script," told him that "he [Ruskin] had Lana Turner dressed in white so that the public understood that the girl's pure. She may be playing around with the guy, but she's not taking her pants off for him."[63] Leonard Leff and Jerold Simmons, in their book *The Dame in the Kimono*, repeat Cain's remarks and also cite "an MGM press release [that] stated that Lana Turner (Cora) would wear forty-one different costumes, each one white."[64] What made the use of white so compelling, of course, was that Cora *was* a doomed femme fatale, and while Turner is actually dressed in black in two scenes, in all the rest her platinum-blonde hair and white clothing, while certainly making her alluring, confound the stereotypical association of the sexual woman with darkness.

Despite Carey's and Ruskin's claims to be the source for the "white idea," a 2013 book on MGM's head designer at the time, Irene, argues that it was Irene's idea, and hers alone; moreover, she had to work hard to bend others to her vision. As her longtime assistant, Virginia Fisher, puts it, "I'll never forget her excitement about her idea for this project. . . . Irene had come up with the idea [of] doing all of Lana's costumes in white except for two scenes. I listened to Irene's reason—the idea was to have a color associated with the character's wardrobe so the color theme of the clothes could work in a movie just like the theme music in an opera."[65] Irene had already designed movies for Tay Garnett, and he always, according to Fisher, gave Irene free rein "to design as she wished since he knew little about clothes. His main concern was that his leading lady be happy with what she wore." In fact, Garnett was most worried that Turner, a "rising star," would object to wearing "one color throughout the entire movie." But Turner was acquiescent, the film was a big hit, and "stores were deluged with customers wanting all white summer wardrobes." (The actual color of white costumes in Hollywood films was usually a very light gray, because pure white, in Max Factor's words, "simply throws back a characterless glare, and contributes only artificiality to [a] picture.")[66]

On the one hand, the newer account simply supports the Hollywood film as a collaboration among all the crafts necessary to get any vehicle onto a film screen. But the point is also that we have only begun to understand the contributions of costume, makeup, and hair to film history. By including Irene "in the picture" we have a much richer understanding of how her craft supported the overall project of an individual well-known film, but her story also shows how easy it was for her employers to shift credit for those contributions to other people, if only for publicity purposes; or how eager they were to recharacterize her color theme, designed to work similarly to leitmotifs in an opera, to one that instead focuses on the girl's sexuality. It also returns us to the tension between invisible storytelling and the nondiegetic or extratextual meanings that elements like costume, hair design, and makeup could acquire, a tension that arguably informs this volume more than any other in the Behind the Silver Screen series. One can easily imagine women all over the country roaming cities and towns and even the countryside dressed all in white or sporting shorts and turbans, as well as lipstick and blonde hair, à la Lana Turner the following summer; and there are any number of ways in which this dynamic plays out with other films as well—indeed, Turner's platinum hair and "sun-tan makeup," in the words of the *New York Times*, were apparently suggested by the hair and makeup of Jean Harlow in the 1930s.

Film historians must always contend with the melancholy but familiar fact that the industry's neglect—sometimes accidental, sometimes careless, sometimes intentional—of its own past means that there are holes in the record that can never be filled: see the loss of many if not most early films, some existing now only as titles in a catalogue; the lack of complete credits, along with the practice of including only the names of department heads onscreen in the studio era or, too often, not including makeup and hair credits at all; a paucity of archival material devoted to costume, makeup, and hair as such, or else weighted heavily toward one or two designers or filmmakers (if Cecil B. DeMille seems to loom large in these pages, it is partly because of his outsized archival presence); and the frequent unreliability of much secondary materiality, such as the biographies or autobiographies of survivors of the studio system who may have images to protect or scores to settle.[67]

Nor are there studio-era trade journals for costume, makeup, and hair, although the associated guilds publish them now. Even film credits themselves are not always reliable; Helen Rose was given screen credit for Irene's designs for *The Stratton Story* in 1949.[68] Added to these are the difficulties with circumscribing such an enormous topic given the intersections of costume, makeup, and hair with the fashion world more broadly. But if this volume inspires its readers to attend more carefully, whether in a movie theater or through the newer media by which films are circulated now, to what Hollywood took for granted or simply did not think to look at for so many decades, it will have done its job.

Chapter Preview

Drake Stutesman's chapter covers the earliest years of commercial filmmaking, from 1895 until the transition to sound in 1927, a period during which film rose from lower-class amusement and curiosity to a position of prestige and huge financial clout. To get to the formation of the industry itself, Stutesman works from the outside in, from analysis of the art and popular culture in which filmmaking and spectating were born and codified as part of American life. She takes costume, makeup, and hair to be both the "underpinnings of cultural allure in everyday life" and "a conduit through which the nascent film industry took hold of its public," especially with the formation of the star system. The first filmmakers imported techniques, as they did actors, from the stage, but soon learned that what worked well across the footlights did not always translate into the much more visually intimate photographic medium of film, which had its own limitations as well as incredible potentialities.

Costume design and fashion, Stutesman writes, "began to enter into a world economy together" in the 1910s and 1920s, and helped to make cosmetic use for women "essential as well as progressive" while also perpetuating more malign stereotypes such as blackface and navigating early attempts at self-regulation in response to fears of federal censorship. In turn, the growth of cinema's influence came from its ability to draw "people who either deigned to work in the new industry in spite of the high positions they had already achieved in other venues, or were novices eager to show they could match the exceptional talent they saw in the theater and other arts." Although archival research material for the early part of the era is especially scarce—as are films themselves—the hierarchical structures and many of the labor routines that she lays out for the industry through the end of the 1920s would remain in place for the next twenty-five years, as would some of its most famous designers and stars.

Mary Desjardins considers classical Hollywood from 1928 through the end of World War II, a period that represents the maturity of the studio system as a vertically integrated industry and that is often called the golden age of American filmmaking. She uses archival documents as well as detailed film analysis to examine the relations among the three crafts and their coordination with others, how they appear in completed films, and, equally important, the "discourses that publicized the labor and material effects of these practices to the film-going public." This is a period in which the industry went from silent to sound, made the change from orthochromatic to panchromatic stock and also began to work with Technicolor, and experienced the imposition of the full force of the Production Code.

Desjardins explores the effects of all these on costume, makeup, and hair design, even as other elements, such as the star system and the organizational structure of individual departments, remained stable. Within these systems, however, she marks the often wide disparities in prestige and pay during a period in which labor union activity roiled the industry as it did U.S. society at large. In classical Hollywood, Desjardins writes, "costume designers and makeup and hair stylists created products of 'flesh and spirit' out of social and cultural struggles that deserve continued historical reappraisal."

At the end of World War II, Hollywood expected not only to continue but to increase its dominance over world filmmaking. But as Prudence Black and Karen de Perthuis discuss in their chapter on postwar Hollywood from 1947 to 1967, instead the studios experienced convulsive upheavals tied to enforced industry restructuring after the Paramount decrees, changing audience demographics and a new youth market, competition from abroad and, especially, from television, the demise of the regulatory structure provided by the Code, and an increase in independent and "runaway" productions. After an immediate postwar resurgence that celebrated the end of the austerity of the war years, the studios' declining fortunes were signaled by the dismantling of the contract system, such that costume, makeup, and hair designers now faced "the insecurity of working freelance along with diminished responsibilities, a lowering of status, and shoestring budgets."

With the exception of certain big-budget films which continued to be made in the new era of uncertainty—some of which were giant successes, others of which were equally large failures—newer modes of independent or youth-oriented films became forms of retail assemblage, with costumers buying clothing off the rack and makeup from drugstore counters. Nevertheless, the period also saw a resurgence in the power of costume, makeup, and hair design to influence fashion, for example the well-known nostalgia for the 1930s created, in part, by the success of *Bonnie and Clyde* in 1967. Black and de Perthuis trace the disruptions as well as the numerous continuities that marked the industry during these two decades, at the end of which films with "name" designers and others with no designers at all shared space at the top of the box office charts.

In her chapter on the auteur renaissance and the period from 1968 to 1980, Robin Blaetz begins by exploring the continued influence of the French New Wave on a Hollywood that was no longer sure of its audience. The socially engaged cinema produced by the film school generation as well as by older but more idiosyncratic late-studio filmmakers continued to reflect and respond to social and political issues and movements, as before on often comparatively tiny budgets. While earlier decades had also been marked by periods of social change and upheaval—including two world wars and economic depression—the 1970s saw the full flowering of primarily youth-based political and social movements involving race, gender, and sexuality. Costuming, makeup, and hair, whether designed or shopped, began to "assimilate changes in notions of propriety" in fashion and behavior as movies increasingly represented people formerly excluded not only from full participation in U.S. society but its commercial films as well.

Indeed, there is a paradoxical relationship of clothing, costuming, and fashion in this era, one that arguably remains with us. While young people often dressed, Blaetz writes, "to reject fashion," and costume designers then created clothing for their characters "in accordance with this cultural (or more properly countercultural) reality," the fashion world in turn co-opted what it saw in the cinema and "sold it back to those who had created it"; thus, "it became ever more difficult" to use clothing "subversively." But the 1970s was also the era of the effects-driven blockbuster, and even studio designers who believed that their careers were over upon the closing of the studios soon returned to work in full force, creating costume, makeup, and hair for period and fantasy films of all kinds, with their influence also felt in the fashion world.

Much like the previous two decades, the later years of the "New Hollywood," from 1981 to 1999, included both small films and blockbusters. Because designers employed primarily established methods during the era—filmmakers were just beginning to tinker with computer-generated imagery to interact with, if not replace, physical modes of character design and manufacture—Tamar Jeffers McDonald focuses on films themselves and the high degree of polish with which the crafts function in the films as expressive texts. Academy Award recognition and attendance figures alike reflect the continued popularity of films that use costume, makeup, and hair, she writes, as Hollywood always has: "to highlight and reveal personality traits, to help actors to develop a character, and to provide visual pleasure."

Jeffers McDonald also points to a new mutability of the costume picture in the 1980s and 1990s, as more and more films were set in a past within more or less recent memory. Working within a self-reflexive stylistic mode, these films construct a past that is partly authentic and partly a pastiche of earlier movies whose glamour and extravagance were designed to set them well apart from their contemporary audiences but are now given quasi-documentary status in relation to that past. Even in films that require "ordinary dress," she argues, the clothing is "no less crafted and carefully chosen than the more elaborate apparel designed for [period films]." In fact, such garments may have more significance to audience members, since they can easily be seen to have equivalents in stores. The tensions she traces in the chapter therefore "illustrate the quandaries all designers must solve, and although the primary one may at first sight seem like a simple binary—historical/current—these then break down, subdivide, and multiply themselves revealing the variety of choices to be made."

The final chapter of the volume covers the years from 2000 through the present. Anyone examining the modern entertainment marketplace, as James Castonguay points out, faces a formidable challenge because of the "sheer scale and ubiquity" of media culture in the twenty-first century (and, of course, because we are still living in it). While many of the era's films exhibit a considerable degree of classicism in relation to their narrative structures as well as marketing and tie-in strategies, the practical work of many costume, makeup, and hair designers is now continually affected by the ubiquity of CGI and the intersection of cinema generally with other media technologies, especially those dependent on and facilitated by the Internet and the plethora of devices through which it can be accessed. While films certainly still use costume designers and makeup and hair artists and employ materials developed in earlier decades, CGI (as well as motion and performance capture) "blurs the line, arguably more forcefully than in the past, separating the three areas from the realm of special effects and animation." This has fomented disputes between "traditional" costume, makeup, and hair designers and those working in visual effects over credit, job descriptions, and remuneration. Ironically, the increasing visual definition and realism of digitally animated films means that animators, who had once themselves been the costume, makeup, and hair designers of their cartoon characters, are now seeking design help from the older crafts.

Castonguay also addresses the relationship between stars and changing conceptions of celebrity on and off the screen. While there are cross-media stars in each of the other periods discussed, the number of platforms across which celebrity travels now, often at lightning speeds, makes older notions about cycles of fashion seem quaint. With films themselves no longer tied to theaters (even home theaters) as sites of exhibition, and with production loosened somewhat from the expensive equipment that formerly made it a rich man's game (in every sense of the term), cinema is now a wide range of intertexts—popular magazines, websites, trade publications, and social and mobile media—and therefore film costume, makeup, and hair are now situated in those intertexts as well.

The six chapters in this volume thus cover a triad of crafts that are at once well known and everywhere, part of our ordinary lives and the business of living, as well as sites of cinematic collaboration, inventiveness and innovation, and art. They have shaped and been shaped by the demands of commercial narrative filmmaking over twelve decades and have never been less than crucial regardless of whether a film was a big-budget studio production or an indie shot on a shoestring budget. Due to the comparative lack of attention paid in the past to costume, makeup, and hair by historians and industry alike, the writers of the following chapters are entering into a conversation that has only just begun. Given the liveliness and passion with which they approach their subjects, it can only be hoped that, regardless of how filmmaking itself evolves in our ever-more-digital and media-saturated age, the three crafts will never again be "politely ignored."

1

THE SILENT SCREEN, 1895–1927   Drake Stutesman

Silent film began in the midst of the tremendous noise of the nineteenth century transitioning into the twentieth. In 1895, cities and towns were crammed with opera houses, theaters, burlesque and vaudeville playhouses, music halls, saloons, circus tents, and minstrelsies. Audiences at this time were well used to the stage as a presence, a literal *place* in which the fourth wall was often breached as performers dazzled, excited, and provoked spectators and fed their Rabelaisian appetites. Performers sang to their audiences—who sang back—or talked to them and made them laugh, cry, or catcall; they threw them acrobatic tricks, dirty double-entendres, and raunchy gestures; they enacted silly, poignant, political, or riveting dramas. This was the stage space that cinema entered, a space with a "here and now" made out of an intimacy full of power.

By holding time in an eternal repetition, cinema created new perceptions for these audiences. By the mid-teens a breathing person could sit in a crowded movie house, intoxicated by a narrative that unrolled as a moving diorama, the fascinating actor now a gigantic face beaming gigantic feelings onto a mesmerized viewer. Cinema manufactured a literalness that, though two-dimensional and usually black and white, was all-enveloping. It embodied theatrical flesh and theatrical flash because cinema's people never aged. But it also dimmed theater's organic life into a ghostliness and made time into a present that was unreachable and inexplicable. How could the enticing world of live and symbiotic theater be remade for film, whose actors could no longer talk with, sing to, or eroticize an adoring audience? The answer much depended on the below-the-line crafts of costuming, makeup, and hairdressing (the last two initially grouped together as "makeup" by the industry) to transform cinema's hypnotic but empty space into a surreal and successful reality.

These arts helped to humanize the alienating cinema "stage." Costume, makeup, and hair, so often the underpinnings of cultural allure in everyday life, too, were a conduit through which the nascent film industry took hold of its public. In the 1890s storefronts, the 1905 nickelodeons, and the movie palaces of the 1910s and 1920s, who was looking at the screen? In 1900, a fifty-year-old American—whether of African, European, or Asian descent—would have lived through the Civil War or revolutions, enslavements, plagues, diasporas, and purges around the world. What appears as a period drama to an audience now could have had personal meaning to a cinemagoer in the silent era. Something as specific as the eighteenth-century French powdered wigs worn in Georges Méliès's *Cinderella* (1899), in the Theda Bara vehicle *Madame Du Barry* (1917), or in D. W. Griffith's *Orphans of the Storm* (1921) might have evoked fear, loss, comfort, or longing. On the screen, people saw things they had never seen before; they may have envied, loved, or despised what they saw; or they recognized what they already knew and felt deeply about.

Even tiny details could have been triggers. Did the spectator own a comb? Use oils, pomades, henna, or hairpieces? Braid her hair into elaborate styles? Have lice or alopecia? Was she suspicious of bathing (as many were in royal and society circles) or grimy from lack of water for washing? Were his clothes rotting? Made at home or fitted at the tailor's? Did he powder with talc (newly invented in the nineteenth century, replacing lethal lead-based powders)? Did she rouge her cheeks with hot red carmine or wish for Sarah Bernhardt's crimson lipstick?[1] And most crucially, what could cinema's arts of costume, makeup, and hairdressing do with the influence implicit in these connections and the reactions they inspired?

Costume, Couture, and the Clothes Rack

In cinema's first two decades, theater overlapped with the new screen world. When the 1912 French film *Queen Elizabeth*, starring Sarah Bernhardt and costumed by French couturier Paul Poiret, became a hit in the United States, Adolf Zukor, the distributor, capitalized on its success. He had created his first company, "Famous Players in Famous Plays," with the idea of drawing "famous players" into prestige cinema. Initially stage luminaries refused to participate, though many young ones (Mary Pickford, the Barrymores) as well as vaudevillians (Marie Dressler, Charlie Chaplin, W. C. Fields) embraced film and made their fortunes. But once Zukor and Jesse L. Lasky drew American opera star Geraldine Farrar into a successful film career with a full-length *Carmen* (1915), directed by Cecil B. DeMille, other established stars followed.

It was not just Farrar's star appeal that was important but her cultural persona as an actor who could, in film scholar Anne Morey's words, "make a claim for the upper-middle-class carriage trade at the same moment that she helped to domesticate a cadre of risqué 'brothel play' roles."[2] As such, Farrar, and others like her, was indispensible to film's emerging identity, in part because she had theatrical gravitas and in part because her roles were ones already bridged by the nineteenth century's courtesans and stage actresses and actors. In the 1880s, fashion-conscious European courtesans set the trends. With dizzyingly high social positions, they were esteemed as sophisticates by both men and women and were the precursors, historian Susan Griffith argues, of celebrities as diverse as Greta Garbo, Gracie Allen, and Madonna.[3] By the end of the nineteenth century, actresses such as Bernhardt, Lillie Langtry, Cécile Sorel, and Gaby Deslys—each one a household name with record-breaking international popularity—led the styles and broke the rules, a role that would be filled by screen stars within two decades. The industry learned how to blend new world attractions with those of the old, blends that helped lead to costume design's centrality.

Cinema emerged just as fashion was shifting from an exclusive customer base into a large retail market. Early Hollywood films provided an unprecedented opportunity to view new clothing as fashion because the movie industry's newly anointed stars[4] initially wore their own clothes on set, often couture they had purchased themselves if they could afford it. As film costuming, no less than the actors who wore it, became vital to the studio system and the stories that films told by the late teens, American fashion and film costume design began to enter into a world economy together.

That said, at the beginning of the twentieth century, style revolutions continued to come from Europe. In the 1910s, Poiret rid fashion of the corset with his empire-waisted, loosely draped dresses, a look augmented by Leon Bakst's extravagantly colored and widely admired Ballets Russes costumes. Stage and screen stars wore clothes from the top couture houses such as Poiret, Doucet, Paquin, Worth, Callot, Vionnet, and Lucile, and actresses often liaised with these couturières/couturiers for their costumes. Deslys's were made typically by Maison Paquin (designer, Étienne Drian) or by Landolff, renowned for stage costume. But Deslys took fashion as a starting place. She wanted, as her biographer put it, "exaggerated adaptations of all current styles," and she personally redesigned costumes for an "outrageous" and "bizarre beauty that bore a personal stamp."[5]

Cecil Beaton's rapturous remarks about Deslys (on whom he modeled his costumes for *My Fair Lady* decades later) and her own 1915 style—for instance, a magenta outfit and magenta makeup—point toward what became film's formula of star glamour, "the most elusive of all qualities": "Vulgar? Perhaps, but by whose standards? The gesture seemed to transcend vulgarity and create it own allure."[6] This formula, which could be said to be something through which cinema itself was created, would find its way into film costume design. Within the second half of the silent period, costume design both became integral to the story, in ways both fantastical and realistic, but also was specially suited to the actor's body and character on and off the screen. Foundational to the new industry, costume also, in its ability to dazzle vast audiences, began to influence fashion rather than follow it. In a letter to Gloria Swanson, one of her era's style setters, a fan relayed how important that appeal was: although the writer was "in hock," she spent her "last fifty five cents / before pay day / to see you on screen!" (figure 1).[7]

By the twentieth century's second decade, pushed by the sense that the United States lacked sophistication, American film producers began to spend money on European couture's artistes. After Zukor's success with Bernhardt and Poiret, others, such as Coco Chanel, Erté, Paul Iribe, and Jeanne Lanvin, were hired to design stars' costumes. One of the most dynamic and complex bridges between fashion and costume (stage and screen) was the internationally successful British couturière Lucile (a.k.a. Lady Duff-Gordon). Lucile, whom Beaton called a "delicate genius,"[8] was novelist/screenwriter Elinor Glyn's sister and a progenitor of fashion promotion and runway shows. She clothed many theater stars, on and off the stage, and was at the forefront in cinema design, dressing Pearl White in *The Perils of Pauline* (1914),[9] Clara Kimball Young in *The Rise of Susan* (1916), Billie Burke in *Gloria Romance* (1916), and Mary Pickford in *Rebecca of Sunnybrook Farm* (1917), to name only a few.[10] *Dressed* is the operative word. These clothes were rarely costumes per se but rather gorgeous fashions.

It is thus somewhat difficult to create a full picture of early silent film costume design history because so many different methods coexisted through the late

FIGURE 1: Gloria Swanson in a publicity photo for *Zaza* (1923), designers uncredited.

1910s. For period pieces (westerns and eighteenth-century themes were as popular in film as on the stage), there was "wardrobe," which was not a department but rather a clothes rack or, at best, a room that held special items. In 1910, Alice Guy Blaché's Solax Studios opened in Fort Lee, New Jersey, and was one of the first to incorporate costume into studio premises. Along with a film processing lab and multiple stages, Solax had workrooms for dressing, sewing, and designing, a template similar to that followed by the Hollywood studios during the classical era. But many "period" costumes had little authenticity. Costume houses, where quality period costumes could be rented or reproduced, began to be founded on the West Coast in 1912. One of the first, Western Costume Company (still a major business), began with an inventory of genuine Native American clothing. The first prominent studio to amass a large permanent collection of reusable costumes was Selig, in 1912, then based in Chicago with a studio in Los Angeles. This enabled them to control the clothing condition (some clothes brought in by actors needed fumigation), have costumes readily accessible, and keep down rental costs.[11]

For films set in the "present," most actors in the swiftly made one- and two-reelers of the early silent era wore their own clothes. Thus, actresses wanting the job learned to dress well, knowing good clothes would make the film look better. (Swanson attributed her first film jobs to her style sense.)[12] Some now-iconic costumes were adaptations of preexisting forms; the baggy pants, too-small jacket, bowler hat, and long shoes of Chaplin's signature tramp outfit—the creation of which he claimed was the "turning point" in his film career—took elements from clowning, minstrelsy, and music hall that were well-known comedy staples (Bert Williams used similar tropes, as did W. C. Fields and others). However, Chaplin so perfected both the look, at once vulgar and refined, and the identity it afforded him that the costume was touted as the "clothes that saved Chaplin" (figure 2).[13]

Cross-dressing, also integral to identity and with a history dating back to antiquity, was another staple

FIGURE 2: Charlie Chaplin as the Little Tramp.

of virtually every kind of entertainment, including early cinema. It is hard to define what cross-dressing meant in silent film—it was used across multiple film genres—but vaudeville and music hall had many cross-dressing star sensations, such as Vesta Tilley and Julian Eltinge, who were world famous. For a female silent star to dress as a man—especially either as a swell, in top hat and tails, or a boy—was so common that it is almost easier to name those actresses who did not. Deslys, Bernhardt, Swanson, Mabel Normand, Pickford, Louise Brooks, Garbo, and later Dietrich and Katharine Hepburn—among others—all performed in male costume, typically tails, onstage or on film. Almost all male film comedians wore women's clothes at some point, among them Buster Keaton, Chaplin, and Roscoe "Fatty" Arbuckle.

Beyond famous cases like Chaplin's, or the memoirs of this or that star who claimed they wore her own clothes to the set or created their own sartorial identity, it is difficult to be sure who actually designed many of the costumes in the early studio era. As is the case for all of film's component crafts, there are few records of the earliest years (as there are comparatively few surviving films); even actors and directors were not always credited. But what information is available shows how herculean the costume demands quickly became once Hollywood started to become the locus of U.S. film production in the early teens, regardless of who was making the costumes or simply renting or purchasing them for a particular film. If a film did employ designers, directors often required rush work that meant "wardrobe" would have to complete a complex garment in two days that would take a couturier three weeks. There was also variable studio support for costumers and much career movement between studios as designers transferred from one to another. Because of this uncertainty, dates and titles can be difficult to fix. Credits were (and still are) especially in dispute when more than one designer worked on a film, which was often the case; sequence films were popular in the silent era and typically contained fantasy or period vignettes that were often designed by multiple artists. Mitchell Leisen, Clare West, Paul Iribe, and Natacha Rambova, for example, designed together for more than one film but their work has often been attributed to one name; and West, Iribe, and Leisen all worked on DeMille's *Male and Female* (1919) but are credited differently in different sources, sometimes as sole designer, sometimes as collaborators.[14]

As Hollywood began to rely more and more on "experts" in other fields as well, fashion designers were sought for leading ladies at least; Ince Studios sent out publicity about the hiring of Melville Ellis, "designer and fashion expert of International reputation," in 1915.[15] But studios began to build serious costume collections with the success of full-length "period" features such as D. W. Griffith's *The Birth of a Nation*, and the costume designer thus could emerge as a singular role, one distinct from "wardrobe mistress" and whose job was to manage, collate, and advise on all matters relating to costume—although the wardrobe mistress and costume designer also, in those years, could be the same person.

Lucia Coulter (1861–1936), also called "Mother," began at MGM as one of the key wardrobe mistresses, and is often identified as the progenitor of the costume/wardrobe room as a serious enterprise.[16] The records vary on her start date. Fashion historian Michelle Finamore claims Coulter began in 1919 and Elizabeth Leese claims it was in the mid-1920s. Both credit her as designing, with a focus on period and "character" clothing and a special talent in the artificial "aging" of garments, some twenty-two films between 1926 and 1929.[17] Jane Lewis worked for Vitagraph from 1915, caring for wardrobe but also designing as many as "eight to ten frocks for the star of each picture"; her name was featured in fan magazines.[18] Mme. Violette (often credited as Mrs. George Unholz) worked for Keystone/Sennett Productions, possibly soon after it began in 1912 and until at least 1923. Finamore identifies her as having "designed and personally supervised" every Sennett short and feature during that time.[19] Biograph's first wardrobe manager, German-born Curt Rehfeld, who later became an actor and director, kept detailed records, showing that he conceived costume design as a field with a future.[20]

In 1916, Clare West was assigned the title "studio designer" at Triangle, after she completed Griffith's mammoth *Intolerance* (1916), with a storyline crossing from antiquity to modern times; it was the first feature to costume extras in detail—and *Intolerance* employed thousands of them.[21] George James Hopkins, coming from the Ziegfeld Follies, began heading costumes at William Fox Studios, starting with Theda Bara's *Cleopatra* (1917).[22] Alpharetta Hoffman was a designer at Lasky Studios in 1917 when press releases were sent out to showcase her as costume "director" and claiming the studio made only original costumes (thereby eliminating rental costs).[23] Ethel P. Chaffin, head of wardrobe (with Clare West) for Famous Players–Lasky from 1919, costumed superstars Pola Negri, Nita Naldi, Swanson, and others, completing 3,000 star outfits in 1920 alone.[24] Although Chaffin was publicly known and consulted by the press, she was often uncredited in her films. She left for MGM in 1925, where she designed for only five films.[25]

Goldwyn Studios employed Sophie Wachner for many films until she left for Fox in 1924, staying until 1930; on occasion, she collaborated with Leisen as well as Dolly Tree. Irene Duncan began at Universal in the mid-teens and by 1919 oversaw eleven wardrobe departments.[26] Harry Collins also worked for Universal in 1915.[27] Gertrude Thanhouser costumed at Thanhouser, and also edited and was a production designer; and Mrs. Frank Farrington (first name unknown) worked there by 1917.[28] Farrington came to cinema from an august position, having costumed the notorious (and banned) Broadway play *Sappho* in 1900; one of Hollywood's most powerful players, Alla Nazimova, the actress-producer-director with an acclaimed career (a Broadway theater was named for her) and her own film company, Nazimova Productions, had tried to adapt the work for film.

Michele Finamore places 1917 as the year that a costume design credit became a regular feature of film press coverage. As the industry, its prestige, and the clear fame it could accord its practitioners grew—the names of costume designers, or at least that of the studio's head of costume, were regularly featured in credits by 1925—film designers came more frequently from couture houses or strong careers in theater and revue, whether in costume or production design. Lucile was the most prolific import; the Russian Erté (Romain de Tirtoff) and the French Paul Iribe and George Barbier also created many cinema costumes. But it was rare for those with an outside career to stay longer than one film or one year; the aims of couture and costume were too different. Couture aimed for gorgeousness, or splendor, while costume design had to characterize, beautify or uglify, tell a story, and suit cinematic lighting, shot scale, and action, all in black and white rather than color. Tricky details had to be accomplished such as anticipating a future look in designing for a chic modern story, as any current vogue used would be out of fashion by the film's release.[29] (By the 1930s, outré couturière Elsa Schiaparelli stated, "What Hollywood designs today, you will be wearing tomorrow.")[30]

But couture itself, especially the understanding of America as a location for high-quality fashion design, would change because of costume's importance to early cinema. As is well known, in the 1910s Americans were not considered fashionably smart by the rest of the western world. In 1917, Emily Burbank, in her *Woman as Decoration*, a dress history and style guide, wrote, "The criticism by foreigners that Americans, both men and women, never appear really at home in evening clothes, that they look as if they felt *dressed*, is true of the average man and woman of our country and results from the lax standards of a new and composite social structure. America, as a whole, lacks traditions and still embodies the pioneer spirit."[31] But within less than a decade, Hollywood costume design began to have what would become a radical effect on international fashion, as designers at some studios, initially Triangle and Famous Players–Lasky and subsequently most of the majors who replaced them, promoted the importance of film costume and, by extension, American fashion design.

The Studio Designer and "Filmland Fashion"

Two early designers, Peggy Hamilton and Clare West, were particularly instrumental in shifting the focus from Europe to America, especially the West Coast. Hamilton (1892–1984), who worked primarily at Triangle, became well known across the country in the teens, beginning as a costume designer but branching out to write a fashion column for the *Los Angeles Times* and moving into fashion design. While at Triangle, she costumed fifteen films between 1917 and 1919, but only four films from 1921 to 1938, which reflected her departure from costume design into a career in fashion.[32] Hamilton wrote about European couture too, but Finamore argues that she was instrumental in promoting Hollywood costume as fashion, or at least promoting stars wearing designs by costume designers as fashion.[33] It is difficult to draw lines between fashion and "filmland fashion" (the promotional term for stars wearing designs by film costume designers as fashion) and even, in this case, costume, but Hamilton's experience in both professions helped to create a new perspective on what costume design was or could be—crucial to telling a story, but also alluring in its own right.

Clare West (1879–1961), who claimed a background as a fashion illustration student in Paris (though she probably started as a seamstress in Los Angeles), was working, uncredited, with Robert Goldstein by 1913 or 1914 and at Triangle on Griffith's *The Birth of a Nation*.[34] It is probable that West created costumes for the women in *Birth of a Nation* and Goldstein for the men, as this subsequently became routine with two in-studio designers. Many of the costumes were made at Fine Arts Studio (1915–1918), owned by Triangle; the Western Costume Company made the Civil War uniforms.[35] Though a meticulous researcher, even in this early film West's attractive costumes seem lived in and not just "in period."[36] West is arguably one of the first costume designers to merge historical precision and tailoring that appealed to a modern audience. In 1916, West's *Intolerance* design concepts were advertised as influencing offscreen fashion trends; an April 1917 *Photoplay* article was entitled "Back to Babylon for New Fashions."[37]

By 1918, West ran DeMille's well-financed costume department (Chaffin ran the non-DeMille productions), working under his injunction that the costumes "make people gasp."[38] Although the over-the-top style of his twenties' films was criticized by some as crass compared to his earlier work, in his racy bedroom dramas—with teasing titles such as *Why Change Your Wife?* (1920) and *Manslaughter* (1922)—West's cutting-edge style (on and off the screen) for Swanson, Pola Negri, Bebe Daniels, and other stars began to rival couture with such edgy costumes as the patent leather swimsuit for *Saturday Night* (1922) or the flowing octopus dress and cape in *The Affairs of Anatol* (1921). A public figure, West spoke out in the press against fawning after European taste.[39] In 1923, *Screen News* quoted her opinion that Hollywood led Paris in fashion. At a time when women's styles were swept with new changes because "American and European women [had] shed more than three quarters of their prewar clothing,"[40] and as film costumes increasingly influenced public taste, designers like West were important.

West moved to First National in 1924, designing only for the Talmadge sisters and other big stars—Mae Murray in Erich Von Stroheim's *The Merry Widow*, Katherine McGuire in Keaton's *Sherlock Jr.*—and, in 1925, she returned to Paramount to costume, along with Lucile, Adrian, Travis Banton, and Howard Greer, the fashion show in *The Dressmaker from Paris* (Paul Bern, 1925). After that, she left the film industry. But by now other costume designers, such as Greer and

Adrian, shared West's endorsement of American fashion, and film costume was a recognized and formidable fashion force. In 1927, the profession had acquired such stature that designer Kathleen Kay, who took over the large costume department at Fox, was involved in a studio bidding war for her services.[41]

Not all studios had the commitment of DeMille, but in the 1920s Paramount, MGM, and Fox built good costume departments with large permanent collections (Paramount's contained 50,000 items). It was not uncommon for the bigger studios to spend lavishly on costumes. DeMille spent $10,000 on Leatrice Joy's furs for one film. Some costumes had real jewels, such as a gown by Sophie Wachner and Mitchell Leisen for Mary Pickford in *Dorothy Vernon of Haddon Hall* (1924, produced by her own Mary Pickford Company) that cost $32,000.[42] Paramount paid $125,000 for Swanson's wardrobe each year. However, many other studios operated throughout the silent period much as they had in the beginning—on a shoestring, or an improvisatory basis. Walter Plunkett, at FBO (the Film Booking Office) in 1926 and later at RKO and MGM, worked in what he described as "part of the drapery department." The costumes were rented or even made from uncut bolts of cloth pinned on a body into a costume and then dismantled at the end of the day. If the cloth was used again, and the costume did not match, Plunkett stated "nobody cared that much"; the method, even in 1926, was "customary," he said.[43] (In 1929, RKO took over FBO and built a department that could compete with other studios.) Howard Greer (1896–1974) had worked for Poiret and Edward Molyneux in Paris, then costumed the Greenwich Village Follies.[44] He ran the costume department at Famous Players–Lasky/Paramount from 1923 to 1927 and was also at RKO (1932 to 1933, and 1938).

The influx of designers from couture continued as well, although some, such as Gilbert Clark, who joined MGM for 1927–1928 and had worked for Lucile Ltd., at first disdained film work.[45] René Hubert, who worked for Patou, joined Famous Players–Lasky in 1925. Texan Travis Banton (1894–1958), a genius with difficult textiles such as satin and who dressed Clara Bow, Louise Brooks, Mae West, Carole Lombard, and Marlene Dietrich in often bias-cut costumes that became iconic silhouettes, began at the New York couture house Madam Francis. Banton came to Paramount as Howard Greer's second in 1924 and took over as head of costume when Greer left three years later.[46] Banton marked a new autocracy for designers in the studio system. Edith Head noted later that Banton "was a god [at Paramount]. Nobody dared oppose him about anything including budgets."[47] Clement Andreani, known as André-Ani, who was at MGM from the mid-1920s and worked with Gilbert Clark, was seen by some as another Erté. He most notably costumed Garbo in her early American films *Torrent* (Monta Bell, 1926) and *The Temptress* (Fred Niblo, 1926). Max Rée, who worked on wardrobe for those films (his exact role is difficult to determine), had been a stage designer for Max Reinhardt in Berlin. He costumed major revues, then became head of costume at First National and, in 1929, went to RKO working in both costume and art direction.

But some of the most famous film costumes of the era also seem, still, the product less of a system or even a department than of individual genius, arising from interests not only in costume (including jewelry and other accessories) and its associated crafts makeup and hairdressing, but production design as well. DeMille, for example, hired Natacha Rambova (1897–1966), born Winifred Shaughnessy, a dancer in a small Russian American troupe and niece to decorator Elsie de Wolfe, to design costumes and décor for the Aztec sequence in his *The Woman God Forgot* (1917), and then sequences in *Why Change Your Wife?* (1920) and *Something to Think About* (1920).[48] In 1919, Rambova began an artistic relationship with Nazimova by contributing designs for Nazimova's first film, *Billions* (1920), going on to design all the sets and costumes for Nazimova's 1921 (unfinished) *Aphrodite* and her productions of *Camille* (1921), *A Doll's House* (1922), and the Oscar Wilde *Salomé* (*Salome*, 1922). Rambova created a homogeneity for these films, using shimmering shades of silver, white, and black in every area of the frame and mixing *moderne* lines and Bauhaus aesthetics with ancient Asian geometries. Costume historian and designer Deborah Landis regards

Rambova's white rubberized cling tunic (made in a tire factory) for *Salomé* as one of the "most memorable [costumes] in the history of motion pictures" (figure 3).[49] In his book *In a Glamorous Fashion*, W. Robert La Vine views Rambova as one of film's "most inventive designers . . . ever" and one of the few to create both production design and costume.[50] Her streamlined perfectionism was very influential on designers such as Adrian, whom she hired for his first film.

By the early 1920s, Rambova managed her husband Rudolph Valentino's career, often negotiating his contracts. In 1923, they sued Famous Players–Lasky, gaining pay and artistic control, which led to the making of three art-driven films: the critically acclaimed

FIGURE 3: (Alla) Nazimova in *Salomé* (1922), art and costume design by Natacha Rambova.

box office failure *Monsieur Beaucaire* (1924), costumed by George Barbier and Rambova;[51] *A Sainted Devil* (1924), costumed by Rambova and Adrian; and the unfinished *The Hooded Falcon* (1924), also costumed by Rambova and Adrian. The battles with Famous Players and also United Artists resulted in Rambova's being barred from Valentino's professional life. The studios feared her power over Valentino, but Emily Leider, his biographer, argues also that his male fans, made uneasy by his sexuality in powdered wigs in period pieces like *Monsieur Beaucaire*, targeted Rambova. The couple divorced just before Valentino died. In 1925, Rambova produced both *What Price Beauty*, which she also scripted, designed, and starred in, and *When Love Grows Cold*, in which she starred. Although her Hollywood career was brief, Rambova's unique, elegant work represented great advances in costume design, especially employed as a tandem to production design.

Mitchell Leisen (1898–1972) was another of DeMille's great finds, hired by him in the late 1910s to work in the costume department and who went on to design films such as *The Thief of Bagdad* (1924). Leisen worked with West, Rambova, and others, but with a background in architecture and dance he quickly expanded into set design and by the early 1930s was directing his own films. His work had an off-kilter beauty that incorporated patterns and unusual ideas into wild plots, well exemplified by his *Murder at the Vanities* (1934), which he directed. (Importantly, by the end of the decade Hollywood was growing its own designers; Edith Head, with little design experience, was hired at Paramount in 1923 as an assistant, and replaced Travis Banton as Head of Costume in 1938.)[52]

But it was MGM, which abundantly funded its costume department, that would offer some of the greatest costumes and tailoring to cinema and fashion, led by Adrian, one of the twentieth century's major talents. Gilbert Adrian (1903–1958), born Adolph Greenberg but known professionally by his surname alone, was a New York Parsons student who studied for a year in Paris and then began his career designing for *George White's Scandals* on Broadway. In 1925, he was hired by Rambova to work on Paramount's *The Hooded Falcon* in their New York studio. He went to Hollywood in 1926 and worked there for DeMille for two years, ultimately designing for thirty films before going to MGM to become head of costume in 1929; he stayed there until 1941.[53]

Adrian was also one of American fashion's most generative designers (with more fashion "firsts"—the first padded shoulders, the first pattern-blocked suits for women, etc.—in tailoring than any other U.S. designer, in or out of the film industry). He exemplified a tremendous work ethic, and although he did not find his stride until after the silent era, his qualities were visible from the outset. His tailoring used old-world quality such as silk linings (in all his costumes), yet his ideas and his costumes' lines and silhouettes had a streamlined modernity. As did many later costume designers (Greer, Banton, Head, Irene, and others discussed in the next chapter), Adrian created couture fashion lines but was also among the first to mass-market a close facsimile of a film costume (a white ruffled dress worn by Joan Crawford in *Letty Lynton* in 1932); its success was a catalyst in placing American style into world competition.

Makeup and Modernity

By the beginning of the twentieth century, society at large was teeming with new excitement about cosmetic use. As Aileen Ribeiro notes in her history of western beautifications, makeup had become an "essential element of modern life" especially in urban environments, where it pervaded all classes; by 1910, the *New York World* reported "the widespread adoption of makeup in the workplace, encouraged by employers who wished staff to look vivacious and actively engaged."[54] Cinema played a large part in making cosmetic use essential as well as progressive.

But the first years were not easy. Before 1910, the wigs and makeup used on film sets were theatrical and disastrously inadequate, as film and its lights intensified detail and theater was not made for detail. Nevertheless, stage greasepaint, a heavy congealed substance, was standard in early cinema and froze actors' faces even as the material baked, cracked, or ran with sweat under the hot lights. Continuity was erratic because, until the mid-1910s, actors applied their own makeup and their image was often incongruous from scene to scene. Photographing the complexion was especially difficult as orthochromatic black-and-white film stock picked up skin tones inaccurately. White skin and its reddish hues could photograph as dark, even black; tawny or black skin and its many gradations could photograph as light. In early silent films very little was done (or was able to be done) to address this, and most actors' skin showed little to no tonal nuance. Caucasians overcompensated by wearing pink greasepaint (Stein's #2) and opaque red lipstick (which, if applied too lightly, appeared white onscreen), resulting in smudges, dark black holes for eyes, and pasty faces.

In films made by companies owned by whites (which was most film companies), African Americans, Asians, Indians, and Native Americans who appeared as their own races in minor roles were painted in uniformly dark shades. Any principal character, however, who was scripted as African American, Asian, Indian, or Native American (for example, any actor who played Uncle Tom in *Uncle Tom's Cabin*, a story often remade in early cinema) would be played by a white man who was darkened or "blacked up." Blackface, in and out of cinema, has been an American racist identifier with, at times, strange purposes to do with American identity—both individual, as in its use by performers such as Bert Williams (figure 4) and Sophie Tucker,[55] and national. As film scholar Anna Everett argues, blackface was "formidable in popularizing and reifying American politics of racial white supremacy,"[56] carried by the many one-reelers of the

FIGURE 4: Publicity photo of Bert Williams.

early 1900s made by Vitagraph, Essanay, Pathé, Lubin, Selig, and the American Mutascope and Biograph Company, which played on racism through titles like *A Nigger in the Woodpile* (1904).

Although film blackface, for extras or leads, was common, it also made the face appear rigid and unrealistic. Even African American actors often wore blackface, a practice known as "double blacking." This meant that a black cast could consist of whites and blacks in blackface as well as African American actors not in blackface. As film makeup became more sophisticated, the nonwhite complexion remained marginalized, the problems it presented in photography addressed particularly only among black filmmakers. In Oscar Micheaux's films from 1919 onward, a light-skinned black actor might wear makeup to appear even lighter, or a light-complexioned black actress, such as Fredi Washington, wear dark makeup because she photographed too "white." To further complicate these issues, there was violent intolerance toward people of different races appearing onscreen together, if in any way intimate, as was famously the case with Griffith's 1915 racist *Birth of a Nation* (Griffith insisting that black characters appearing in intimate scenes with white characters be white actors in blackface). This intolerance extended to tones of lighter and darker skin even if all the actors involved were African American.[57] There are few makeup records for race films but it makes sense that the thriving commercial cosmetic lines for African American hair and skin care, started in 1909 by Madam C. J. Walker (who made a fortune) and a few other entrepreneurs, would have been involved in the race film industry. However, it is not certain if they were ever employed or hired officially to do makeup and hair, whether for individual films or by studios.

For all the buzz in the 1910s about cosmetics, makeup, as it evolved in cinema, began with a history of gender biases. Contrary to popular belief, cosmetics have rarely played one role in society; rather, they have had a volatile history with one vogue often contradicting the next. Men's use of cosmetics has remained fairly level (either in style or out of style) but women's makeup has been subject to fickle associations—sordid, refined, whorish, wholesome, sophisticated, rural, girlish, vampish, rich, poor, tasteless, genteel, often all at the same time.

Until the late nineteenth century, the courtly face, male or female, led the fashion. The fresh, bare, seventeenth-century face became, by the eighteenth century, so artificial it was called a "grotesque beauty" of "painted porcelain."[58] At that time, the prostitute's face was plain but, by the nineteenth century, the whore was heavily made up and the "respectable" woman unadorned.[59] The latter did wear makeup but the divide was so strict that even royals had to apply their cosmetics surreptitiously.[60] However, society men, especially military sports, dyed their mustaches, sideburns, and hair, flaunted rouge, and reeked of perfume. Langtry, Bernhardt, and Deslys defied Victorian sanctions by wearing rouge, kohl, mascara, and nail polish; further, they endorsed cosmetics in advertising.[61] Their obvious use of makeup for beauty had a great effect on its reception—both hungered for and moralized against, sometimes both at once. But, with their leads, women of means openly bought cosmetics again and, during the Edwardian period (around 1900–1914), makeup became *de rigueur* for the fashionable and titled.[62]

In 1910, the cultural world was on fire with flamboyant cosmetics, led by Serge Diaghilev's Ballets Russes and its brashly colored Asian-themed décor and costumes as well as its on-the-edge choreography, music, and sets. This vogue was not easily interpreted in cinema's black-and-white palette, however, and when the Ballets Russes's principal dancer Lubov Tchernicheva's green and gold eyeshadow started a craze, cinema could not imitate it.[63] But as the close-up became a cinematic mainstay and makeup successfully adapted to the hugely magnified face, makeup became key to cinema's major break from theater's thrall. By the late 1910s, the film face, not the theater face, was the great beguiler. It would take the genius of Max Factor (1877–1938) and George Westmore (1879–1931) to achieve this, through a symbiosis of lens, stock, light, complexion, movement, detail, and distance. Both men were European immigrants and experienced wigmakers and barbers, arriving in the United States with important skills, as hair care was, as today, expensive but crucial to those seeking social status.

Factor came to Hollywood with a career formed by servitude to the Russian opera and the czarist courts. He was born Maksymilian Faktorowicz in 1877 in Lodz, Poland.[64] At nine, he apprenticed to a Lodz wigmaker/cosmetician and later to another, Antek Cierplikowski, who, after moving to France, became the groundbreaking coiffeur Antoine of Paris.[65] For four years, from age fourteen, Factor worked for Korpo, head of hair and makeup for the Imperial Russian

Grand Opera in Moscow, after which Factor served at the czarist palace. There he was, as were most palace servants, a virtual prisoner, on immediate call for courtiers and royals and barred from marrying or leaving the grounds without armed guard. He secretly married and, in 1904, he, his wife, and their three children escaped to America.

Factor's understanding of faces that wished to look beautiful, healthy, enticing, and rich, often seen in the buttery, wavering, pale light of a candlelit hall or the cold blues of a Moscow winter, would have given him some sense of cinema's special needs. He saw how the painted face and coiffed hair changed in different kinds of still and moving light, and this same interaction was in the cinematic process. He had had to make the seething underworld of court intrigue function at the only level at which the courtier could prosper or even avoid death: the level of attractiveness. The attractive courtier lived large; the dissipated one lived small or not at all. Actors faced similar crises, as did the film industry itself.

By 1908 Factor opened Max Factor's Antiseptic Hair Store ("antiseptic" was often used in advertising as people were afraid of disease) on Los Angeles's South Central Avenue, catering to theaters, at a time when film studios were building in California and leaving the East Coast and Midwest. Factor immediately recognized the important market that cinema offered as it dealt so poorly with the transition from theater to film. Theatrical recipes of Vaseline, flour, lard, cornstarch, cold cream, paprika, or ground brick dust photographed as badly as greasepaint. The wigs of "straw, mattress stuffing, excelsior, Spanish moss, wool, tobacco leaves" or "mohair stuffing from Model T Fords" and stubble beards of mucilage "dabbed with sand and tobacco flakes," as his biographer puts it, were equally lacking.[66]

Factor broke into the film business in 1910 and, in his laboratory, moved quickly to solve its many problems with multiple inventions. His own greasepaint, a thin (thus flexible) cream applied from a tube or jar (not a stick), was the first makeup made directly for cinema as it covered inherent skin color but was lightweight enough not to photograph as paste. He launched it in a screen test for Charles L. Gaskill's 1912 *Cleopatra* and then created thirty-one tints, a "color harmony" Factor later marketed as a retail cosmetic able to complement any "ensemble."[67] By 1914, Factor had made a twelve-toned face cream, subtle enough to obliterate the use of a harsh chiaroscuro method of darkening to diminish and lightening to bring forward, a theatrical trick that only made the film face lifeless.[68] The greasepaint used by comedians like Keaton, Chaplin, Harold Lloyd, Normand, Dressler, Arbuckle, and others had a comic effect of its own; but with Factor's supple cream, for the first time their expressions had intimacy while their makeup stayed resistant to slapstick's pounding (pies in the face, sweaty runs, and falls in water and dust).

Factor also created henna shampoos, liquid skin dyes, and artificial wounds. Leading from the Color Harmony line, Factor made Supreme Liquid Whitening, which purportedly "did not rub off" and was lead-free. He pioneered film wigs made from real hair, previously considered too expensive, when he fitted hundreds of hairpieces for DeMille's 1914 hit western *The Squaw Man*.[69] Also, as he had learned in Russia, he knew that a new look could mean a new job and he accommodated actors' career moves. He is credited with many other firsts, from makeup dispensers to false eyelashes to waterproof makeup. Factor's work meant that cinema's artistic viability became increasingly important. By 1917, makeup and its concomitant craft hairdressing were, like costume design, key to the industry, and makeup departments, in consultation with cinematographers, arbitrated all products and applications; actors no longer made up their own faces or did their own hair, which meant reliable continuity.

By the 1920s, the thriving and wealthy film industry was dependent on the glamorous "star face," and hopefuls and new recruits resorted to plastic surgery as well as intense makeovers, from altering hairlines to dental work, to achieve it.[70] And both inside and outside of the film industry, cosmetic empires were being built; the word *makeup* began to replace *cosmetics* in general usage when Factor promoted it (always as "make-up," with the hyphen), linking the cachet of the word's film associations to the broader beauty market. Makeup's dissemination meant it was accessible to all, a universality that the press often linked with women's rights and issues of the workplace and the vote.[71] No longer considered morally dubious, in the early 1920s makeup was considered "empowering" and, by the late 1920s, *de rigueur*: 90 percent of adult women used face powder, 83 percent used talcum, 73 percent used perfume, and 55 percent applied rouge.[72] Factor recognized the market's potential for film-associated products. Having always had a retail business, even in Russia, it was inevitable that in the 1920s he would sell his makeup commercially (Color Harmony Make-up debuted in 1927), capitalizing on and easily adapting to film and its stars the nineteenth-century convention of stage actresses endorsing products in advertising campaigns.

Panchromatic film stock was gradually replacing orthochromatic stock in the late 1920s, but, in 1927, with synchronized sound's arrival, the requirement for more quiet tungsten lights rather than loudly crackling carbon arc lamps made panchromatic the industry norm.[73] Tungsten was too hot for Factor's makeup, however, and panchromatic film made the faces appear shadowy. Factor had to invent new materials to deal with both problems and by 1929 had trademarked Panchromatic makeup, in many hues, that were all based on the brown tones that panchromatic film translated to nuanced and "natural" shades of gray. Though it has been argued that Perc Westmore created a blend of Stein Pink greasepaint and eye shadow that preceded Factor's Panchromatic makeup, for whatever reason George Westmore, the patriarch of what would become the Westmore dynasty of Hollywood makeup artists, acceded to Factor's talent. In a personal letter, he stated that for "special makeup needs" that had "perfect results in photography and reliability," he used Factor "exclusively."[74]

Creating the Star Face

Lipstick was the last cosmetic element to conquer public favor. Until about 1924 it was considered "deplorable" for use by ordinary girls and women.[75] But, in film, lipstick was an intoxicating female signifier, and screen sirens' mouths were symbols. The 1910s had bee-stung lips (the Gish sisters, Mary Pickford), the 1920s had the cupid's-bow mouth (Clara Bow, Gloria Swanson), and the 1930s had full "hunter's bow" lips (Greta Garbo, Joan Crawford). Until the late 1930s these were usually accompanied by the slender eyebrow—plucked, with slight variations, into barely more than a line of single hairs.

All these women set styles or typified the vogue of their time. But it was Greta Garbo who defined a new look with her makeup, in the view of historian Kate de Castelbajac so influential that "her look changed the idea of femininity in the twentieth century."[76] In her first feature, the hugely successful German film *The Joyless Street* (G. W. Pabst, 1925), her eyes were rimmed with a strong, simple black line and her lids shaded, but she still had the heavily darkened, bee-stung mouth of the time. By her move to and establishment in Hollywood in the late 1920s and early 1930s, her thin eyebrow's line followed the bone beneath it, accentuating her eyes' curve, and her mouth was given a natural wide form. But her eyes became the focus of her mystery when a dramatic dark line (using the newly perfected eyebrow pencil)[77] was drawn through the eye furrow (between brow and lid) (figure 5). The era of the lush Edwardian, pseudo-Eastern kohl eyes popularized by Orientalist vogues ended as much with Garbo's look as with any other fashion shift. Her makeup's arresting, precise, stark lines symbolized both the twentieth century's future and the late 1920s woman as modern, urbane, and Western and, like Garbo's image, sleekly mature.

FIGURE 5: Greta Garbo, by Ruth Harriet Louise, in *The Mysterious Lady* (1926). Costumes credited to Gilbert Clark, makeup and hair uncredited.

Marking a new era in film consciousness, Garbo's was the iconic cinematic face as cinema moved to become the modern "lively art." Garbo would define it, but cinema's part in the democratization of cosmetics meant the image was available to everyone; her use of shadow and line dissolved the old connection between the painted eye and the "fast" woman represented by Bara, Negri, Swanson, and Nazimova. Now, as a contemporary wrote, "even the nicest people" had this look.[78]

As Factor ruled makeup's consistency, George Westmore ruled its application. Westmore, an English wigmaker, founded the first (and very small) makeup department at Selig Studio in 1917 but moved to Triangle. Soon, he started another first—freelancing across the major studios, with special attention to specific stars, ultimately building his business into a Hollywood dynasty.[79] The oldest of his six sons, Mont (1902–1940), was by 1921 Valentino's sole makeup artist (the actor had been doing his own makeup and hair), modifying Valentino's heavy black eye makeup and softening and shining his hair. Westmore claimed to have invented custom makeup for Valentino to complement his Italian complexion, in itself a risk as every dark complexion was conventionally covered by a uniform white in keeping with the era's racism. However, Emily Leider states that Westmore only whitened Valentino's face and left the hands dark.[80]

Others assert that Valentino came to Factor for help, exhausted by the dull overall white he had to wear, and that Factor gave his face shading and detail, trimming his eyebrows and slicking back his hair.[81] Westmore worked with Valentino on *A Sainted Devil* (1924), *Monsieur Beaucaire* (1924), and the unfinished *The Hooded Falcon* (1924), all filmed in Paramount's New York studio, and followed him to Hollywood in 1925. In 1926 Valentino died, and Mont, with his father George, worked on DeMille's biblical epic *The King of Kings* (1927) and then went to Selznick International where he died of complications from a tonsillectomy after completing *Gone with the Wind* (1939).[82] In 1923, Perc (1904–1970), only nineteen, went to First National and established the studio's first makeup department, running it for twenty-seven years. His work was legendary. Bette Davis once said, "I owe my career to Perc Westmore."[83] Wally (1906–1973) headed Paramount's makeup from 1926 to 1967. Ern (1904–1968) was at RKO from 1929 to 1931.

George Westmore did establish methods that would become routine in the industry, partly through his sons. Although Pickford had already experimented with retail cosmetics and worked with her cameraman to see how they looked onscreen,[84] Westmore understood that makeup offered even more. Stars such as Pickford and the Talmadge sisters had to uphold mega-careers with mega-images and he started a routine of applying their makeup in their homes before work, both for their comfort and so they would always be public-ready.

The Westmores did not, however, rule MGM. In 1925, Englishman Cecil Holland (1887–1973) was appointed head of MGM's makeup department, where he stayed until the 1950s. In England, Holland had been a versatile actor known as "The Man of a Thousand Faces" before actor Lon Chaney inherited the title. In 1927, Holland wrote one of the first books on screen makeup, *The Art of Make-Up for Stage and Screen*, published in Hollywood with Chaney's introduction.[85]

In her book *The Artificial Face*, Fenja Gunn argues that, by the 1920s, the vogue of the mature woman was replaced by a desire to look young and that this occurred, in part, because in the 1920s women's "youthful faces and boyish figures . . . replaced the men who had been killed in the war."[86] In the years following World War I (1914–1918), grief and war-consciousness affected every aspect of life. War films such as *J'Accuse* (Abel Gance, 1919), *The Big Parade* (King Vidor, 1925), and *Wings* (William Wellman, 1927) were prominent releases, but audiences also rushed to the new horror films. The industry was producing some of the genre's best—*Dr. Jekyll and Mr. Hyde* (John Robinson, 1920) with John Barrymore, and *The Phantom of the Opera* (Rupert Julian, 1925) and *The Hunchback of Notre Dame* (Wallace Worsley, 1923), both with Lon Chaney, who not only acted the roles but created his own makeup.

Chaney worked with the available materials—greasepaint, putty, plasto (mortician's wax), fish skin, gutta percha (a natural resin), collodian (liquid plastic), and crepe hair. Leading the box office in the 1910s and 1920s, his makeup and prosthetic skills created so distinct a look, most notably as the Phantom and the hunchback Quasimodo for which he constructed agonizingly heavy makeup and body harnesses, that the characters' faces and figures are still recognized today (figure 6). As the Hunchback, Chaney's face was smashed in with eyes on different planes; and as the Phantom, his nose was missing, mouth gaping, teeth jagged, and eyes wide and almost lidless. He also played amputees in

FIGURE 6: Lon Chaney, above as Quasimodo in *The Hunchback of Notre Dame* (1923), below in the title role of *The Phantom of the Opera* (1925). Makeup by Lon Chaney, wigs by Zan (both uncredited).

The Penalty (Wallace Worsley, 1920) and *The Unknown* (Tod Browning, 1927).

Chaney's genius in disguising himself as a monster and his attention to clinical realism would become one of Hollywood's primary means of rendering horror and the grotesque of war's terrors and its maimed soldiers, returning home missing much of their bodies, wearing prosthetics.[87] Postwar audiences were drawn to Chaney's frightening faces (less frightening in 1923 than today). Veterans could identify with his characters' physical pain and many more could identify with their more ordinary problems of unrequited love and alienation. Through Chaney's realistic makeup and his characters' stories, the audience could absorb, more easily, their own everyday stress.

However, the extremes to which Chaney went in creating his characters were the exception, not the rule. In Hollywood's pantheon of stars, most men as well as most women were constrained by ego, the studio, or fans to always "look good" and they were loath to let go of what worked. Makeup and hairdressing, as much as costume design, were key to an actor's appeal in a film and sometimes off the screen as well. It worked both ways—subtle or limited makeup could sustain a career as much as Chaney's comparative excesses did. In 1925, King Vidor, director of the World War I film *The Big Parade*, insisted that the lead, John Gilbert, use "no make up and wear an ill-fitting uniform"; at first Gilbert refused but, once he tried it, loved what it did for the character and "never used make-up again."[88]

Parsing Hair in Early Cinema

Hairstyles and their meanings also underwent profound changes across cinema's first two decades. Mary Pickford's corkscrew curls, for which George Westmore was apparently responsible, became among the most familiar in the world until the advent of child star Shirley Temple's perfectly formed ringlets in the 1930s. Having been an actor for David Belasco in 1907 (at fifteen), Pickford, as an adult, remained famous for her "girl" roles and her real success began at Biograph in 1909, where she became known as "the girl with the golden curls" (figure 7).[89] Hairpieces were common and much advertised, and Westmore capitalized on this. Instead of arduously coiffing her hair daily, he attached the curls as pieces, and this method became an industry staple.[90]

Pickford's curls were deliberately girlish, to suit the character she played as "America's Sweetheart," but her audience would have seen the style in a context that is impossible for today's audience to grasp. Women's curls had been popular since the Restoration's hairstyle "*à la Ninon*" (named for the celebrated courtesan, Ninon de Lenclos), and there were many versions over the subsequent centuries.[91] But it is the nineteenth-century favorite, the "Alexandra curls," a French style of the Second Empire (1852–1870)—a period considered the courtesan's "golden age"—that has bearing on Pickford's look.[92] These long,

FIGURE 7: Mary Pickford and her trademark curls.

silky, tightly rolled neck curls, associated with the era's courtesans, had some resemblance to Pickford's hairstyle.[93] Jeanine Basinger, in her book *Silent Stars*, notes that Pickford's screen identity was not really that of a put-upon child but instead a resourceful "clever minx who solved problems"; and as an actor with sharp timing in comedy and melodrama, she became the industry's highest paid star and ran her own career, providing a "fairly astonishing role model for women, a modern woman before such a concept was fully understood."[94] The smart, beautiful, self-sufficient woman who triumphs has echoes of the not-so-distant courtesan and her even closer stage icon. Pickford's audience would have viewed her through, and had experience with, a variety of these connotations—fashionable/unfashionable, girlish/womanly, chaste/sexual.

Because actors were not perceived as being "made up" to the same degree as actresses, men relied on their hair almost more than stars like Pickford did. Matinee idols and *hommes fatales*, such as Valentino, usually had hairstyles that rarely varied and were their trademarks. Cinema men built their looks on the past meanings of hair as the innumerable styles of haircut, sideburn, and mustache were full of connotations, which the public recognized.[95] The suggestively upturned mustache of the military dandy found its way to the silhouette of cinema's venal landlord. The clown with distinctive wig was as old as recorded theater and a burlesque and vaudeville must for many comedians. Comics often had telling hair: Chaplin's was rumpled, Harold Lloyd's slicked, Stan Laurel's tufted, and Marie Dressler's lank and stringy. These hairstyles would give the audience an unconscious sense of superiority, empathy, and camaraderie. Hair, and problems with it, was something everyone had.

Mack Sennett often emphasized that comedy's success was based in the messy "fall of dignity," as all people are alike in such a class obliterator.[96] An example of this, showing hair's immense clout, can be seen in a Max Linder one-reeler where Linder, the internationally famous French comedian who set the bar for male cachet and skillful timing, used his hair to great effect. *Le Baromètre de la fidélité* (*The Barometer of Faithfulness*, Georges Monca, 1909) is a six-minute comedy about a barometer, able to measure marital fidelity, that suddenly registers an alarmingly high level and panics both philandering wife (Jeanne Marnac) and philandering husband (Linder). This terrifies Linder, and his combed back, voguishly styled hair suddenly stands on end and breaks into three parts in his shock.

More than the silliness of the story and brilliance of the actors, the hair—so weird a look on impeccable man-about-town Linder, smug in his tails, top hat, and spats and safe in his bourgeois household and its bourgeois routines (which include afternoon dalliances)—is not only hilarious but creates a subtext about what is beneath the appearances of the respectable world. The hair tells us that Linder is just like anyone else, poor or rich. His slick life comes apart just as his hair does and his appearance of the have-it-all dandy vanishes. He is like anyone in the street whose disheveled hair, if only because he cannot afford a good pomade, betrays the situation in which he has to live.

The improvement of hair dye also brought about a significant shift in attitudes. Not common in the west, hair dye was popularized, for men and women, in the 1870s by opera singer Adelina Patti. Peroxide, which lightened hair, was also in use by men and women but dye's downside—that it didn't always leave a beautiful result—gave it a bad reputation. By the early 1900s French chemist Eugène Schueller developed a reliable synthetic dye, naming it Aureole, which was shortened to L'Oréal in 1910, forming the base of the giant cosmetics firm.[97] Bright blonde, as a color, photographed badly and needed special filters with orthochromatic stock; so it was not until the arrival of the more light-sensitive panchromatic that the blonde bombshell, exemplified later by Mae West, Jean Harlow, Betty Grable, and Marilyn Monroe and one of cinema's most exuberant stock characters, was truly born.[98]

As lip shapes had done, then, hairstyles also marked decades, often symbolizing not just the industry's but that period's social change. The silver screen's long-haired, virginally seductive beauty or man-eating vamp emerged from nineteenth-century models like the tragic Delacroix odalisque and the Symbolist siren. Theater had embraced both, as did cinema, and the seductress, adorned with cascading hair, was a long-lived craze. Often Orientalized as Cleopatra, Salome, the Queen of Sheba, and the like, she was played over and over—by Lillie Langtry in 1883, Ida Rubenstein in the Ballets Russes in 1910, and movie star Betty Blythe in 1920 (her hair piled up), to name only a few.

One of her most famous incarnations was Theda Bara in the early 1910s, who appeared many times as the seducer, with blackened eyes and four-foot-long hair. Bara was costumed often, in nearly nude bejeweled fabrics (at a thousand dollars a yard), by George James Hopkins, who also created suitably extreme production designs, setting a style that became a mark of cinema.[99] The late 1910s saw a shift in the vogue when feminists protested this bizarre "ideal woman." She was replaced in the 1920s by DeMille's smart, urbane woman, as played by Swanson, Negri, and Daniels, who wore shortened cuts of the sort popularized by ballroom dancer Irene Castle in 1915 and based on the Marcel technique. Swanson's shingle cut in *Manhandled* (1924) was much discussed in the press.[100] But it was the iconic "flapper bob" that outdid all others.

Styling the Flapper

The flapper rage was not long, 1923 to 1928, but Colleen Moore, Louise Brooks, and Clara Bow, flapper superstars, were young women in shimmying sheath dresses, with stockings rolled and thighs exposed and, in Bow's and Brooks's cases, representing a nation of girls drinking, driving, and having sex. With the flapper came "The Look," which mostly focused on hair. Moore was, in 1926 and 1927, at First National and the "number one box star attraction in America," outdoing Pickford and Chaplin.[101] Her signature was a Dutch-boy bob, which Moore claimed her mother cut, though it is likely that Perc Westmore, head of First National's makeup department by 1926, did or at least perfected it.

Bow, sexy and fun-loving with a shingled, often wildly disarrayed cut, played the more quintessential flapper roles; but few embodied its look as Brooks did, whose straight, severe yet louche bob was so sleek and whose sex appeal was so strong that they still feel contemporary. Barry Paris, Brooks's biographer, describes her hair as defining her "like the hood of an ornament of a car."[102] Many took credit for the cut—most notably Brooks herself, Perc Westmore, Walter Wanger, and Travis Banton.[103] Antoine of Paris (who taught Factor about hair) pronounced on

FIGURE 8: Louise Brooks and her iconic bobbed hair and cupid's-bow mouth.

the hairstyle's *pas raffinment* (unrefined) Americanism, which also reflected how Brooks's look became both an era's icon and a national one; according to Barry Paris, Brooks's "powerful *American* essence" ensured the hairstyle's impact and also made her an American original (figure 8).[104]

The clever, sexual, active woman's "glossy bob" haircut—best represented by Brooks—was arguably the first haircut for women perfected for and by cinema, viewed and discussed in the press as an emblematic break from the socially constructed role of women in the past and their symbolic long hair. Though women who fought hard for access to contraception, unions, votes, wages, and equality all had flowing long hair (pinned into a bun), the flapper bob was, and still is, always linked to women's suffrage and the right to vote (legalized in 1920) and all that went with it. The sensual, buxom, boudoir-loving Edwardian fatale was now the slender, bluntly sexual, hard-drinking 1920s flapper.

The zenith of the flapper image also helped move cinema into a new position in the arts. Zelda Fitzgerald, a flapper among literary modernists, was a power player from theater and literature who, although involved in cinema through her novelist-turned-screenwriter husband, was ambivalent about cinema flappers. But historian Judith Mackrell argues that although Zelda disliked their "uniformly scarlet lipstick and glossy bobs, . . . their manufactured sass and smart opinions," she could see they were "in control of their destinies." (Zelda also wrote that she felt "very stupid" next to their "very clever" talents.)[105]

This shift in the representation of women's agency was potently visualized in Nazimova's 1922 *Salomé*, where Salome's mother, Herodias (Rose Dione), drips with long dark frizzy hair while Salome (Nazimova) wears a bobbed platinum wig (then in vogue as the height of sophistication).[106] Herodias's heavy weight, gaudy rings, and early silent film costume of burdensome leopard skins are set against Nazimova's lithe, gymnast's body clothed in Rambova's ground-breaking clinging rubber tunic. Nazimova made her Salome (a role typically rendered as coldly cruel) into a young woman troubled, defiant, curious, questioning, and risk-taking as well as spoiled. Her shining short hair subliminally offered the audience a rapport with this character as a modern woman, struggling and in the mode.

Thus, while the American film industry and its costumes, makeup, and hairdressing evolved out of the nineteenth century's theatrical spectacles of attraction, they also evolved from another source: the attraction of everyday life. The familiar body, its accoutrements and its clothes, gave the silent era a foundation upon which to create a new form that was neither a stage nor a light show. Costume, makeup, and hair, disseminated through film into increasingly urban ordinary lives, were, in part, responsible for modernizing cinema itself. Created by immigrants as a business of bourgeois entertainment, film became a novel art form despite, or perhaps because of, its initially poor production values when compared to the urbane, spectacular, and sophisticated live theater available, even in the hinterlands, in the early years of the century. Cinema's power was that it both attracted and was attractive to top quality, and thus could hire people who either deigned to work in the new industry in spite of the high positions they had already achieved in other venues, or were novices eager to show they could match the exceptional talent they saw in the theater and other arts.

In short, cinema's costume, makeup, and hairstyling helped the industry, arguably more than live theater, to represent and concretely visualize many of the nation's social problems. The film industry, run within a new and "unformed" society, was a micro version of the larger struggle of the United States to find its way in what Emily Burbank, back in 1917, had described as a "new and composite social structure [that] lacks traditions."[107] These three arts became places where complex and quintessentially American questions about authority and identity could be submerged or subverted, such as racial hatred; or confronted, such as war trauma or the rise of women's rights. In this way, the country's international identity, in part, began to emerge, through cinema's ingenious and swift productions, as both classical and, above all, modern.

2

CLASSICAL HOLLYWOOD, 1928-1946 Mary Desjardins

Scholars broadly understand the classical studio period of American film as *classical* in at least two senses. First, the films produced during this era follow classical principles of storytelling: plots of clarity and continuity based on goal-oriented and more or less well-rounded characters. Second, this period represents the mature phase in the film industry's status as an oligarchy with an efficient and predictable system of mass production, distribution, and exhibition that resulted in economic profits for management and (relative) work stability for labor. An examination of the relations among practices of costuming, hairstyling, and makeup and their coordination with other filmmaking processes, the textual evidence of these practices in the completed film, and the discourses that publicized the labor and material effects of these practices to the filmgoing public help us to understand the powers and interrelated facets of this system.

As in the silent era, costume designers, hairstylists, and makeup artists worked with producers, directors, cinematographers, set decorators, art directors, and actors, and sometimes with color process experts (the first Technicolor feature, *Vogues of 1938*, was released in 1937), to ensure that films were successful at the textual level—specifically, that audiences would not only comprehend but sustain emotional investment in storylines and characters as well as in visual spectacle. In reality, work relations among individuals and departments representing the aforementioned production labor categories were often characterized by conflict as much as by cooperation. Failures in communication, deadline stresses, competing demands, differences in interpretation, and tensions within labor or professional hierarchies, or between management and labor, all characterized the conditions in which costume, makeup, and hair design contributed to a film as a finished product. Furthermore, costume, makeup, and hair—like performance, direction, cinematography, editing, and other creative shapings of Hollywood and its products—could contribute to narrative and ideological contradictions, or even incoherencies, as well as support the clarity and continuity that characterize what is known as the "classical text."

However, the conventions governing the productions of film texts and publicity campaigns emerged from, and helped to construct, mutually reinforcing beliefs about audiences and films—most significantly, the beliefs that "going to the movies" was one of the most meaningful cultural experiences of the American public, and that the industry enabled long-term affective investments in films, particularly in film stars, through the coordination of labor in mass production. Studio publicity departments depended on the labors of the departments most associated with any star's iconic status to ensure that audience members would become fans. For this reason, costume designers, makeup artists, and hair stylists achieved prominent positions in classical-era film publicity, especially in fan magazines, in which the names and images of Adrian or Travis Banton or Edith Head or Irene (costume designers), the Westmore brothers or Jack Dawn (hair stylists and makeup artists), and Max Factor (makeup artist and cosmetics developer) were more frequently invoked than those of directors and producers. Both fan magazines and internal studio memos suggest that these creative talents had, like the stars they designed for, affective relations to their work and its contribution to film pleasure for viewers and to success for the industry.

Three large categories are relevant to the era: the role of costume, makeup, and hair in production and preproduction practices, in the textual meanings of films, and in film publicity and promotion campaigns. Each of these categories reveals the affective investments of studio workers in production processes, which, like investments that audiences make in films they watch, have to be understood in relation to struggles and contradictions within social and cultural contexts. The experiences, meanings, and goals of creative labor and product are often fragmentary, partial, unstable, and exploitative as well as shared, and the practices of, and images produced by, costume, makeup, and hair reflect and constitute a contested and polysemous interpretive field for historians and theorists of today, as they did for workers and audiences of the original period of a film's production.

"9:45 and Am Still Waiting for Costumes"

Cecil B. DeMille fired off a memo with words of annoyance ("9:45 and am still waiting") over the delay of costumes arriving from Paramount's wardrobe department to the set of his 1935 production *The Crusades*. It was one of three terse memos about wardrobe, makeup, and hair that he composed to Fred Leahy, assistant manager of production at Paramount studios, within a sixty-five-minute period on the morning of February 15, 1935. The content of the first memo is structured by a timeline listing what happened on the set during each of the three fifteen-minute increments between 9:15 and 9:45. At 9:15, a half-hour before expressing his exasperation at missing costumes (clarified in the morning's third memo at 10:50 to be costumes for four drummers), DeMille claims that he has been "spending the morning costuming the people, illustrating the manner in which Arab women wear veils. They are all hung on them in a haphazard manner. . . . On asking for jewelry for men and women, I am informed by the wardrobe that we have South Sea Island stuff only."[1]

Leahy's written response, if there was one, is missing from the extant Paramount production files, but DeMille had been exchanging memos about the film with a number of Paramount and DeMille Productions personnel since the fall of 1934. The tone of the missives had quickly become demanding after shooting began in January 1935, as the labor and management of two co-producing companies (Paramount and DeMille Productions) dealt with the complications of an expensive period film using hundreds of extras as well as multiple featured players. Frank Richardson, the head of Paramount's wardrobe department, had responded on February 2 to DeMille's earlier complaints about wardrobe and wigs with a reminder that the director's late evening call for additional extras had caused delays in the department's preparation of appropriate items for the next day's shooting. Furthermore, Richardson scolds,

> The men's wardrobe staff of nine men worked until Tuesday 4:00 AM, Wednesday 2:00 AM, Thursday 3:00 AM, Friday all night and returned each morning at 6:30 AM. All available dress-makers of about 100 have worked two solid nights. [Extra free-lance] makeup people and hairdressers are not available because of the rush at other studios. There are eight other companies shooting on the lot. Coupling this with our NRA [National Recovery Administration] regulations [concerning maximum work hours and compensation for overtime], it is a great injustice to criticize the present results. Calls must come in earlier or there is going to be a bad holdup for one of your sets.[2]

These memos concerning costume design and on-set wardrobe and makeup practices point to several key characteristics of studio production in general and DeMille productions in particular. First, during a film's production, time is money as far as management is concerned—that is, studio processes need to follow sequences that make efficient use of time and work before and within an actual shooting schedule. Second, studio labor divisions and hierarchies—as well as federally legislated regulations—mandate that particular departments are responsible for specific on- and off-set activities and when and how long these take place. Third, department responsibilities and processes (such as preparing wigs or costumes) of the wardrobe and makeup and hair departments must be coordinated with other studio departments (such as the studio casting office and Central Casting) and with individuals (directors, production managers, actors) responsible for getting images on film. Fourth, costume, makeup, and hair contribute to the goal of historical and cultural accuracy in period films; interpretations of historical and cultural accuracy, as well as aesthetic effect, can be sources of conflict among creative and other production labor on and off the set. And finally, director-producers of a film have more creative and decision-making power than other studio labor, but behind every demand for particular aesthetic and material effects there are perhaps hundreds of workers laboring to the brink of human endurance within working conditions over which they have little control. Much was at stake for DeMille and Paramount—this was an expensive film, employing 1,500 people, 800 horses, and, just in terms of wardrobe and hair materials, 18,000 yards of cloth, 2,500 pounds of crepe hair for beards, and several thousand wigs.[3]

More will be said later about what DeMille's production practices, aesthetic and ideological ideals, and memos can tell us about the role of costume, makeup, and hair in the history of this period of filmmaking. However, since these memos allude to or illustrate a number of principles about how those roles and departments were supposed to work in the course of a film's preproduction and production, it is useful to first enumerate what were considered the ideal sequence of events in which plans for costumes, makeup, and hairstyles went from design and planning in preproduction to their realization on-set during production. During the preproduction phase of a film, the head of every production department would receive a script from the film's producer or the studio production manager. They would then base the processes, materials, and work flows of their departments on a breakdown of the script—that is, dividing the script into increments based on how many scenes, locations, performers, etc. would be used during production. The picture had already been given a budget and each production area head had to estimate one for their area within that figure. Area budgets needed the approval of the producer and others higher up in the studio hierarchy before firm decisions about materials and work assignments were made.

Costume designers usually worked at least nominally under the head of the wardrobe department.[4] While heads of wardrobe officially assigned designers to pictures, powerful designers with supervisory responsibilities, such as MGM's Adrian, were usually considered de facto designers for the top female stars. Makeup and hair stylists also worked under a department head who, during pre-production, consulted with other department heads as they planned according to their script breakdown what kind and color of hair dyes, wigs, cosmetics, and other accoutrements would be needed to coordinate with costumes, settings, casting, film stock (Max Factor's Panchromatic makeup for black-and-white film was made up of shades of brown that created "natural" skin tones photograph-ically, but was not suitable for Technicolor; for that Factor developed Pan-Cake makeup, which became a successful consumer product as well), and probable lighting choices, as well as how many stylists would be needed in the department and on set during the actual shooting.

While the makeup and hair department would engage in research, ordering of materials, and experimentation during preproduction, its busiest work period was during the actual shooting of the film. The wardrobe department, however, was divided into separate work functions—manufacturing (involved most heav-ily in the preproduction phase or at the start of production) and finished wardrobe (involved most heavily at the end of preproduction and during production)—and had to manage work-flow issues for long periods of time, across many special-ized categories of expertise (figure 9). The studios' mod-ern business efficiencies mandated time- and money-saving strategies which would work by ensuring that many work functions of individ-ual departments could take place simultaneously rather than sequentially. The major studios spent time and money training performing talent through diction and movement lessons, as well as grooming it through such practices as enforced diets and exercise, often delaying casting decisions concerning a performer until he or she was "ready." However, time and money could be saved in future productions by coordinating many of these

FIGURE 9: A fitter in MGM's costume department works on a dress, designed by Adrian, for Jean Harlow in *The Girl from Missouri* (1934).

grooming tasks with the wardrobe and makeup and hair departments in advance of any specific casting decisions.

For example, a dressmaker's dummy would be made according to the measurements of actors as they were first put under contract. As in the silent era, male performers were often expected to supply their own clothes for films with contemporary settings, and while costumes were frequently designed for them for period or specialty films, local costume houses, such as Western Costume in Hollywood, might also serve as resources for generic cowboy or military garb. The processes involving the dress dummy were especially important for female acting talent, as actresses cast in leading or supporting roles had most of their costumes designed by in-house or contracted freelance designers. The dummies served as "stand-ins" during some of the costume manufacturing processes of a film, especially after approved costume sketches had been handed over to pattern cutters. To free up an actress from every time-consuming fitting so she could be available for other labor, patterns were fit on her stand-in dummy, and after any readjustments were then cut in muslin, fit on the dummy again, and then fit (by "fitters," or "drapers," not "cutters") on the actress to pick up any discrepancy between her human form and the dress form before the pattern was cut in the fabrics specified by the designer and then actually put together by "finishers."

Wigs, made from human hair imported mainly from Europe (the United States forbade domestic sales of human hair), could be ordered (often from makeup developer and wigmaker Max Factor) or custom-made by wig artists in-house and repurposed for multiple uses in a single or many films. "Hair lace," the small hairpieces that would be placed on the front parts of the head to frame the face, had to be especially realistic because of the importance of facial close-ups in studio-produced film narratives. While sections of hair were crocheted (known as "ventilating") into the gauze base of the rest of the wig, individual hairs were ventilated into the more delicate and flexible netting of the hair lace. This, together with the wig, would rest until in use on top of a plaster or wooden bust made according to the head measurements of lead performers. Like the kind of bead and embroidery work done by specialists in costume manufacturing, wigmaking was a time-consuming, physically demanding job, and it is not surprising that the Westmore brothers were documented as working fourteen-hour days six days a week as they supervised wigmaking (done mostly by women) as well as makeup design and application.

In wardrobe, the designers' sketches and script breakdown were central guides in manufacturing and finishing costumes, although the "key costumer" had his or her own script breakdown to keep track of which costumes had to be on the set at particular times and what needed to cleaned or altered for the next day's shooting. In makeup and hairdressing, lead artists would designate their plans for makeup color, type, and application and hair style and color using illustrated forms that detailed where and how certain cosmetics or hair parts were to

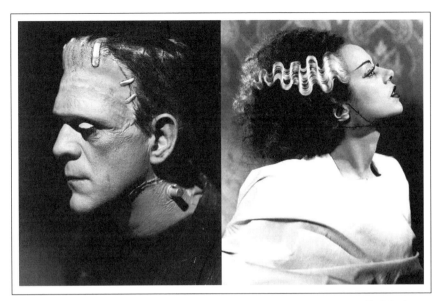

FIGURE 10: Boris Karloff in *Frankenstein* (1931), uncredited makeup by Jack Pierce, and Elsa Lanchester in *The Bride of Frankenstein* (1935), costume design by Vera West, makeup by Pierce and Otto Lederer, and hair by Irma Kusely (all uncredited).

be applied or manipulated on actors' faces and heads. Character makeup and hair were the most time-consuming to apply, especially when the goal was complete transformation as occurred with Jack Pierce's creation of Frankenstein's monster (as well as Frankenstein's bride) at Universal in 1931 and 1935 (figure 10). It took hours each day for Pierce to transform Boris Karloff into the now-iconic creation, and the combination of multiple appliances as well as heavy costuming were agony for the actor to wear.[5] Because Mary Shelley's novel does not contain a detailed physical description of the monster, Pierce could give his imagination free rein.

Other kinds of character makeup turned white people into different ethnicities or races, or into well-known historical figures. For example, Jack Dawn (lead makeup artist and sometime hairstyle designer at MGM in the 1930s) and his assistant William Tuttle chose appropriate hairstyles for the actors cast as characters in *The Good Earth* (Sidney Franklin, 1937) based on photo booklets depicting hundreds of hairstyles worn by Chinese people of different ages and classes that were provided to them by department researchers. Next to photos of the selected hairstyles for the story's characters, Dawn and Tuttle sketched detailed instructions about how wigs needed to be combed, parted, and pinned to approximate the particular image.[6]

Similarly, makeup forms illustrating actors' faces designated where and what type and color of cosmetics makeup artists needed to apply on the actors for each scene of the film. Tuttle marked up a chart and illustrated template detailing the face of Robert Morley, who played King Louis XVI in *Marie Antoinette*

(W. S. Van Dyke, 1938), one for each of the various sequences in which his character appeared in the film—for example, one form illustrated with a template
of his face was marked with pencil shadings and a numbered list of cosmetics
to guide the makeup and hair stylists in scenes depicting the king's early married life with Marie Antoinette; another form was created for scenes depicting
how stress registered on the character's face at the beginning of the Revolution; and yet another was needed for the scenes showing him in prison. Details
included those concerning the eyebrows, wig, and cheeks of the character, as
well as instructions on how to apply makeup to shade and shape Morley's face
into what was needed to convey the king's character arc across the temporal
unfolding of the story.

The contribution of the wardrobe, makeup, and hairdressing departments to
a film's visual design and storytelling emerged out of the rationalized business
and labor procedures outlined above. However, given the contingencies of the
human body, the variety of involved personalities (with their differences in taste,
positioning in power hierarchies, temperaments, senses of professionalism, etc.),
and the social conflicts and contradictions that emerge out of systems of capitalist labor practices and production, it is not surprising that full rationalization
of the decision making and creative labor involving costume, makeup, and hair
encountered resistances. Indeed, James Cagney, frustrated with Warner Bros.'
typecasting of him as a gangster, decided to take makeup and hair into his own
hands and "really give them a mug."[7] He reported to the first day of shooting
Jimmy the Gent (1934) with a "convict look": a shaved head, complete with scars.
The production shot around Cagney until his look could be remedied to producer
Hal Wallis's satisfaction. Claudette Colbert delayed the shooting of DeMille's
Cleopatra (1934) because she had a disagreement with designer Travis Banton
over costumes. Once she finally approved the costumes, her tardiness at costume
fittings resulted in further production delays and budget overruns.

Buddy Ebsen, who was originally slated to play the part of the Tin Man in The
Wizard of Oz (1939), was severely allergic to the blend of makeup for his character
and a new actor (Jack Haley) had to be cast so that production could continue.
Bette Davis fought director William Wyler over the makeup concoction (a calci-
mine-zinc oxide combination) she designed with makeup artist Perc Westmore
for her character of Regina in The Little Foxes (1941). Ginger Rogers was unable
to dance in the original glass-beaded, fur-trimmed costume made for her character in Lady in the Dark (Mitchell Leisen, 1944) because it was too heavy for her
athletic but trim body. A copy of the gown had to be made for the dance segment
using lightweight sequins.

Most of these "resistances" to the rationalization of production were not even
evident in finished films—for example, Banton's designs for Colbert, and her
way of wearing them, were spectacular, and contributed greatly to the success of
Cleopatra—but they suggest that film costume, makeup, and hair practices were

sites in which the human body became vulnerable to the demands of labor management and creative decisions; in which tensions among laborers and between labor and management could be performed; and in which affective investments were expressed by workers in creative and professional activity. Bette Davis had professional and artistic stakes in making choices she thought were best for the character she was playing. Costume, makeup, and hair were crucial elements in her constructions of characters, and she found an ally in Perc Westmore, head of the Warner Bros. makeup and hairdressing department and its lead artist. He had helped her to enact her interpretation of an older Queen Elizabeth I in *The Private Lives of Elizabeth and Essex* in 1939, in which her forehead and eyebrows were shaved (color plate 3), and he helped her again with the characterizations of Regina in *The Little Foxes* (1941) and Fanny Skeffington in *Mr. Skeffington* (1944).

The Davis-Westmore team came up with the idea of the ultra-white, mask-

like face to suggest that both Regina and Fanny dealt in deception—Regina deceiving others (about business, inheritance, and family) and Fanny deceiving herself (about beauty, age, love, and money). Westmore created Regina's look cosmetically with liquids and powders; he designed Fanny's look mainly through cosmetics, but for the last scenes of the film, when the character is ravaged by illness and age, he created a latex mask that conveyed the sagging cheeks and neck of an older woman, alarming director Vincent Sherman with its "hideousness" and irritating Davis's skin (which caused at least minor delays in production), even as she relished its contribution to the film's visual look and to the emotional impact of her performance.[8] Davis had to submit to twenty-four steps of makeup, mask, and wig

FIGURE 11: Bette Davis in two versions of old-age makeup and hair in *Mr. Skeffington* (1944), costume design (gowns) by Orry-Kelly, makeup by Perc Westmore, hair (uncredited) by Margaret Donovan.

application for these *Skeffington* scenes. The process started with her upper eyelids stretched and kept in place with application of full-strength latex, and her lower eyelids, nose, upper lip, and jaw line then covered by various strengths of latex, continuing with powder and makeup pencil applied to eyelids, nose, and cheeks, liquid and powder rouges applied to cheeks and lips, and ending with head and hair wrapped for proper placement of the wig (figure 11).[9]

Paul Muni, Davis's colleague and sometimes co-star at Warner Bros., also invested much of his professional identity as an actor in a style heavily indebted to character inhabitation through costume, makeup, and hair design.[10] Like Davis, he was willing to undergo hours in both the makeup planning stage (for example, having plaster molds made of his head) and in the daily makeup before shooting (for example, for *The Story of Louis Pasteur* [1936], which meant three to four hours each day of makeup artists using makeup pencil to provide shades and highlights to make Muni's face look broader, shaving to raise his hairline by two inches, applying liquid makeup to create fake skin suggesting wrinkles and lines for the upper part of his face, and using spirit gum to add a beard and sideburns).[11] Warner Bros. production head Jack Warner is reputed to have exclaimed, in reaction to the commitment of Muni to character building via makeup and hair alteration, "We're paying Muni all this dough and we can't even recognize him [onscreen]!"[12]

The Warner studio was a hotbed of actor discontent about working conditions and control over creative decisions, which may have intensified some of its acting talent to so avidly invest in artistic craft to satisfy their affective relations to their profession. It is telling that Muni thanked only Perc Westmore, who also designed the makeup for Muni's roles in *The Life of Emile Zola* (1937) and *Juarez* (1939), when he accepted his Best Actor Oscar for playing the role of Louis Pasteur: "I looked in the mirror and didn't see myself. I saw Louis Pasteur. . . . I did the lines, but was no longer Paul Muni. I was Pasteur. Perc Westmore deserves as much credit as I for this award."[13]

For female stars, especially, the costume design and fitting processes also became arenas in which to gain professional and emotional satisfactions, forge relationships to other creative individuals, and at times express anxieties about their status at the studio and their feelings about their bodies as these related to performance and image—all of which could affect film production and work assignments. Barbara Stanwyck, already a major star by the time she was cast in *The Lady Eve* (Preston Sturges, 1941) at Paramount, was given so much self-confidence by Edith Head's costume designs for the film that she requested the designer for films from that point on (consequently, Head was frequently loaned to other studios, as Stanwyck freelanced). Head had already solved the actress's figure "flaws" (a long waist and low rear-end) in her designs for earlier Stanwyck films, but it was her simple and sophisticated clothes for *The Lady Eve*, subtly referencing the current Latin American style, that advanced Stanwyck to the ranks of best-dressed Hollywood stars while suiting the film character's lively sense of humor, athletic movements, and wily motives.

Clothing's enveloping forms give them a spatial proximity to the outer form of the wearer—and thus to her inner subjectivity. Mary Astor, a veteran of many roles, films, and studios, recalls in her memoir how much her "feminine pleasure in clothes was completely satisfied" in MGM designer Irene's fitting room. Before taking over from Adrian as lead costume designer at MGM in 1942, Irene (a.k.a. Irene Lentz Gibbons) had been couturière at the Bullock's Wilshire department store. Many female stars patronized her services there for their personal wardrobes, which led studios to occasionally hire her to design costumes. Astor sums up the appeal of Irene's costumes and how they could inspire, through their fit, detail, and sensuousness, creative performances on film: "She paid special attention to shoulder and neckline detail, so it wouldn't detract from the face in close-ups, and still have an interesting line that would compose well. Her evening clothes had great movement, material that would flow around the thighs, revealing and relaxing; she paid attention to accessories . . . just the right pin or a clasp for a bag, earrings that would shape the face and not waggle and detract from the face."[14]

Astor's evocation of the comfort and ease of Irene's costumes underscores

FIGURE 12: Paramount costume designer Travis Banton confers on a costume design with Marlene Dietrich.

how much actresses valued not only clothes that flattered, but ones that enabled relaxed fittings behind the scenes and performances onscreen. Actually, fittings could go on for hours, well into the evening after a day's shooting had ended (additionally, actresses were often required to fit for costumes for their next film while still shooting another). Uncomfortable foundation garments not only had to be worn under costumes during shooting but in these fittings as well. While Marlene Dietrich had a reputation for expecting control over her image, she was admired by Travis Banton not only for her sense of style and her beautiful embodiment of his designs, but because she had the willingness, the energy, and the discipline to withstand long and complicated fittings even if, as Edith Head (Banton's assistant at the time) claimed, it took thirty-six hours to get details on one costume just right (figure 12).[15]

Colbert, like Dietrich, believed protection of her star image relied on control over behind-the-scenes production processes as much as over acting craft and publicity campaigns, and eventually contractually stipulated specific conditions for being made-up and photographed. Extremely knowledgeable about fashion (she had once studied fashion design) and yet insecure about her own looks, Colbert battled Banton before he became the only in-house designer at the studio she trusted to create clothes she considered flattering. Nevertheless, she sometimes resisted costume fittings and thereby delayed shooting. Adele Balkan, a Paramount sketch artist under the supervision of Banton and Head, recalls that the actress was distrustful of other Paramount designers and costume employees—she witnessed Colbert become furious upon learning that sketch artists, rather than Banton, were rendering detailed images of her costumes for *Cleopatra*, although this kind of practice was standard at all studios at the time.[16] No doubt this was what at least partially motivated Colbert's refusal of the first set of costumes for the film, which cost the production thousands of dollars in delays.[17] If the star was profitable enough, studios tolerated such tantrums and looked the other way when some pulled rank on employees lower in the power hierarchy. For example, Paramount was willing to spend more money to bring in Irene to design Colbert's costumes for *Midnight* (1939) than they would have spent using their own Edith Head because the popular actress refused to work with the latter (this was after Banton's contract was not renewed in 1938).[18]

Although anecdotes about behind-the-scenes behaviors, especially bad behaviors in wardrobe and makeup, may be dismissed as merely idiosyncratic, sexist, exaggerated, or even apocryphal, they should be taken seriously as symptoms or evidence of the material realities of labor conditions in the studio system. From the studios' point of view, activist labor unrest, particularly strikes, were the greatest threats to a smooth rationalization of business. When non-contract employees of makeup and hair departments (that is, all workers in those areas, excluding head designers and supervisors and other contracted house employees) went on strike in April 1937 under the umbrella of the Federation of Motion Picture Crafts (FMPC), thirty-three films were in production throughout Hollywood and studios worried about meeting planned release dates promised to exhibitors. Newspapers reported Barbara Stanwyck applying her own makeup on the set of *Stella Dallas*, in production at the Goldwyn Studio (which relied entirely on non-contract makeup artists), and described the models for Walter Wanger's Technicolor *Vogues of 1938* struggling with makeup typically applied by experts who understood the new Technicolor process. The Westmore brothers' Sunset Boulevard beauty salon, the House of Westmore, was vandalized, a sign of their position as symbols of the power hierarchies and wage disparities among studio employees (strikers claimed that studio or competing union "goons" were trying to frame them for the violence).[19]

The Studio Basic Agreement of 1926 had established open-shop policies and recognized five key unions for collective bargaining. The Brotherhood of Painters, which included makeup artists, had withdrawn from the agreement in 1932 and by 1937 had formed a coalition with other local studio labor groups, including hair stylists, as the Federated Motion Picture Crafts union. Both studio producers and IATSE (International Association of Theatrical Stage Employees), the largest and most powerful of the unions recognized by the agreement, were threatened by this autonomous coalition of local laborers, and worked to break the strike by immediately bargaining with unions or guilds potentially supportive of the FMPC, such as the Motion Picture Costumers union and the Screen Actors Guild, and by dividing the members of the crafts coalition itself. Ultimately, the individual member groups struck individual wage and work-hour deals with the studios, which effectively dissolved the coalition (eventually absorbed by IATSE).[20]

The memos flying between DeMille and Paramount's wardrobe department during the production of *The Crusades* in 1935 should suggest some of the reasons costume, makeup, and hair workers sought better wages and working conditions through collective bargaining. Even though the industry was at that time following labor practices established by the National Industrial Recovery Act (ruled unconstitutional later in 1935), with its goal of increasing employment and supporting collective bargaining, low pay and outrageous work hours were still typical in studio productions. The DeMille memos, which implicitly demanded that costume, makeup, and hairdressing laborers do whatever necessary (including work hours beyond NRA stipulations) to satisfy the director, also expose how he ignored crafts departments' own labor divisions based on skill hierarchies, divisions that eventually would be mandated by union rules.

For example, DeMille's anger that designer Ralph Jester was not on the set "to coordinate costumes, wigs, and makeup" for the costumer Joe Kaplan, "as was the habit of Leisen, Adrian, and other costume designers that I have used in the past," denied divisions between costume manufacturing and finished costuming that now characterized studio labor and work flows. His ignorance might only have been annoying if not for the fact that DeMille was not merely indulging in nostalgia for earlier modes of production, but laying a paper trail to fire Jester for problems partially out of the designer's jurisdiction.[21] Paramount production memos concerning the film also suggest that the studio was investigating Banton, their lead costume designer, who was in charge of the costumes for the film's major female characters played by Loretta Young and Katherine DeMille (Cecil's daughter); the studio was calculating the ratio of Banton's costume sketches for the film to the number of cocktails consumed with Colbert, Dietrich, and Carole Lombard as he was working on designs for their personal wardrobe.[22]

After Paramount elected not to renew Banton's contract in 1938, Jester was kept on and Natalie Visart became lead designer for DeMille's Paramount films until she retired in the mid-1940s, at which time Head, collaborating with a number of other designers, took on the challenge of the DeMille spectacle film. Visart was one of the costume designers Banton supervised on *The Crusades* and the protégé of DeMille's former art director and sometime costume designer from the silent and early sound era, Mitchell Leisen, by the mid-1930s one of Paramount's top directors and an excellent collaborator for the contentious Colbert. The kinds of conflicts at Paramount that cohered around performers, directors, and costume, makeup, and hair workers perhaps could have been more successfully contained at other studios, such as Twentieth Century–Fox or MGM, which had more stable—but not necessarily more benign—executive leadership and more harmonious wardrobe and makeup departments. The Paramount problems exemplify in more extreme form the behind-the-scenes struggles out of which film texts and images were produced at all studios during the classical era of Hollywood.

Spectacle and Storytelling

Despite preproduction issues and problems, on the screen the costumes in *The Crusades* register as relatively accurate historical referents, and, in the case of the women's costumes, as straightforward symbolic visualizations of good and evil. These conceptual categories tend to loom large in DeMille's work and, indeed, in this film the female leads' costumes convey the most primary oppositions between light and darkness—for example, the pure heroine Berengaria (Loretta Young), whose purity will inspire King Richard's greatness, is mostly dressed in bright white or other light-colored, diaphanous, bias-cut, silk or silk-chiffon gowns, while the scheming Princess (Katherine DeMille), whose filial alliances will bring Richard down, is costumed in dark velvet gowns with necklines and sashes trimmed with jeweled embroidery. The princes, kings, knights, and other soldiers wear armor differentiated by varying crests, chain mail, and head gear that approximate what the average filmgoer might have seen in storybook illustrations or in previous films about knights of the Middle Ages. The veiled Arab women with whom DeMille was so concerned are seen briefly and conform to a generalized Orientalist stereotype.

What is perhaps most startling from our perspective is that the severely tweezed eyebrows, rouged mouths, manicured nails, and hair bangs and waves of Young and DeMille are decidedly 1930s glamour rather than characteristic of the Middle Ages. The practice of combining design elements of both contemporary and period styles of costume, makeup, and hair was typical of period films made during the classical era, as it had been during the 1920s.[23] However, the blending of different temporal moments is relatively subtle in the costumes for *The*

Crusades (for example, bias-cut, rather than straight-cut, gowns). The makeup and hair are egregiously out of period—worth mentioning if only because DeMille repeatedly publicized his professional persona as a producer-director who was devoted to detail and strictly adhered to accuracy in period films. He was so invested in publicizing his great concern for detail that, during the preproduction of *The Crusades* when he was briefly hospitalized for a virus, he had the studio take publicity photos of him going over costumes and sketches while in his sick bed (figure 13).

Hollywood Extra Girl (1935), a film short made to advertise the feature, narrates the day in the life of an alleged extra in *The Crusades.* DeMille himself appears in the film, which is set in the Paramount soundstages; he sits on the seat of the camera crane, and, from his godlike position high above the convened extra players, calls out a young woman—the "extra girl" of the title—for not wearing the "correct" period wig. In a scolding tone, he informs her that, despite all the researchers who strived "to get accurate and authentic detail . . . [Central Casting] gives[s] me a girl that looks as though she just walked out of a beauty salon." Later in the film, lecturing less loudly but in no less hyperbolic terms, he tells her that the "art of the screen isn't just . . . looking . . . like a tomato-mouth blonde. It's learning a great art and to express that fire within. . . . [We] need faces there that show souls in their eyes."

The costumes for *The Crusades* do contribute to telling the film's story and conveying its themes, and even the obvious costume, makeup, and hair anachronisms

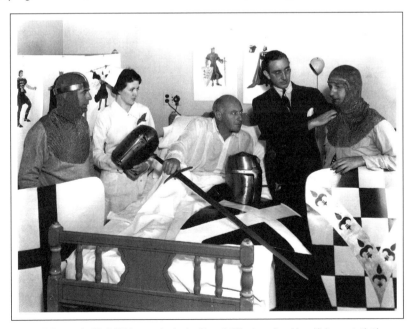

FIGURE 13: Director Cecil B. DeMille's reputation for detail in period films is confirmed by publicity reports that he checked costume designs for *The Crusades* (1935) while hospitalized. Gowns for the women stars by Travis Banton; wardrobe for men by Joe Kaplan and for women by Edna Shotwell (both uncredited).

support those themes by sexualizing the female characters as potential mates for King Richard (Henry Wilcoxon), the hero of the film. However, Banton, Mont Westmore (uncredited makeup artist and supervisor for the film), Nellie Manley (uncredited hair stylist), and their peers at other studios usually had opportunities to create designs that would make contributions to storytelling and characterizations in more complex and sometimes more subtle ways.

For example, Samuel Goldwyn's production of *Dodsworth* (1936), with costumes by Omar Kiam and direction by William Wyler, also constructs a hero's crisis in terms of an opposition between two women, but the film refuses a simple binary, at least one divorced from believable social contexts and individual psychology. Industrialist Sam Dodsworth (Walter Huston) goes on a European tour with his wife, Fran (Ruth Chatterton), to celebrate his retirement and a renewal of his marriage. Fran sees the journey as an opportunity to climb the social ladder and reinvent herself sexually, taking younger lovers from the European social set of gigolos and counts. Sam eventually agrees to a divorce and, while traveling again in Europe, re-meets and falls in love with divorcée Edith Courtland (Mary Astor). Although she is wealthy and the same age as Fran, she is egalitarian, sincere, and graceful—everything that Sam once thought Fran was. The female characters are contrasted by costume—Edith always looks feminine and chic but wears the dark colors and understated jewelry that complement her age and convey her modest assumption of high-class status, while Fran progressively changes from an attractive, unassuming, and classically dressed woman to an

FIGURE 14: The divergent social values held by *Dodsworth* (1937) characters Fran Dodsworth (Ruth Chatterton) and Edith Cortright (Mary Astor) are contrasted by costume and hair style. Costumes by Omar Kiam, makeup and hair uncredited.

overdressed one whose dyed hair, form-hugging lamé gowns, and faddish accessories (slave bracelets, hair clips) betray her wish to be younger as well as her desire to show off wealth (figure 14).

As Jane Gaines notes, costume in classical Hollywood film must "*register* at the same time it must *recede*," that is, must solicit the spectator's desire and interest via conveyance of significant meaning even as it must not call too much attention to itself and risk breaking the text's illusionism.[24] Fran's increasing social pretentiousness and denial of her age is clearly registered through costume and hair (which keeps getting blonder as the story progresses), but rather than turning to binaries, caricature, or exaggeration, the film sets up the opposition between Fran and Edith within a carefully crafted verisimilitude. Before her clothes start to reveal her pursuit of youth and social acceptance, Fran demonstrates her belief that class, in both meanings of the term—as manners and as social and economic status—is a matter of showing off knowledge of foreign phrases, dressing for dinner, expensive taste, and the latest styles. At the start of their trip she abandons the unadorned crepe hostess gowns she wore as the dutiful wife who entertained her husband's business clients. Her alienation from Sam is first indicated when she scorns his casual dismissal of the need for formal dinner dress on the voyage's first night, and is finalized when she refuses him—her husband of twenty years—the sight of her in a state of undress after she has been out with one of her lovers. Fran's change, however, slowly unfolds in the narrative via small visual details, such as her placement of a diamond clip on a graceful gown's neckline in a way that ruins the beauty of its curve, or the way she adds a largish bow to an otherwise flattering hairstyle, or a slave bracelet to her arm when her formal gown's drape elegantly references timeless classical refinement until the added piece of jewelry adds connotations of sexual vulgarity.

Dodsworth is not concerned with questioning the industrial capitalist success that is responsible for Sam's wealth and freedom—in fact, it romanticizes it by contrasting his self-made, hands-on wealth with the inherited wealth of European nobility and Fran, the brewer's daughter. The text elevates the virtues of experience and unpretentious self-knowledge, identifying them with the self-made (Sam) and the gracious (Edith). While at Edith's Italian villa overlooking the sea, Sam and Edith decide to share worldly adventures. She is wearing peasant-influenced garments—a simple linen dress, with rolled-up sleeves and large pockets on a long skirt, unadorned espadrille flats on her feet—while Sam is in white linen with the sleeves of his white cotton shirt also rolled up. At the villa, they are romantically identified with the earth, the sea, and the work and leisure rhythms of an unpretentious peasant life. Their costumes register, but they recede as costumes so that these are just people wearing clothes.

This "recession" of costumes into "character[s] merely wearing clothes" in effect naturalizes the virtues associated with Sam and Edith so we do not see the class difference between them and the Italian peasants who serve them.[25]

Our last glimpse of Fran is when she attempts to lure Sam back—she has been rejected by the aristocratic mother of her younger paramour because she is on to Fran's real age (that is, unlikely to give her son an heir). When Sam returns to Edith, Fran is left behind on a boat going back to America, wearing a print-patterned day dress reminiscent of her earlier wifely garments. Her hat is capped with a feather that looks something like a question mark, suggesting that the future direction of her life is uncertain. The film has a "good woman" and a "bad woman," but both are human: they are opposed not by their adulterous sexual desires (Edith, for instance, is surely the lover of the still-married Sam) or wealth (both have money left to them by men), but by their social values, and it is their costumes that help to tell the story of Sam's slow realization that it is Edith's values that are closer to his own.

While DeMille demanded stereotypical and simplistic costuming, hair, and makeup for *The Crusades* that visually suggest the kind of binaries Kiam's designs in *Dodsworth* eschews, his speech in *Extra Girl* emphasizes both historical "accuracy" and something other than that—the dreamy pseudo-spiritual qualities of film that enthrall audiences, that enable them to believe in spectacle and film narrative because, through performance, costume, makeup, and hair, they are allowed access to the "souls" in the actors' eyes. Putting this less floridly than DeMille, and with greater consciousness about the ideological role of film, we can say that Hollywood films of this era were meant to be "pleasure machines"— that is, texts that involve spectators and naturalize representations by producing meanings that work on affective as well as cognitive registers. Elements of a film narrative's visualization, such as costume, makeup, and hair, convey to spectators what is at stake in watching, and why they should care about watching. Classical Hollywood films also affectively connected to audiences through their relevance to contemporary social conflicts and challenges. Sarah Street argues for the role of film costume in securing this connection: costume "frequently operates as a 'system' governed by complex influences that relate to notions of realism, performance, gender, status, and power."[26]

Designing the "Rightness" of Love

Paramount's Technicolor *Lady in the Dark* explores gender and power in its story of fashion magazine editor Liza Elliott (Ginger Rogers), whose recent nightmares, inability to make decisions, and difficult relations with three men—co-worker Charlie (Ray Milland), benefactor and married lover Kendall (Warner Baxter), and movie-star model Randy (Jon Hall)—lead her to undergo psychoanalysis. The costumes were designed by the studio's chief designer Edith Head, director Mitchell Leisen, Raoul Pène du Bois (also one of the film's art directors), and Mme. [Barbara] Karinska, a designer and stylist for New York ballet companies and brought to Hollywood during the 1940s.[27] The film uses the course of the character's psychoanalytic treatment as a structuring device, with each of Liza's visits to the analyst contributing to her final psychological breakthrough. The therapy sessions are structured according to Liza's recounting of the previous night's dream. The dreams are coded by color and costume—a "blue dream" in which Liza dances in an ultra-feminine blue chiffon gown with a sequined dark-blue bodice, for example, ending with the unveiling of a caricature of her in a masculine professional suit not unlike what she wears to work in waking life; and a "white and gold dream" in which she happily dances in a white wedding gown and huge medieval-looking veiled headdress before scaling a large wedding cake as her dress falls to pieces around her.

In the final dream, which is rendered in a spectrum of bright, saturated colors, Liza is on trial before a kangaroo court for her inability to make choices about either men or about magazine covers. Liza dances in the most elaborate gown of the film—a paisley-patterned, red-and-gold-sequined, long-sleeved, V-necked body-suit over which a floor-length mink skirt opens to reveal a matching lining as well as Liza's shapely, bare legs. The dream's judge is the magazine's effeminate fashion photographer Russell Paxton (Mischa Auer), who repeatedly calls attention to the outrageous behaviors and styles in the waking-life office with a cry of "This is the end, the absolute end!" The jury members are the magazine models and female secretaries who have aggressively gazed at the men who come through the office—the magazine office functions in both waking and dream lives as a theatrical arena for women to look at and judge men as well as their female co-workers. The tailored, richly colored suits and hats the women wear as work clothes in waking life have been re-versioned in the dream's visual logic as garishly colored grotesqueries (too short or too long, exaggerated details, etc.), transforming the wearers into clowns who inspire both laughter and horror.

Lady in the Dark's elaborately costumed dream sequences lead to Liza's "cure." In the scene of her final therapy session she wears a mustard-colored, sheer organdy blouse with a frilly jabot instead of her usual buttoned-up, dark-colored, broad-shouldered work suit. Significantly, the dream's fantastic mink and sequined dress, or at least how Liza remembers it through the secondary revision process, enables the "breakthrough" that allows her to wear the organdy blouse with apparent sincerity (figure 15). That is, her repetitive opening and closing of the mink skirt to display her legs reveals the genital area that, in Freudian terms, signifies woman's "nothingness," her lack of the phallus. With the psychoanalyst's help in dream interpretation, she embraces a "normative" femininity she discovers through a realization that she cannot replace her mother in her father's affection and that she needs a man to dominate her.

Liza still wears the light, frilly blouse when she invites Charlie—the magazine's cynical and misogynist advertising director—to be her business partner. Their kiss in the final shot (after he has literally taken her chair from under her and then

FIGURE 15: The expensive sequined-lined mink skirt and jacket worn by Ginger Rogers in *Lady in the Dark* (1944) was the most publicized of the film's many lavish costumes. Costume design by Edith Head, Raoul Pène du Bois, Mme. (Barbara) Karinska, and uncredited Mitch Leisen and Babs Wilomez. Makeup by Wally Westmore, hair uncredited

helps her off the floor) suggests she is also inviting him to be her sexual and marriage partner. In other words, her cure is both achieved and symbolized by an alignment of her inner desire to be an appropriately "feminine" woman with her outer sartorial display that suggests delicacy as well as her willingness to be the object of the male gaze. This alignment would seem to confirm the warning of Liza's wise-cracking editorial assistant Maggie (Mary Phillips): psychoanalysis "can scare the pants off you."

However, the fashion-world setting also supports the film's obvious self-reflexivity about the "storytelling" function of film costume and its relation to a naturalized and supposedly unified self. The excessive color, texture, and even size and volume of the costumes, which contribute to the theatricality of both dream and office, expose gender as performance. Liza's song in the final dream recounts the story of "Poor Jenny," who "would make up her mind" and, like Pandora, unleash disaster upon all she touches. The song communicates one of patriarchy's "double binds" for women—that is, how women are put down for not being able to "make up their minds," but blamed for the consequences when they do.

Liza's alternation of revealing and concealing legs and crotch in the accompanying dance—making the fur-as-fetish, as well as her "nothingness," appear and disappear—suggests she can control the play of signifiers that will either assuage or terrify her male partners. Her therapeutic breakthrough and adoption of "feminine" clothing leaves us to wonder, if Liza was once masquerading as "masculine" to hide the "femininity" inside her, could her new fashion be hiding a residual inner masculinity? While Liza turns down the proposal of movie star Randy Curtis after he declares he wants a woman who will take care of him (rather than one whom he can dominate), she does not give up the magazine. Her subsequent offer of a *co*-editorship to the domineering Charlie suggests that she will not abandon all "masculine" prerogatives even if their kiss and her more feminine costume suggests her willingness to embark on a sexual relationship.

This reading of the film's end as ambiguous or ambivalent is supported by the effeminate photographer Russell, who "queers" the kiss between Liza and Charlie with a repeat of "This is the end, the absolute end!" He declares the obvious—the story is over—but also conveys that *this end is unbelievable*. The film's costumes are unbelievable—fantastic, made of fabrics that teeter on exceeding the limits of what was allowed by World War II rationing of materials—and so is the possibility that Liza would entirely give up the magazine and her "masculine" controls over it for the price of a kiss. Russell's exclamation seems to summon the historical context of the film's production—the war home front needs women to be "masculine," but women have to be ready to have their "pants scared off," with fashion masquerades providing the materials and performances in which to negotiate these contradictions. Secure closure is unbelievable in these terms. Despite its lack of subtlety, *Lady in the Dark* queers what had become by the mid-1940s a conventionalized way for costumes to tell a certain kind of women's story. Rosalind Russell, who often portrayed such career women, later wrote, "[After the male character says] 'Underneath it all, you're very feminine' . . . [I reply,] 'Please Richard, I must go on with my work, so many depend on me.'" This narrative set-up led Russell to tell "Jean Louis, Adrian, Irene or Travis Banton, 'Make me a plaid suit, a striped suit, a grey flannel, and a negligee for the scene in the bedroom when I cry.'"[28]

Adultery and female sexual awakening are central to both *Dodsworth* and *Lady in the Dark*. While costume design harnesses the close alignment between subjectivity and clothing to convey and justify character motivation and story developments in classical Hollywood films, representational restraints on sexual expression were imposed by "The Code," both the list of "Don'ts and Be Carefuls" guiding the Studio Relations Committee until mid-1934 (the "pre-Code" era) and the revised and more strongly enforced Code administered by the Production Code Administration (PCA) from late 1934. Costumes were subject to self-regulatory surveillance and, at the same time, served as the possible vehicles for conveying what the text could not more explicitly represent through dialogue and action.

In *Mandalay*, released in early 1934 before the PCA was established, Tanya (Kay Francis) lives on a boat in Rangoon with her lover Tony (Ricardo Cortez). In the typical fashion of a Warner Bros. pre-Code film, romance between sexually adventurous characters is expressed through hints of nudity or partial undress. From outside a window above the lower cabin of their houseboat, Tony watches Tanya as she showers—she runs over, wrapped only in a towel, to scold him. However, she instead raises her arms to embrace him, and the towel falls (a close-up of her arms and face as she moves into the embrace is followed by a cut to a close-up of the towel slipping to her feet). These shots exemplify pre-Code visuals, naughty through suggestiveness.

Orry-Kelly's costumes convey Tanya's sexual power while charting her development from a sensual innocent to a hard-driving, disillusioned prostitute. The night Tony sells Tanya to Nick, a "nightclub" owner to whom he is indebted, she wears a simple, form-fitting gown of ivory silk crepe. The bodice consists of a "tropical" off-the-shoulder neckline, but a sophisticated look is affected by tight, off-the-shoulder straps adorned with large, heavily-starched cloth tropical flowers. The dress has an easy flow, and to create curves for the willowy Francis, a wide, sequin-appliquéd sash reminiscent of a bandana or sarong is tied around her hips. The total effect is an exoticism that combines the natural and lush beauty of a tropical flower with a sophisticated, womanly sexuality.

The word "prostitute" or a prostitute's activities are precluded even by regulations adhered to pre-Code, but through costume, the film can allude to Tanya's commodified sexuality after she is unwillingly transformed by the brothel women into the dazzling star of the nightclub/brothel. The climax of her makeover—when she finally realizes she can make the situation work to her advantage only by embracing the power of her sexuality—is signified by her grand entrance into the nightclub as "Spot White." She descends the long staircase into the club wearing a stunning curve-hugging gown of sparkling gold sequins, topped with a white tulle boa. The soft, dark waves characterizing her former hairstyle have been straightened and slicked down so that she appears to be wearing a black helmet. As the gazing male customers murmur comments about Spot White's formidability, we believe it (figure 16).

Anna Karenina (Clarence Brown, 1935), made according to the stricter Code regulations, emphasizes the romance and tragedy of Anna's affair, rather than exploits its sexual nature. In his designs for Garbo's films with contemporary settings, MGM's lead costume designer Adrian successfully identified Garbo with modernity. His costumes—including oversized slouch-coats and hats that sit partially over one eye—projected not the girlishly young women who were Garbo's contemporaries, but

FIGURE 16: The transformation of innocent Tanya (Kay Francis) into the sexually powerful Spot White is signaled by the form-hugging gold sequined dress and black-helmet hairstyle she dons midway through *Mandalay* (1934). Gowns by Orry-Kelly, makeup probably by Perc Westmore (uncredited), hair by Ruth Pursley (uncredited).

the aloof, modern woman of experience who might also be androgynous. Adrian's costumes for Garbo's period films, on the other hand, emphasize the feminine softness of her characters, also women of experience, but whose longing for intimacy makes them vulnerable to tragic romance. The costumes for these films are often made of lightweight fabrics or layers of sheer materials, many with frills, ruffles, bows, and off-the-shoulder necklines, and convey the romantic feminine desires and delirious happiness that her characters experience before they realize the impossibility of their loves.

In the black-and-white *Anna Karenina*, the costumes convey the "rightness" of the love between Anna (Garbo) and Count Vronsky (Fredric March), but work within Code regulations limiting the terms of its representation. When the characters first meet exiting a train in winter, they both wear coats that frame their faces in fur; dancing at a ball they stand out from the crowd in their starkly contrasting black (Anna's gown) and white (Vronsky's uniform tunic) costumes.

At a turning point in their affair, they play croquet at a summer garden party where other characters are gossiping about the propriety of their relationship. Anna and Vronsky, both dressed in bright white and lit in full sunlight, are centered in the shot's back plane, framed by the gossiping, darkly dressed characters in the foreground. Anna, wearing a wide-brimmed white hat slightly curving over her right eye, is dressed in a white organdy dress whose ruffles and bows reference a playful femininity. Vertical ruffles extend from a frilly collar and silk bow at the neckline to a bow that sits atop the band of horizontal ruffles that brings in the skirt's slight fullness just above the knees, below which the skirt breaks away into a ruffly, slightly A-line flounce ending in a long train. Although the back of Garbo's neck is framed by the dress's frilly stand-up collar, the front of the neckline is slightly open, in direct contrast to the tightly closed neckline of the dresses Anna wears in her home, which, by this time in the film, is increasingly her prison. The fundamental role of sexuality in both these films, and the differences between Tanya's and Anna's experience of sex's power, is not conveyed just by performances, locales, situations, and expected conventions of class behavior, but also by costumes of sumptuous excessiveness that work within Code restraints.

Blending "Flesh and Spirit": Promotion and Publicity

Kay Francis and Greta Garbo were favorite subjects of fan magazines and other kinds of publicity and promotion at the height of the studio system. Fan magazines were crucial vehicles of connection between studios and audiences, especially the female audience, during this era. Articles and photo layouts constructed narrative and visual discourses about marriage, work, beauty, and fashion, articulating a relation between stars and the ordinary young woman assumed to be the ideal movie fan. They strengthened the symbiotic relations among studios, female fans, and the consumer industries that relied on star testimony and a visualized glamour to sell their products. Paid advertisements for cosmetics and other beauty products supported the magazines financially and complemented typical fan magazine stories or photo spreads thematically oriented around star "transformations." Film costumes as worn in films, or personal wardrobes as examples of the fashion influencing or influenced by costumes, were often worn by stars in fashion photo spreads or in portraits that illustrated magazine stories. Although studio photographers usually photographed stars in costume specifically for use in fan magazines, the publications might also rely on materials from the studios' campaign or pressbooks, which compiled the materials most typically used by exhibitors and newspapers: camera-ready layout for theater advertising, articles, potential product and business tie-ups, order forms for stills and lobby cards, and so forth. Makeup artists and hair stylists, often represented by Max Factor or one of the Westmore brothers who headed makeup and hair departments at several of the major studios, frequently authored, or were quoted in, magazine and newspaper features about beauty makeovers.

It is beyond the scope of this essay to enumerate and analyze all the ways fan magazines and newspapers used film costumes or makeup and hairstyles in their features. However, several publicity and promotion strategies concerning them were particularly evident at the height of the classical era: stories about the "authenticity" of costume, makeup, and hair in particular films; features that documented or suggested street fashion adaptations of costumes worn in film or ways that readers could approximate star makeup and hairstyles; and stories about film stars whose careers were made or transformed by fashion (worn both in and out of films) or by cosmetic changes. But fan magazines and other journalistic outlets could intentionally or unintentionally trouble the efforts of studio publicity departments to create normative ideals and smooth over struggles and contradictions in these ideals and the labor processes of making pictures and stars.

The importance of makeup in the films of Paul Muni and Bette Davis, and of historically "accurate" makeup, hair, and costumes in DeMille's period films, exemplifies typical subjects for film and star publicity, in particular those invested in discourses about "authenticity." In all these cases, the control and care over those elements of behind-the-scenes labor elevate the individuals involved into significant authoring agents and their films into culturally prestigious productions. Yet promoting "authenticity" as key to the appeal of these films and stars involves certain risks during the era of the contract star. There is a potential conflict between advertising a specific "historical" film, which requires actors to be physically transformed into a well-known figure, and the need to create a consistent transmedia image for stars that will be put to the service of other, future films—hence, Jack Warner's worry that Muni (and the studio's investment in him) won't be recognized under all the makeup. However, the implied economic risks are mitigated by the prestige accruing to the acting and design artistries publicized and, in the case of Muni and *The Story of Louis Pasteur*, by clever advertising graphics produced by the studio publicity department. For example, the film's pressbook makes available to exhibitors one ad layout featuring a "before and after" of Muni: a small photo of Muni's face without makeup, and, to its lower right, a much larger image of Muni's face in character as Pasteur, enabling audience contemplation of two aspects of Muni's star persona.

The interrelation among star personas, film characters, and makeup, hair, and costume as they relate to a promotable "authenticity" must also be seen in terms of the racist assumptions that characterized the film industry and American society at this time. Fan magazines were not just obsessed with the flashy makeup, hair, and costume transformations, such of those of Muni and Davis, which they connected to a notion of "great acting." They were also particularly fascinated with cosmetic and sartorial wizardry that enabled cross-racial transformations; between the 1920s and 1940s, articles about the "yellowface" transformations of Caucasians Muni, Luise Rainer, Edward G. Robinson, Loretta Young, Myrna Loy, Nils Asther, Gale Sondegaard, and Warner Oland into Asians appeared with some regularity in entertainment news outlets. Loretta Young's transformation into a Chinese character by Perc Westmore for *The Hatchet Man* (1932) was the subject of at least three fan magazine articles or pictorials in the same month. As Yiman Wang argues, white actors playing the racial "other" not only attracted praise for their skill at playing someone "not like him- or herself" (as might happen with other significant cosmetic or sartorial transformations), but also contributed to the marginalization of nonwhite performers within the system.[29] The fan magazine pieces on Young made to look Chinese is typical of the promotional displays of racial transformation through movie makeup. They predict that Young *will* be mistaken for being Chinese, but conclude in a fashion characteristic of fetishistic processes: saying, in effect, well, she is not really Chinese but could *almost* be mistaken for "a yellow-skinned, slant-eyed Chinese gal."[30]

However, fan magazines could also circulate discourses that countered the racist fetishism inspired by the yellowface makeup articles and pictorials. Chinese American film actress Anna May Wong used them to speak against racist miscegenation laws (which made it impossible for her to kiss a white male actor onscreen), racist behaviors toward her in social interactions, and studios favoring white actors made up in yellowface for Asian characters. Wong had lobbied hard for the role of O-lan in *The Good Earth*—in one interview, she speaks frankly about her disappointment over Rainer's casting as the character, complaining that the studio would only consider her for the unsympathetic role of Lotus, eventually played by Tilly Losch.[31]

Sarah Berry argues that Hollywood makeovers of white actors into yellowface or other exotic beauty looks could function as white fantasies of liberation from the strictures of western social prohibitions, such as sexual prohibitions. However, by the late 1930s, fan magazines and makeup companies (such as Max Factor) started to market "cosmetics in terms of a spectrum of colored features [that] helped to displace nativist beauty norms that non-Anglo-American women had long been seen as inferior to."[32] Examples from film pressbooks expose some of the challenges for the system's attempts to coordinate the use of film costumes, makeup, and hair to represent a particular film character's narrative arc with their representations in promotion and publicity, which must reach a mass female audience who may or may not be seeking fantasies of the sort Berry describes.

While the role of Tanya in *Mandalay* might inspire connections between Kay Francis and stereotypes assigned to nonwhites (such as a loose sexuality), the character is supposed to be white, so yellowface makeup was not used on Francis. The film's Orientalist exoticism is conveyed by costuming, hair, and the character's association with nonwhites at Nick's nightclub/brothel, that is, the Asian prostitutes and dancers who work there and Nick himself, played by Warner Oland, the Swedish yellowface actor mentioned above. The film's pressbook offers poster and newspaper advertising layouts and cardboard theater lobby displays that emphasize Francis in costume, with the spectacular gold-sequined gown and the dress referencing tropical flora figuring prominently in the graphics. Articles for use in entertainment and women's pages of the newspaper articulate Francis's fashion advice, the film's setting in the Orient, and even such filmic devices as the series of lap dissolves that convey Tanya's movement from innocent to queen of the underworld through sartorial transformations. Yet the pressbook's copy has to avoid associating the stunning film costumes with aspects of the film's actual story—that is, that Tanya becomes a white slave sold into prostitution and that the film shows some of these clothes to be tools of the trade. Consequently, most of the suggested tie-ins are related to fashion items—clothes, jewelry, shoes—that have a generalized Orientalist flavor and that can stimulate fantasies of "exotic" travels and peoples, while at the same time avoiding the nasty realities/fantasies of economic exploitation and racism that serve both as the narrative's pretext for Tanya's eventual liberation and as support for the studio's policy of employing nonwhite stars in token fashion only.

Evidence for how much box office fruit was produced out of such promotional campaigns is difficult to find. The costumes for *The Crusades* were featured in both *Screen Play* (July 1935) and *Movie Classic* (September 1935). The latter magazine structured its spread on the film's costumes in terms of their possible influence on street fashion; it suggested that "skirt fullness" and "metallic cloth" will be in vogue, but the proposal that the "close-fitting hat with an upturned and shiny band brim, face veil, and chin strap" (patterned after the medieval metal headband and veil worn by Young in the film) will surely "appeal to glamor-conscious moderns" seems improbable.[33] Paramount's attempt to promote *The Crusades* in terms of the costumes' relevance to fashion may have brought some of the female audience to the theater, but since the film lost money, this was not a sufficient strategy. The studios must have believed that this type of strategy worked, for all cooperated with fan magazines for many years by providing film stills and photos of film stars to create promotional and publicity features that made associations between film costumes, makeup, and hair and contemporary fashionable street styles.

The promotional strategy that might have provided the greatest inspiration to the female film spectator/fan magazine reader whose "psychic life" had been internalized by studio publicity and promotion directors was the story of the "actress whose career is made or changed by collaboration with a designer."[34] All the major studios had at least one or more designer–female star collaboration which might work for this narrative—Travis Banton's work with Dietrich, Colbert, and Carole Lombard at Paramount; Orry-Kelly's work with Davis, Francis, and Delores del Rio at Warner Bros.; Walter Plunkett's work with Katharine Hepburn at RKO; the collaboration between Adrian and Garbo, Norma Shearer, Joan Crawford, and Rosalind Russell at MGM; Edith Head's work with Dorothy Lamour and Barbara Stanwyck at Paramount; and Rita Hayworth's work with Jean Louis at Columbia.

The design philosophy of Adrian, whose work was linked to a great number of major female stars, was summed up in press interviews in which he was always quoted as speaking variations on "It is the mind of a woman [I costume] that counts." He advises the fan magazine reader to know herself in order to look stylish and "smartly gowned whether she wear gingham or velvet." He explains that he designed simple lines for Garbo when he took over her costuming in 1928 because she takes a straightforward approach to the world. In dressing her according to her personality, "everyone else began to see a dynamic and powerful actress in the place of a mere decorative feminine figure."[35] To most fans, Garbo became identified with Adrian more than with her directors, photographers, and even co-stars (with the exception of John Gilbert). When MGM sponsored a contest for UCLA art students to compete in designing modern fashions inspired by the Adrian-gowned Garbo in the period film *Conquest* (1937), it was clear the contestants had internalized the Adrian look, most of all the broad-shouldered costumes that contributed to the image of Garbo as a "powerful actress."[36]

Garbo had strong support from her studio in addition to Adrian's costuming. Carole Lombard's collaborations with Travis Banton at Paramount represent the case of a contract player who recognized her studio was not providing a context for her to develop into a major star. In response, she crafted a successful career trajectory for herself through alliances with receptive creative types, shrewd contract renegotiations (including rights to make films at other studios, with Banton in tow), and assertive press agentry. Banton's designs were at the center of her strategy, and he found in her one of the few stars at Paramount who was always a pleasure to design for.

Fan magazines probably showcased the two more than any other designer-star duo; articles with titles such as "How Carole Lombard Became the Best-Dressed Star" (*Movie Classic*, May 1935), "Be Modern or Be a Wallflower" (*Motion Picture*, August 1935), "How Carole Lombard's Clothes Match Her Moods" (*Movie Classic*, September 1935), "Portrait of a Self-Made Woman" (*Movie Classic*, December 1935), "The Evolution of a Wow!" (*Movie Mirror*, December 1936), "Studio Designer Confesses" (*Motion Picture*, December 1938), and "Hollywood's Goofy Gal Goes Glamorous" (*Screen Book*, February 1939) narrated Lombard's move away from the status of blonde starlet whose main attributes were humor and a good body to a sophisticate with the individuated glamour necessary for stardom. According to fan magazines, she created a unified star image by paradoxically multiplying the facets of her "personality," which were made visible by the designer's clothes for her film characters and her personal wardrobe. These personalities were united in an image of her as the orchestrator who knows herself and selects the appropriate clothing, makeup, and hair to suit her choice of film roles and the aspects of her private self she wants as part of the public image.[37] Her comments about clothes, work, creativity, and fun suggest that the form of glamour she produces with Banton comes from their knowledge of how to make the effort seem effortless, how to create the perfect "blend of flesh and spirit."[38]

There were many processes and individuals, named and unnamed, involved in creating and promoting Hollywood's costume, makeup, and hair—behind-the-scenes artists, workers, and activities underpinning a large and complex industrial system. Within that context and the promotional and publicity stories by which Hollywood emphasized the ease with which glamour could be achieved, we must note the concomitant ease with which Lombard's "self-made" woman image could be appropriated by the ideologically motivated American success stories that the industry told so well. In actuality, costume designers and makeup and hair stylists created products of "flesh and spirit" out of social and cultural struggles that deserve continued historical reappraisal.

3

POSTWAR HOLLYWOOD, 1947–1967

Prudence Black and Karen de Perthuis

When the costuming unit for Cecil B. DeMille's 1956 remake of his 1923 epic, *The Ten Commandments*, arrived in Egypt with costumes for three thousand extras, they were told these would not be nearly enough—the legendary director wanted costumes for fifteen thousand extras.[1] To design the costumes for the film, the team of Edith Head, Dorothy Jeakins, Gile Steele, Ralph Jester, and the religious artist Arnold Friberg had drawn on sources as diverse as the Bible, the Koran, ancient Egyptian art and jewelry, and nineteenth-century paintings of the Pre-Raphaelites.[2] The result was an eclectic, if inauthentic, mix of biblical referencing, historical imagining, fashionable silhouettes, and sexual display (figure 17). A biblical spectacle on a grand scale, *The Ten Commandments* was filmed in Technicolor using DeMille's dominant scheme of reds, greens, and blues, and with Paramount's new widescreen process, VistaVision. Attention to detail counted. Dan Striepeke, who worked under Hollywood veteran Wally Westmore, was a young makeup artist on the film and later recounted DeMille's response to seeing extras wearing hook-on whiskers: "Dissatisfied with their cheap appearance [he] shut down the movie for three days while real hair beards could be procured."[3]

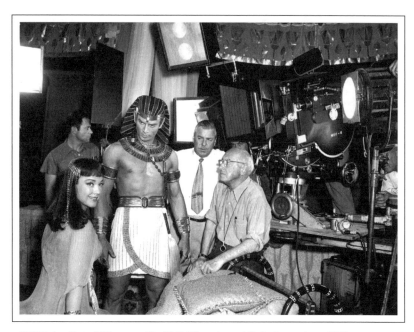

FIGURE 17: Anne Baxter, Yul Brynner, and Cecil B. DeMille on the set of *The Ten Commandments* (1956), costume design by Arnold Friberg, Edith Head, Dorothy Jeakins, John Jensen, and Ralph Jester; makeup by Wally Westmore, Frank Westmore, and Frank McCoy; hair by Nellie Manley. IMDb.com lists some sixty uncredited wardrobe personnel in addition to an equal number of uncredited makeup and hair artists on the film.

Once released, DeMille's film would earn more than $100 million worldwide and gross $26.5 million in the United States alone, surpassing the box office record held since 1939 by *Gone with the Wind*.[4] This huge success ensured that *The Ten Commandments* strongly influenced the future direction of Hollywood on a number of levels, including overseas production, which by 1960 accounted for "forty per cent of all movies financed by the Hollywood majors."[5] Behind this statistic stood the grim reality of an industry in decline. Traditional Hollywood movies with extravagant wardrobe budgets—such as Douglas Sirk's melodrama *Imitation of Life* (1959), the religious epics *Spartacus* (Stanley Kubrick, 1960) and *El Cid* (Anthony Mann, 1961), the ill-fated *Cleopatra* (Joseph L. Mankiewicz, 1963), and *My Fair Lady* (George Cukor, 1964), starring Audrey Hepburn and designed by Cecil Beaton—were still being made and, to varying degrees, still drawing people to cinemas. But 1963 proved to be the worst year for Hollywood production in fifty years and, in 1964, foreign releases outnumbered U.S. releases by two to one as Hollywood commercialism fell casualty to the growing niche market of art house sophistication.[6]

The sensational success of Twentieth Century–Fox's musical *The Sound of Music* (Robert Wise, 1965) seemed to offer hope when it achieved a new box office record, displacing even *The Ten Commandments*. But if studio executives, anticipating a return to the good times of an earlier era, saw in the von Trapp family's story a metaphor for their own ability to climb mountains and come out the other side, they were kidding themselves. Rather than the new horizons of *The Sound of Music*'s final scene, a more accurate metaphor of the current state of Hollywood was to be found in the earlier scene where Maria (Julie Andrews) makes the von Trapp children a new set of clothes out of old curtains. This "make and make do" attitude was a product of Maria's initiative and rebellion in the film, but for the costume designer Dorothy Jeakins, as well as for the rest of Hollywood, it represented the new reality.

A Slow Dissolve

When Bette Davis as Margo Channing delivered the legendary line "Fasten your seatbelts, it's going to be a bumpy night" in *All About Eve* (Herman J. Mankiewicz, 1950), she could have been prophesying Hollywood's future. In 1947 there were over 18,000 movie theaters in the United States; by 1956 almost a quarter of these had closed, with the impact only marginally offset by an increase in drive-ins.[7] Census Bureau figures show film attendance declined sharply from a high of 90 million in the years 1946–1948 to a new low of 40 million in 1960 and falling steadily to 20 million in 1970.[8] Along with the general decline in audiences, a major blow came with the Paramount antitrust decision of 1948, which went into effect on January 1, 1950, and precipitated the dismantling of the studio system that had more or less been in place since the 1920s. Throughout Hollywood's classical era, this system had been an efficient and profitable method of producing and releasing large numbers of films, with individual companies owning and controlling all aspects of production, distribution, and exhibition. But once such vertical integration became illegal and the monopolistic link between production companies and movie theaters was broken, the market power of the Hollywood studios was curtailed and, for producers and exhibitors alike, writes Peter Lev, "Every film became a risk."[9]

Contributing to Hollywood's decline were significant changes in American society. The dramatic increase in marriage in the postwar period and the resultant Baby Boom saw the United States reach a population of 163 million in 1960 (forty years earlier than the Census Bureau had predicted in 1946). This was accompanied by the shift of families to newly created suburbs and a lifestyle focused on outdoor leisure activities.[10] With the antitrust laws in place, exhibitors struggled to fill cinemas in downtown areas that now became deserted at night.[11] American films were still popular overseas and the lucrative international market might have promised an alternative income stream for Hollywood. However, hopes here were disappointed by restrictions imposed on the importation of American films by foreign governments, especially the British and French, which needed their precious foreign exchange reserves for the enormous task of rebuilding nations that had been devastated by the war.

By any measure, the greatest threat faced by Hollywood at the beginning of the 1950s was television. In 1948, *Fortune* magazine estimated that 90 percent of U.S. citizens had not yet seen a television program.[12] By 1950, more than 7.3 million sets were sold across the United States, with never fewer than 5 million new sets added to homes annually up to the end of the decade.[13] Over the same period, the number of commercial television broadcasting stations increased fivefold in the two years from 1948 to 1950 and, by the end of the decade, 440 stations were transmitting the formulaic comforts of television to audiences in living rooms across the nation. Eventually, a symbiotic relationship developed between the two ostensibly competing industries of television and film. In the meantime, the threat to Hollywood was real. In 1949, Samuel Goldwyn of MGM confronted the challenge faced by the studios when he wrote in the *New York Times*, "The future of motion pictures, conditioned as it will be by the competition of television, is going to have no room for the deadwood of the present or the faded glories of the past."[14]

Making the Cut

Those who worked behind the scenes in the making of films were among the first to experience the harsh reality of the new era. Across the board, studios cut costs by trimming back creative and technical personnel and releasing stars, directors, and writers from long-term contracts. In the 1940s, studio costume departments were run with assembly-line efficiency and according to a strict, formalized, three-tiered hierarchy.[15] Costume designers created the overall look for the film's costuming with supervisors or heads of department often working on several films at once, handling the costumes of lead actresses; they were acknowledged with the onscreen credit "Gowns by."[16] Costumers assisted with the budget, organized production details, and dressed actors on set. At the least glamorous end of the scale, "thousands of seamstresses, cutters and fitters, milliners and wardrobe men and women . . . made the brilliant concepts reality."[17] It was those responsible for the "low paid, low status, and backbreaking work" of wardrobe finishing or manufacture that were hit hardest by the changes as they lost the security of being on the full-time studio payroll.[18] As film historian Elizabeth Nielsen writes, "People who had worked at the same studios for more than thirty years found themselves adrift as freelance workers."[19] In this atmosphere, the role of the Motion Picture Costumers union (Local 705) became increasingly important.[20]

Employees at companies such as Western Costume Company were also affected by the changes. Set up to trade in Native American wares and costumes in 1912, Western held maybe a million costumes in stock, boasted a vast research archive, and could manufacture anything upon request. Employees, including experts in a variety of specialist fields, such as hats, police uniforms, and weapons, both modern and ancient, commonly dressed extras with little supervisory control. The director of research at Western, Baston Duval, was even "decorated by the Counsel General of France for his 'true representation and accurate research on the national costumes of the Republic of France.'"[21] Of course, Western also provided costumes for the important genre of western films. But in the postwar period, these too were experiencing a time of transition, becoming more reflective and less formulaic, a shift that carried through to wardrobe departments. During preproduction of *Shane* (1953), director George Stevens insisted that he didn't want any "Western Costume Co. nonsense or wardrobe department nonsense" and that "whatever Shane wears should look 'store bought' or homemade."[22] The costumes for the film, designed by Edith Head, are testament to the success of this approach, but this was little comfort to the employees who had been laid off at Western after it was bought out in 1947 by a consortium of Warner Bros., Fox, Universal, and Columbia, cutting staff from 300 employees to 140.[23]

More generally, the situation for workers continued to deteriorate throughout the 1950s due to a number of factors. Falling audience numbers, combined with increased local production costs and shrinking profits, encouraged the shift to filming overseas (or elsewhere in the United States)—known as "runaway" production—where subsidies and tax breaks, as well as exotic locations and cheap labor, were on offer. Great Britain, France, and Italy, as well as Spain, North Africa, and even Australia, all became partners in convoluted financial deals that saw the erosion of the distinction between, in Paul Monaco's words, "what was technically considered an American movie or a British, Italian or French film."[24] The widespread trend toward runaway production was controversial and created labor unrest and picketing outside theaters, but in the end this was of little consequence. Massive cuts to technical staff working on films continued, and in the second week of March 1960 alone, the major studios laid off some 3,400 workers.[25]

Costume designers were not exempt from these cuts, and even long-term contracts dissolved as the studio system broke down.[26] Nonetheless, supervisors and heads of department generally fared better. During the war, articulate, career-oriented women had contributed to changing the status of women on set. The immediate postwar period also saw a resurgence of extravagant costume design that signaled the end of austerity dressing and wartime rationing. This potent combination set the stage for the rise to prominence of designers such as Edith Head, Helen Rose, Irene Sharaff, and Dorothy Jeakins, replacing the old guard of Adrian, Travis Banton, and Howard Greer.[27] Both Sharaff and Rose had honed their craft on Broadway and brought to Hollywood the practice of the designer taking responsibility for the entire cast and the concept of integrated design.[28] This was in contrast to the Hollywood tradition where the designer's focus was primarily on the costumes of female stars.

New developments in color production and widescreen technologies also made the technical expertise of costume designers indispensable. Their contribution to creating the look of a film was belatedly recognized with an inaugural Oscar for Best Costume Design instituted at the 1948 Academy Awards. As in the categories of cinematography and art direction, initially two Oscars were awarded, one for black and white and one for color.[29] The first designers to win the Oscar were Dorothy Jeakins and Barbara Karinska for *Joan of Arc* (Victor Fleming, 1948), color, and Roger K. Furse for *Hamlet* (Laurence Olivier, 1948), black and white (figure 18).[30]

In the same year, the contribution of costumers working down the line was recognized by their own when the Local 705 began sponsoring the Costumers Ball, awarding an "Adam and Eve" statuette, The Figleaf.[31] Five years later, in 1953, Shelia O'Brien, who started at Paramount working in the manufacturing workroom and ended up at Warner Bros. designing costumes for Joan Crawford, established the Costume Designers Guild (CDG) with thirty founding members.[32] O'Brien had long been part of the Local 705 negotiating committee and was, in Elizabeth Nielsen's words, "a powerful behind-the-scenes force in Hollywood labor circles."[33] Although the guild did not initially participate in collective bargaining with producers, it did help members with individual contracts and the negotiation of conditions such as a minimum wage and a health plan.[34] This proved crucial as individual studios adapted to the new era. MGM, Fox, and Columbia maintained, respectively, Helen Rose, Charles LeMaire, and Jean Louis as head of their costume departments until the late 1950s, and Edith Head was under contract at Paramount until 1967.[35] But these were the exceptions, and Deborah Nadoolman

FIGURE 18: Elizabeth Taylor presents Dorothy Jeakins with the first Oscar for Best Costume Design (color) for *Joan of Arc* (1948), shared with Barbara Karinska. The black-and-white award was won by Roger K. Furse for *Hamlet*.

Landis writes that "for most others, costume design became a freelance career," with costume designers contracted one film at a time.[36]

Onscreen, a glamorized version of the fashion industry was portrayed in films such as Vincente Minnelli's *Designing Woman* (1957) and Stanley Donen's *Funny Face* (1957) but, not surprisingly, strong ties between Hollywood and the fashion industry also existed offscreen. After the Hollywood Pattern Company ceased production in 1947, the role of providing patterns of styles worn on film was filled by the fan magazine *Photoplay*, as well as by Advance Patterns and a number of other pattern companies with "screen" or "star" in their name that used movie fashions as "a major marketing tool."[37] In the process of costuming a film, designers would experiment with material not normally used for specific garments, influencing industry trends. This was the case when Helen Rose designed a sheer lace and satin lastex bathing costume for Esther Williams in *Million Dollar Mermaid* (1952), creating a shift toward new and lighter fabrics for retail swimwear.[38]

Tie-ins between studios and the fashion industry also continued. In the case of the science-fiction hit *The Day the Earth Stood Still* (1951), the fashion editor of *Look* magazine, Perkins Bailey, was recruited to design the costume of the film's hero, Klaatu, and then adapt his jacket for earthlings in order to have it ready for sale in time for the film's release.[39] The exchange worked both ways with a number of established Hollywood designers building on their reputation as "designer to the stars." In 1947, while still under contract to MGM, Irene (the working name of Irene Lentz Gibbons) established boutique-salons in department stores across the country with an extremely successful wholesale line,[40] and Jean Louis embarked on an equally successful venture when he left Columbia in 1961. When Helen Rose retired from MGM in the late 1960s, she also went into private business with a ready-to-wear label and a custom-made clothing range, even taking some of her costumes from MGM on tour with "The Helen Rose Show." Her most popular design was the white chiffon dress worn by Elizabeth Taylor in Elia Kazan's *Cat on a Hot Tin Roof* (1958). Known as "The Cat Dress," it sold in the thousands.[41]

New Technologies: Cranking It Up

While Hollywood in the 1950s is often identified with what film historian Peter Lev calls "beatniks, Method Acting, film noir, [and] teen films," for most of the decade the industry focused on producing escapist entertainment that reflected the values of an increasingly affluent, suburbanized, and conservative America.[42] Certainly, the films that attracted an Oscar for Best Costume Design tended to fall into this category, with musicals, historical dramas, bitterly realistic portrayals of Hollywood, religious epics, and anything starring Audrey Hepburn dominating as winners throughout the 1950s and into the following decade. The religious epic was attractive for a number of reasons, not least because, in Hollywood's ongoing battle with television, it provided grand-scale spectacle against which the small screen could not compete. In this regard, new technological developments were a crucial element in the formula for survival. The Academy Award–winning costumes of DeMille's *Samson and Delilah* (1949)—most memorably Hedy Lamarr's spectacular cape made from thousands of peacock feathers—were filmed in three-strip Technicolor, a relatively expensive process that had been used in live-action film since 1934 and required special camera equipment. But with the announcement of Eastman Kodak's one-strip process in 1950, filming in color became less expensive and more easily available and, by 1955, color production accounted for 50 percent of Hollywood releases.[43]

The other major technological innovation of the period was the widescreen process. In the early fifties, experimentations with new kinds of motion picture vision had created a short-lived craze for 3D filmmaking, followed by the "one-of-a-kind" multitrack sight and sound experience of Cinerama.[44] The major studios had a number of successes with 3D, including effective use of the technique by Alfred Hitchcock in the crucial scene of *Dial M for Murder* (1954) where Grace Kelly kills an intruder with scissors, but the format had multiple problems and was soon dropped. Cinerama, which required purpose-built theaters for its wraparound screen, was destined to be limited in its reach. Nonetheless, the appeal of widescreen was obvious and Twentieth Century–Fox released the biblical epic *The Robe* (1953) and the romantic comedy *How to Marry a Millionaire* (1953) in its new format, CinemaScope. A relatively simple process, based on French technology invented in the 1920s, CinemaScope used an anamorphic lens in both the camera and the projector but used regular 35mm film stock. Advertised as widescreen "without glasses," the impact of Fox's innovation in terms of intensity, vibrancy, and cost was immediate and its competitors quickly developed widescreen formats of their own, among them VistaVision, Todd-AO, and Panavision, along with numerous others.

These new technologies had a considerable impact on how costume could influence the look of a film. Nicholas Ray was three weeks into shooting *Rebel Without a Cause* in 1955 when Warner Bros. realized the enormous star potential of James Dean and switched production of the film from black and white to the more expensive color format.[45] For Ray, it was a chance to break away from the conventional black-and-white documentary realist style used by "social problem" films of the time. Taking full advantage of the potential offered by the new technologies, he combined elements of jarring red (Natalie Wood's dress and lipstick, Dean's jacket) with a widescreen visual style and tilted angles to achieve "a psychological realism" that matched Dean's angst-ridden plea: "How can a guy grow up in a circus like this?"[46] Designer Moss Mabry accentuated the effect. Upon discovering that high school kids shunned new jeans, he aged and dirtied Dean's blue Levis.[47] Worn with a white undershirt played against the striking red of his nylon windbreaker, the look immediately became a teen sartorial classic that provided a counterpoint to the more hard-edged symbol of rebellion that Marlon Brando had created when he wore a T-shirt, jeans, and black leather jacket in Laslo Benedek's *The Wild One* (1953).

Others also took advantage of the heightened effect of Technicolor to achieve maximum emotional and symbolic impact. Alfred Hitchcock, one of the few directors in Hollywood with enough box office clout to exert artistic control over every frame, was meticulous about color, paying fetishistic attention to the details of the hair and costume of his leading ladies. Golden-haired Grace Kelly was dressed in blue chiffon and muted pastels in *To Catch a Thief* (1955); the narrative twist of *Vertigo* (1958) turns on Madeleine/Judy's platinum blonde chignon and gray suit; and Tippi Hedren is a cool blonde in a green woolen suit in *The Birds* (1963). Working with less autonomy, Douglas Sirk nonetheless managed to imprint his now celebrated signature style on melodramas renowned for their vivid use of color and a visual strategy that Peter Lev states "revels in phoniness."[48] In Sirk's *All That Heaven Allows* (1955), an idealized image of suburbia is subverted by being too picture-perfect, the costumes by Bill Thomas too matching. Again, red is key. Jane Wyman's Cary wears a scarlet dress that signals her emergence from widowhood as she rediscovers sexual desire with the wrong person—the working-class Ron (Rock Hudson), whose outdoor working clothes complement the bold autumnal tones of the film's opening scenes.[49]

Working out how to use the new technologies to the best advantage was often a case of trial and error. Billy Wilder's *Some Like It Hot* (1959) was a box office hit, despite the fact that it was filmed in black and white, a decision made after the thick makeup worn by Tony Curtis and Jack Lemmon was discovered to cause a green tint. For the famous Ascot scene in *My Fair Lady*, Cecil Beaton had numerous problems with reds turning orange, blacks and whites turning to green and yellow in long shots, and tweeds "strobing."[50]

FIGURE 19: Publicity shot of Marilyn Monroe, Lauren Bacall, and Betty Grable in *How to Marry a Millionaire* on the cover of *The Australian Magazine* (November 24, 1953). Costumes designed by Travilla, makeup by Ben Nye, hair uncredited.

The Robe was equally, if not more, nightmarish for Charles LeMaire, who had originally designed for shooting in black and white; the studio's decision to switch to color meant that many costumes needed to be bleached, dyed, or remade.[51] CinemaScope also caused design problems when tests showed that it magnified every detail, including machine-stitching on biblical-era costumes, which now had to be pulled apart and resewn by hand.[52]

As David Chierichetti tells it in *Hollywood Costume Design*, LeMaire also faced opposition from the three stars of *How to Marry a Millionaire*—Lauren Bacall, Betty Grable, and Marilyn Monroe—over the distorting effects of the widescreen technology. William Travilla, who designed the costumes for the film, was aware of the widening effect of CinemaScope onscreen, but LeMaire as costume supervisor at Fox wanted to use the fashionable full skirts of the French-based "New Look" for the film. In the end, Grable and Bacall compromised for a few scenes, but Monroe refused to budge and insisted on her signature figure-hugging skirts (figure 19).[53]

Hollywood's New Looks

LeMaire's concern with the silhouette of his leading ladies represents a dilemma that confronts all designers of films set in the "present": how to make female characters fashionable, but not so fashionable that they date the film when it is released, usually months later. Edith Head learned this lesson the hard way when Christian Dior launched his nostalgic, extravagantly feminine collection on February 12, 1947, to a rapt audience in Paris. Immediately dubbed the "New Look," its soft shoulders, wasp waists, and shockingly full skirts swept away the austerity dressing of the war.[54] Over the span of her long career, Head would costume over a thousand films, and receive a record eight Oscars. With the arrival of Dior's New Look she realized that "every film that I had done in the past few months looked like something from the breadlines. . . . I vowed that I would never get caught by a fashion trend again."[55]

In this Head was aided by directors cautious about fashion onscreen, both for its potential to distract from the narrative (if too spectacular) and its unfortunate habit of constantly changing. With her designs for Elizabeth Taylor as the social-ite Angela Vickers in *A Place in the Sun* (George Stevens, 1951), Head achieved a perfect balance. Audiences thought her designs reflected the latest fashions as worn by high-society teenagers but, she explained, her clothes were "middle of the road in terms of the current fashion trends"; she had simply taken the styles current in 1949 (when the film went into production) and set about "translat-ing them into something timeless."[56] Head was awarded an Oscar for her work on the film, and the Angela Vickers New Look gowns worn by Taylor received maximum publicity and were used as a selling point in the film's promotion;

widely copied, they generated huge retail sales.[57] The most famous was the white, strapless, wasp-waisted gown with a bodice decorated with sprays of violets and layers of extravagantly full skirts that Angela wears to the Eastman ball. Now it appears an uncomfortable example of Simone de Beauvoir's notion of "elegance as bondage," but in Hollywood (and life) the silhouette became the gold standard for wedding, prom, and debutante dresses.

However, unlike these gay occasions, *A Place in the Sun* does not end happily and, to visit her lover George Eastman (Montgomery Clift) on death row, a demure and grave Angela wears a plain black, full-skirted dress with white collar and cuffs. By crossing it with the pared-down aesthetic of Chanel's "little maid's dress," Head proved that the New Look was nothing if not adaptable. Capable of conveying a wide range of emotions, as translated by Hollywood, it became an "essential part of the lexicon,"[58] as Stella Bruzzi puts it, equally associated with youth and elegance as with "safe, not particularly sexual, and quite matronly forms of femininity."[59] By 1957, Orry-Kelly was satirizing the look in *Les Girls* (George Cukor, 1957), but throughout the 1950s it was ubiquitous, worn even by the dwellers of the mystical Scottish village in *Brigadoon* (Vincente Minnelli, 1954), a twirling skirt here and a rustic flounce there adding a touch of authenticity to the otherwise fashionable line that continued to appeal to audiences.

Then, as now, strict adherence to authenticity needed to be weighed against the demands of the film to tell its story. Ingrid Bergman thought that *Joan of Arc* (Victor Fleming, 1948) had the "smooth, glossy quality of Hollywood" and, in fact, her haircut for the film influenced hairstyles into the fifties.[60] At the time, Barbara Karinska and Dorothy Jeakins set new standards for authenticity in costume when designing the fifteenth-century costumes, creating garments on hand looms and copying fabrics sourced from museums.[61] The sheer scale of the grand historical epic meant that costume design on such films was often the responsibility of more than one designer. On DeMille's *Samson and Delilah*, for example, Elois Jenssen, Edith Head, Dorothy Jeakins, Gile Steele, and Gwen Wakeling shared the Oscar for Best Costume Design (color). However, most of the workers who contributed to costuming on a film never received an onscreen credit, despite the crucial contribution of their expertise.

For *The Robe*, the master weaver Dorothea Hulse meticulously researched the relic stolen from Christ's body that gives the film its title, weaving it by hand on an authentic replica first-century loom built with the help of her husband. Although she also created textiles and costume fabrics for *David and Bathsheba* (Henry King, 1951) without receiving a credit, in a surprise twist Hulse herself ended up onscreen in *The Ten Commandments* after DeMille called for the replacement of an extra working at a loom as he wanted someone in the scene who looked like they knew what they were doing.[62] On these huge epics, the research process alone could be daunting. For William Wyler's *Ben-Hur* (1959), the British designer Elizabeth Haffenden began work on the costumes over a year before filming started, researching extensively with her team and making over eight thousand sketches.[63] At Rome's Cinecittà studios where the production was based, the costume department included Italian leather makers and armorers working with traditional materials, as well as seamstresses, tailors, and other wardrobe personnel, all of whom helped create the costumes for the film's massive cast of 50,000 people.[64]

Also filmed in Cinecittà (after an initial failed attempt at Pinewood in England) was one of Hollywood's greatest miscalculations, *Cleopatra* (Joseph L. Mankiewicz, 1963), the hugely extravagant and highly publicized epic that, at a final cost of over $40 million, hastened Fox's descent into a financial abyss. The film featured Elizabeth Taylor, Hollywood's "last great star,"[65] in the title role, wearing scores of staggeringly gorgeous costumes created by Irene Sharaff. In her memoirs, Sharaff recounts a design process that included reference to archeological records and artifacts. But cinematic portrayals of the life of Cleopatra VII are notorious for getting her costume wrong, ignoring her Greek heritage in favor of a fancy-dress Egyptian style, and then combining it with a contemporary fashionable twist that can be easily read by audiences. Sharaff's costumes styled as "purely Egyptian" with "an early 1960s aesthetic" were no exception.[66] The clinging gowns that showed Taylor's sumptuous décolletage and tightly cinched waist to great advantage mixed historical plausibility with Hollywood imagination. Made from silk jersey cloth of "24-carat gold," metallic leather, sequins, and bugle beads, the sixty-odd costumes worn by Taylor were modern enough for the star to inform a reporter that they would make "the most wonderful ball gowns and party dresses," and she planned to "pilfer" them all.[67]

Sharaff had been brought onto the film after the departure of the original designer, Oliver Messel. She also designed the costumes worn by Rex Harrison's Caesar, with responsibility for the remainder of the film's 26,000 costumes shared by Nino Nerovese and Renie (Irene Brouillet), designing for the male and female cast, respectively. Taylor's forty-odd wigs, including the iconic black plaited bob with gold tassels, were made by the famous British wigmaker Stanley Hall, who was known to source the finest hair from Italian convents for his individually woven and hand-knotted "wig creations."[68] Alberto De Rossi was head of makeup on the film, but Taylor's sweeping jet-black kohl and spangly eye makeup was said to be her own invention. "I think I'll set a new trend," said Taylor in an interview during filming.[69] And she did. In 1963, the "Cleopatra look" appeared on catwalks of major fashion houses and Revlon released their own Cleopatra look—Sphinx Pink lipstick and Sphinx Eyes—with a television commercial starring top model Suzy Parker. Adding to the status of Taylor's filmic persona, Andy Warhol created *Silver Liz as Cleopatra* (1963), which, as Suzanne Osmond points out, "conflates the iconic identities of Taylor, Cleopatra and the *femme fatale*."[70]

With casts of thousands demanding elaborate hairpieces and exotic makeup, *Cleopatra* proved to be a boom for makeup artists, though costume historian

Alicia Annas's description of Kubrick's 1960 *Spartacus* as being "quite simply about brown eyeshadow" might be overstating the case.[71] Makeup special effects were also usually required for horror as well as science-fiction films, the latter of which became a major genre in the 1950s, infused with a Cold War mentality and anxieties over communist invasion or nuclear attack dressed up as *The Thing from Another World* (1951) or *Invasion of the Body Snatchers* (1956).[72] In 1948, Guerlain promoted their lipsticks with a campaign depicting a red-lipped Hollywood femme fatale against the backdrop of an apocalyptic, mushrooming atomic cloud.[73] It was not entirely inappropriate: World War II had led to an explosion in beauty products, with a continually expanding range of merchandise that developed out of the "new scientific advances gained in the war."[74] In 1950, cosmetics had grown into a billion-dollar industry and, by 1957, it was estimated that 95 percent of women and girls over twelve used at least one beauty product.[75] Among the new wares was Max Factor's Cream Puff, the first compacted powder, which boasted Ava Gardner as its spokesperson.[76] The looks created had global reach, and in Japan Shiseido promoted its cosmetics with campaigns influenced by Hollywood styles.[77]

By the mid-1950s, half the makeup artists in Hollywood were at least sixty years old. A new wave of young makeup artists was entering the field, with many of them trained in the use of latex and other techniques developed after the war for providing prostheses for injured veterans.[78] Makeup for *The House of Wax* (André de Toth, 1953), the first 3D film to go into production at a major studio, was credited to Gordon Bau, who was head of the Warner Bros. "face-fixing department."[79] Gordon's brother George, who also worked on *The House of Wax*, had learned about the manufacture of foam and rubber compounds while employed at a rubber plant in the 1930s, and is credited with innovations in latex foam appliances and developing now-common latex masks that could be pulled over one's entire head.[80] However, it was not all sophisticated technology. On-set photographs show Marlon Brando doing his own makeup for *On the Waterfront* (Elia Kazan, 1954), and the head of the makeup department at Universal Studios, Dan Striepeke, used paint to suggest Kirk Douglas's rippling muscle tone in *Spartacus*.[81]

In that film, Douglas (who served as executive producer as well) wore unusually brief costumes that emphasized the spectacle of his muscled, oiled body. Whereas traditionally men's bodies in Hollywood films were functional rather than decorative, in the postwar period—from the "inescapable animal bulk" of Brando to the sleekly bare-chested Yul Brynner in *The King and I* (Walter Lang, 1956)—men's bodies were offered up as objects of erotic display.[82] If the exotic virility of Brynner left the corseted and crinolined Deborah Kerr breathless, to look at Brando in *A Streetcar Named Desire* (Elia Kazan, 1951), wearing his T-shirt shrunk skintight, the sleeves cut short and the body ripped, was to celebrate blue-collar sexuality in a manner that refuted the convention of spectacle

FIGURE 20: Marlon Brando in *A Streetcar Named Desire* (1951), costumes by Lucinda Ballard, wardrobe uncredited. Makeup by Gordon Bau and others (uncredited), hair uncredited.

as solely the realm of the female body and female dress (figure 20).[83] Broody and complex, Brando, like James Dean, Montgomery Clift, and, later, the dazzlingly handsome Paul Newman, represented a new type of male hero. Dressed down, they also offered a new way of desiring male stars.

The Hays Code, the Slip, and the South

When it was released in 1963, *Cleopatra* was proclaimed "morally unacceptable" by the Catholic Legion of Decency and given an official "B" rating ("morally objectionable in part").[84] Five years later, in 1968, Hollywood introduced its own ratings system after the suspension of the Motion Picture Production Code (familiarly known as the Hays Code) in 1966.[85] But until then, censors worked in conjunction with the Legion to keep a tight rein on morality. On-site visits by the censor were not uncommon, and working sketches and photographs of costumes had to be passed by the censor's office. Edith Head tells of consulting closely with Paramount's censorship specialist over Hedy Lamarr's revealing costumes for *Samson and Delilah* and working with the censor up until the last day of shooting.[86] Getting around the demands of the Code was an essential part of the costume designer's craft. In this, nude-colored soufflé was a designer's best friend. When combined with transparent materials, wrote Sharaff, "so long as there was a covering, however thin, the studio could claim that the actress was fully clothed."[87] In matters of censorship, biblical adaptations were particularly appealing; under the guise of "historical authenticity," they provided opportunities to push regulations to the limit. In 1956 *The Ten Commandments*, for example, deftly negotiated scantily clad women, transparent, clinging gowns, and scenes of sexual domination with a marketing strategy that appealed to Christian, Jewish, and even Muslim audiences across the globe.[88]

Underlining how out of touch the Code was with broader community standards, in the same year that Fox released *How to Marry a Millionaire* and *Gentlemen Prefer Blondes* (Howard Hawks, 1953), its new star Marilyn Monroe appeared on the cover of the first issue of Hugh Hefner's *Playboy* magazine wearing a black-and-white dress with a neckline slashed to the waist. Inside the magazine, reclining invitingly on a red velvet cloth as the magazine's first "Sweetheart of the Month," Monroe wore nothing at all. Nudity onscreen was, of course, out of the question. Even the hint of a panty line under a costume could be rejected by the censors for "being overly sex suggestive."[89] Underwear was an ongoing problem for the costume designer. For *The Seven Year Itch* (Billy Wilder, 1955), Travilla, who dressed Monroe in many of her films and formed a close relationship with the star, managed to get her into one of only two full skirts she would wear on film throughout her career. His design of an ivory bias-cut halter dress in rayon-acetate crepe with sunray pleats—known as the "subway" dress—was iconic from the moment a fifty-two-foot cutout of Monroe, with her skirts billowing around her in the breeze, appeared in Times Square for the New York premiere of the film. But the famous scene of Monroe standing over a subway vent was cut drastically in the final edit of the film due to censure over a glimpse of her frilled panties.[90]

For the signature number "Diamonds Are a Girl's Best Friend" in *Gentlemen Prefer Blondes*, Travilla was forced to replace a $5,000 gown—made from bands of black velvet, rhinestones, and soufflé dyed to match Monroe's skin tone—with a pink satin sheath lined with a modesty layer of felt to make it stiffer. The felt provided added assurance against any wayward jiggling of curves. The original dress had been designed to transform Monroe into "a giant necklace" and was "a triumph in wires and soufflé."[91] A similar feat of engineering was later achieved by Orry-Kelly in *Some Like It Hot* when he poured Monroe into two bias-cut gowns, one "nude" and one black, made on a soufflé base covered in crystal and jet beads, which barely contained her voluptuous bosom.[92] By the time of the film's release in 1959, interpretation of the Code was increasingly loose; nonetheless, the film was banned in Kansas, although this was less at the offense of seeing Monroe's quivering bust than the appearance of the cross-dressing Tony Curtis and Jack Lemmon.[93]

In view of the restrictions imposed by the censors, it is no coincidence that a number of films portrayed the hot and sweaty South; one way to see characters semi-naked was to have them remove clothes because of the sweltering heat. The opening scene of Elia Kazan's *Baby Doll* (1956) reveals Karl Malden's Archie Lee spying on his teenage virgin bride, Baby Doll (Carroll Baker), who is dressed in a baby-doll nightie, curled up on a crib sucking her thumb (figure 21). The much older Archie Lee is dressed by designer Anna Hill Johnstone in ill-fitting shirts

FIGURE 21: Carroll Baker in *Baby Doll* (1956). Costume design by Anna Hill Johnstone, wardrobe by Florence Transfield, makeup by Robert Jiras, hair by Willis Hanchett.

with buttons gaping, a costume choice that indexes his (metaphorical) impotence and inability to keep things together. Eli Wallach, on the other hand, as Silva Vacarro, the slightly sadistic third party in the love triangle, is dressed sharply in black, a whip often in hand. Baby Doll herself, in turn manipulative and vulnerable, teasing and seduced, is in and out of her clothes, spending one long scene in nothing but a slip.[94]

At this time, with any sight of panties repeatedly censored, it became almost obligatory that female leads appear in at least one scene wearing a slip. For *Cat on a Hot Tin Roof* (Richard Brooks, 1958), Helen Rose had only three outfits to design for Elizabeth Taylor's Maggie, one of which was a slip.[95] It was a garment that seemed made for Taylor's "volcanic" brand of womanliness. In the opening scene of *Butterfield 8* (Daniel Mann, 1960), as "party girl" Gloria, she wanders leisurely around her "date's" empty upscale apartment, wearing only high heels and a figure-hugging ivory slip trimmed in ecru lace. When she finds an envelope with a note and $250 payment in her handbag, her mood turns suddenly and, after angrily scrawling "No Sale" in lipstick on the mirror, she walks out wearing only her slip under the mink coat she has pilfered from the well-stocked closet of her lover's wife. Even the quintessential good girl Doris Day appeared in a black slip in *Please Don't Eat the Daisies* (Charles Walters, 1960) although, in this instance, the sexual implications of the garment were domesticated by the presence of her children; she is simply a woman getting dressed.[96]

Bathroom nudity was given a different treatment in Alfred Hitchcock's *Psycho* (1960) when the female lead (Janet Leigh as Marion Crane) was killed midway through the movie, stabbed to death in the shower. One of the most famous scenes in film history, Marion's nudity was only part of the reason behind calls to censure or prohibit the film, but the fact of its release points to the gradual erosion of the Code that was in evidence throughout the sixties up until its final collapse. Hollywood was quick to take advantage of the new freedom. Hitchcock's script for *Rear Window* in 1954 had been subject to a number of cuts at the hands of the PCA censor, including one scene where James Stewart observes from his window "a young girl . . . wearing only black panties . . . [and] nude above the waist."[97] In stark contrast, the opening scene of *Bonnie and Clyde* (Arthur Penn, 1967) shows a naked Bonnie catching Clyde trying to make off with her mother's car; his first glimpse of her is of her full-frontal nudity framed in a dusty window.

Designing Icons

For Marion Crane's costumes in *Psycho*, Hitchcock instructed costumers Rita Rigg and Helen Colvig to buy her two dresses off the rack, paying only what a secretary such as Marion could afford.[98] In *Who's Afraid of Virginia Woolf?* (Mike Nichols, 1966), Irene Sharaff transformed Elizabeth Taylor into a blowsy, middle-aged alcoholic through use of clever padding and clothes of a particularly unflattering cut. Earlier, for *Viva Zapata!* (Elia Kazan, 1952), Travilla transformed actress Jean Peters into a Mexican peasant by breaking her confident American stride with a pair of shoes half a size too small.[99] And for *The Country Girl* (George Seaton, 1954), Edith Head played down Grace Kelly's beauty by putting her in "dresses that made her feel plain and depressed just to put them on."[100] This was a different type of transformation than had been popular in films of an earlier era when the emphasis was on a glittering star in satin, lamé, and sequins. Instead, with the emphasis more strongly on narrative and character, the intention was less for the audience to see a star in costume than to see someone "merely wearing clothes."[101]

Although in many respects this approach was not new—indeed, film scholar Jane Gaines has argued that it lies at the heart of the cinematic costuming code of black-and-white contemporary dramas of the classical era—it gained fresh impetus when there was little distance between the actor and the role he or she was playing. In the films of Audrey Hepburn, arguably it is this perception that underscores her ongoing hold on the popular imagination. *Roman Holiday* (William Wyler, 1953), *Sabrina* (Billy Wilder, 1954), and *Funny Face* (Stanley Donen, 1957) are all classic transformation narratives of the "Cinderella story" (although the transformation in *Roman Holiday* is reversed); and in *Breakfast at Tiffany's* (Blake Edwards, 1961), Holly Golightly has left behind her earlier identity of Ella May. In all cases, whether "before" or "after," dressed to the nines or casually chic, Hepburn manages to appear equally at home in what she is wearing, apparently never playing anyone but a version of herself.

The relationship between Hepburn and the young Paris couturier, Hubert de Givenchy, who provided clothes for her roles in *Sabrina* (uncredited), *Funny Face*, and *Breakfast at Tiffany's* (as well as dressing her offscreen), is more documented than any other relationship between a Hollywood star and a designer. However, it was not the only instance of Paris couture being brought to the Hollywood screen in this period. In 1962, Pierre Balmain designed clothes for *Tender Is the Night* (Henry King, 1962) (uncredited) and, earlier, Christian Dior had designed Jennifer Jones's costumes for *The Indiscretion of an American Wife* (Vittorio De Sica, 1953), which earned him an Academy Award nomination.[102] As well as being a favorite of Marlene Dietrich, Dior also co-designed (with Pierre Cardin) Elizabeth Taylor's wardrobe for *The V.I.P.s* (Vincente Minnelli, 1963).[103] With Paris fashion the byword in chic and an estimated 70 percent of haute couture clients coming from the United States, the Hollywood-Paris connection made sound economic sense, with both parties standing to benefit.[104] But no one could have anticipated how potent and enduring the combination of Hepburn's gamine European looks and Givenchy's impeccably elegant design would be. Controversy remains over who designed what in *Sabrina*; the wild popularity of ballet flats owes as much to Brigitte Bardot as to Hepburn's "empathical" footwear in *Funny Face*; and the instantly recognizable Holly Golightly look in the opening scene of *Breakfast at Tiffany's* has devolved into a fancy dress favorite. Nonetheless, there is no denying that between the actress, the couturier, and the costume designer a new ideal type was created. As historian Nicholas Drake writes, "Hepburn's every change of appearance and role was recorded in *Vogue*" and, from the glamour of a Givenchy gown to the classic simplicity of black turtlenecks, capri pants, beige trench coats, and a man's white shirt, on Audrey Hepburn many fashion staples were born.[105]

The End of Design?

In Stanley Donen's dark comedy *Two for the Road* (1967), the credits for Hepburn's wardrobe read like the pages of *Vogue*, with names like Mary Quant, Paco Rabanne, André Courrèges, Foale and Tuffin, and others providing cutting-edge ready-to-wear clothes in scene after fashionable scene. Hepburn's acerbic co-star, Albert Finney, was dressed by the British designer Hardy Amies who, at the time, was better known as dressmaker to the queen.[106] Men rarely drew focus around costume, although there are some notable exceptions: Brando in his T-shirt, or Clint Eastwood in Sergio Leone's spaghetti western *The Good, the Bad and the Ugly* (1966), his pants slung low, a Mexican blanket flung across one shoulder like the cape of a rugged super-antihero. And Sean Connery as James

Bond was once described as being just "like a fashion model . . . you'd watch a scene to see what he was wearing."[107] However, as long as the tailored look of the lounge suit was still dominant, male stars were often left to their own devices. For Hitchcock's *North by Northwest* (1959), Cary Grant wore suits from Savile Row[108] (as did Connery in the Bond films) and, while Hitchcock paid meticulous attention to the costumes Edith Head designed for Grace Kelly in *To Catch a Thief* (1954), Grant claimed to have bought his own wardrobe in Cannes, just days before shooting began.[109]

As Hollywood faced up to the economic reality of a "runaway" audience, the number of films in production shrank, budgets were slashed, and the expertise of an experienced costume designer was no longer considered essential. Buying clothes off the rack became common and "shopping" replaced "design." For the first time in decades, films appeared without a costume design credit. This practice was most apparent in the new genre of beach and surf movies that emerged in 1959 to satisfy the growing teen demographic. Almost all the major studios jumped on board. Columbia released *Gidget* (1959) and *Ride the Wild Surf* (1964), Paramount made *Blue Hawaii* (1961), starring Elvis Presley, and United Artists released *For Those Who Think Young* (1964). But it would be a Hollywood outsider, American Independent Productions (AIP), that most successfully exploited the niche, starting with *Beach Party* (1963).[110] Marjorie Corso, whose career spanned over two decades, designed many of the costumes for AIP during the 1960s, including those for *Beach Blanket Bingo* (1965) starring Annette Funicello. Despite a long history designing for film, Corso's work has received little recognition by costume or film historians.

In his book *Hollywood Surf and Beach Movies*, Thomas Lisanti writes about the new genre: "Surfers loathed them, teenagers flocked to them, critics dismiss them, and producers laughed all the way to the bank."[111] While they did prove very popular with audiences, their primary appeal for motion picture companies was that they could be made on shoestring budgets. For example, *Surf Party* (1964), for Twentieth Century–Fox, was filmed a year after *Cleopatra* almost cleaned out the studio. With little money in the bank the film was made in black and white and most of its costumes were off-the-rack. Alternatively, in a return to the practice of Hollywood's early days, actors wore their own clothes, or even bought clothes themselves for a specific scene. As Sue Casey, who played the female lead in *The Beach Girls and the Monster* (1965), commented, "There was no money in this film to do anything. I did my own hair, my own make up and supplied all the clothes I wore."[112] Tie-ins and product placement were another wardrobe solution. For example, in *For Those Who Think Young* (1964), Peter Pan Swimwear International provided bathing costumes and promoted the film in their ad campaign.[113] In terms of costuming, the bikini was without a doubt the garment du jour (figure 22). For *It's a Bikini World* (1967), the costumer carried the entire wardrobe of bikinis and bathing suits around in a little laundry bag.[114] If in the

FIGURE 22: Bikinis in *The Beach Girls and the Monster* (1965). The film has no credit for costume design, only wardrobe, by Bonnie Cole; makeup was by Joann Howard, hair by Adelade Halpern.

1950s Hollywood had helped create and popularize classic symbols of teen style, what was on display here was teen fashion reduced to its absolute minimum.

New Wave Hollywood

In 1966, the first wave of baby boomers turned eighteen. They had grown up on rock 'n' roll and now lived in a world where youth culture was defined by the Beatles, Bob Dylan, the Rolling Stones, Jimi Hendrix, Janis Joplin, and Aretha Franklin—icons for a new generation with whom movie stars could not compete. Television, which had switched to color in 1963, broadcast news of assassinations, the civil rights movement, antiwar demonstrations, and the nascent second-wave feminist movement, none of which made it onto the cinema screen, except in rare instances such as *Guess Who's Coming to Dinner* (Stanley Kramer, 1967) with Sidney Poitier. Hollywood worked hard to catch up and retain what was left of its dwindling audience. With films like *Psycho*, *The Apartment* (Billy Wilder, 1960), *West Side Story* (Jerome Robbins and Robert Wise, 1961), and *Barefoot in the Park* (Gene Saks, 1967), it proved still capable of producing reliable, money-making, entertaining, aesthetically creative, and socially challenging films. With *Camelot* (Joshua Logan, 1967), even some of the aura of extravagant costuming from Hollywood's golden era returned when the Australian designer John Truscott covered the ten-foot train of Vanessa Redgrave's wool and silk wedding dress with dried pumpkin seeds from scores of pumpkins delivered to the Warner Bros. studios and individually sewn on by hand.[115]

However, from the late 1950s, films from France, Italy, and Great Britain were showing in art houses or at film festivals, attracting young and educated filmgoers who openly defined their taste in cinema against the commercialism of Holly-wood.[116] Although the first foreign film to make a box office breakthrough, *And God Created Woman* (Roger Vadim, 1957), starring Brigitte Bardot, was less than highbrow, it was followed by films directed by the leading lights of the French New Wave and European cinema—Jean-Luc Godard, Alain Resnais, François Truffaut, Michelangelo Antonioni, Federico Fellini, and Ingmar Bergman—all of whom would have a lasting influence on cinema and style. Unhampered by cen-sorship restrictions, films such as *À Bout de Souffle* (*Breathless*, Jean-Luc Godard, 1960), *La Dolce Vita* (Federico Fellini, 1960), and *Blow-Up* (Michelangelo Anton-ioni, 1966) provided American audiences with a more mature depiction of sex and eroticism. Often liberal sexual mores were accompanied by provocative costum-ing, as in Antonioni's *Blow-Up* where the model Veruschka seductively writhes, half-naked in a beaded black dress, on the floor for David Hemmings's camera.

The costumes for *Bonnie and Clyde*, one of the first American films with clear ties to the French New Wave (producer and star Warren Beatty had originally hoped that Godard or Truffaut would direct), were designed by Theodora Van Runkle, a sketch artist who had been recommended for the job by Dorothy Jeak-ins.[117] By this stage, Hollywood had virtually ceded any authority it once had on fashionable style to other forms of entertainment and popular culture such as music and television. But *Bonnie and Clyde* was, in the words of David Newman and Robert Benton, the film's screenwriters, a film "about style and people who have style,"[118] and the fashion-plate look that Van Runkle created for her two Depression-era celebrity bank robbers had "a sweeping impact on the American fashion scene."[119] Beatty as Clyde, dressed in pinstriped suits, spectator shoes, and fedora hats, recalled Hollywood gangsters of the 1930s channeled through the cool sophistication of the French New Wave.

But with Faye Dunaway's Bonnie, it was the look of textured knits, silk neck-ties, bias cut mid-length skirts, sharp suits, and sensible shoes, worn with a beret as "the final culmination of the silhouette," that inspired legions of imitators on both sides of the Atlantic.[120] These were period clothes made unrepentantly mod-ern, and in his study of *Bonnie and Clyde* Lester Friedman attributes the force of their appeal to "the rising tide of feminist thought in the 60s."[121] Van Runkle is credited with cutting short the reign of the mini-skirt and boosting sales of berets, but the more important legacy of "the Bonnie look," according to Fried-man, was that it gave women an expression of power "while still projecting a distinctive aura of femininity" (figure 23).[122]

The masterly ending of *Bonnie and Clyde*, with its two antiheros meeting a hail of bullets in a violent "ballet of death," was shot on four cameras running at four different speeds to capture the graphic details of Clyde's scalp flying and Bonnie's body being torn apart by bullets—special effects that were achieved with an innovative combination of newly perfected exploding squibs and capsules of synthetic blood.[123] The stylized violence divided audiences and critics but firmly

FIGURE 23: Faye Dunaway sporting Bonnie's iconic look, including beret, in *Bonnie and Clyde* (1967), with Warren Beatty as Clyde and Michael J. Pollard as C. W. Moss. Costumes designed by Theadora Van Runkle (wardrobe for women by Norma Brown, for men by Andy Matyasi), makeup by Robert Jiras, hair by Gladys Witten.

identified the film, and its aesthetic, as part of the cinema of sensation. Its box office success with audiences around the world, along with *Cool Hand Luke* (Stuart Rosenberg, 1967), starring Paul Newman, and *The Graduate* (Mike Nichols, 1967), marked a turning point for American cinema. All three films appealed to a youthful, sophisticated audience and proved, as cinema historian Paul Monaco writes, that "Hollywood filmmaking was no longer a 'conservative' undertaking in any normal sense of the word."[124]

One of the last Hollywood releases of 1967, *The Graduate* was Dustin Hoffman's first starring role; he played Benjamin Braddock, an alienated, angst-ridden college graduate who returns from college to his suffocating, upper-middle-class home in California. "I'm worried about my future . . . I want it to be different," he tells his father, before falling into a soulless affair with Mrs. Robinson (Anne Bancroft), the wife of his father's legal partner, and then falling in love with her daughter, Elaine (Katherine Ross). For every scene, the predatory Mrs. Robinson, her impeccably groomed dark hair streaked with blonde highlights, is dressed in layers of animal prints, from the tiger-striped lamé dress she wears at Benjamin's welcome home party to her leopard-spot satin bra and half-slip. Wrapped in $25,000 worth of furs, including a Somalian leopard skin coat from the furrier Maximilian, and jewelry from Harry Winston, she is a suburban vision of Hollywood glamour, a contemporary femme fatale who belongs to the past (color plate 7). In contrast, her daughter wears a selection of modern-day dresses, skirts, jeans, and jackets—none of which are memorable. The exception, of course, is

FIGURE 24: Katherine Ross and Dustin Hoffman near the end of *The Graduate* (1967), costumes by Patricia Zipprodt (other wardrobe personnel uncredited), makeup by Harry Maret, hair by Sydney Guilaroff and Sherry Wilson.

in the final scene where Elaine, in a white wedding dress, hair flying loose, and Benjamin, in a nylon hooded jacket, khaki pants, and sneakers, run away from the church, leaving the outraged wedding party and guests trapped behind glass doors (figure 24). The lasting image of the film is of the two of them sitting on the backseat of a bus, heading into an uncertain future.

Bleak Realities

In the years between 1947 and 1967, Hollywood designers created some of the most iconic looks of the twentieth century. Working on films that played to a global audience they fashioned costume, makeup, and hair that helped shape everyday fashion culture. But the period was also one of great transitions for the Hollywood film industry as it confronted the dismantling of the studio system, lost much of its audience to television, attempted to address shifting demographics, and struggled to maintain relevance with a new generation more interested in European and art house cinema. By the mid-1960s, writes film scholar Thomas Schatz, "Hollywood was on the verge of its worst economic slump since the War."[125] Despite this bleak reality, in 1966, the incoming president of the Motion Picture Association of America, Jack Valenti, announced that "the American movie is the world's most wanted commodity."[126] Paradoxically, this meant that Hollywood film companies became an attractive target for takeover by larger interests. In what Schatz describes as "a post-1965 conglomerate wave," Paramount was acquired by the oil company Gulf & Western in 1966 and United Artists by Transamerica in 1967. This was followed by the merger of Warner Bros. with Kinney National Services and the buying out of MGM by the real-estate tycoon Kirk Kerkorian in 1969.[127]

By this stage, writes Deborah Landis, "companies like MGM and Twentieth Century Fox . . . eager to leverage every studio asset . . . sold their backlots and auctioned huge quantities of historically significant props and costumes."[128] Thus began a "gold rush" in Hollywood memorabilia that also marked "a low point in Hollywood history" with many items scattered to the winds.[129] In 1992, the collector Larry McQueen discovered a staff in an antique shop that turned out to be the one used by Charlton Heston as Moses in *The Ten Commandments*.[130] Coming full circle in terms of its narrative of excess, garments worn by Elizabeth Taylor in *Cleopatra* were auctioned in 2011, her tasseled wig going for $20,315, her gold cape for $59,375.[131] Earlier, Audrey Hepburn's iconic black Givenchy dress from *Breakfast at Tiffany's* was auctioned by Christie's auction house for £467,200, exceeding by far its expected price of £70,000.[132] Outstripping all was the dress made famous by Marilyn Monroe as she stood above the breeze of a subway vent in *The Seven Year Itch*, which sold at auction in 2011 for $4.6 million.[133]

But this was all in the future. In 1967, after forty-three years at Paramount, Edith Head's contract was not renewed by the studio's new owners, Gulf & Western. Now close to seventy years old, she moved to Universal where she remained under contract until her death in 1981. But she was the exception. For almost everyone else, Hollywood no longer meant a long-term contract but the insecurity of working freelance along with diminished responsibilities, a lowering of status, and shoestring budgets. Things would get worse before they got better. In 1969, Peter Fonda and Dennis Hopper made the counterculture hit *Easy Rider* for $501,000.[134] It had a makeup department of one person, and no costume department at all. For those wanting to carry on the decades-long tradition of Hollywood glamour, style, and creativity that Head's career represented, looking down the road, it was going to be a long and bumpy night indeed.

4

THE AUTEUR RENAISSANCE, 1968–1980 Robin Blaetz

The late 1960s and early 1970s are recognized by film scholars as a period in which the rich traditions and techniques of Hollywood cinema, no longer regulated by the pieties of the Production Code, converged with the auteur-driven art cinema of postwar Europe to inspire some of the most interesting films in the medium's history. Due partly to the intense social and political climate of the era—which included protests against the Vietnam War, the assassinations of Martin Luther King and Robert F. Kennedy, the Watergate scandal, the Stonewall riots, and the continuing force of second wave feminism and the civil rights movement—and aided by the rise of film schools and film culture on college campuses and in cities large and small, younger filmmakers and their audiences approached cinema with deep intellectual seriousness.

The dismantling of the major studios and their elaborate hierarchical structures enabled iconoclastic directors who had worked on the fringes of the industry, such as Robert Altman, Hal Ashby, Stanley Kubrick, and Arthur Penn, as well as the new "film school generation" of George Lucas, Martin Scorsese, and Francis Ford Coppola, among many others, to seize the chance to move into the center and to re-create the film industry in their own images. The success of Penn's *Bonnie and Clyde* (1967), made for Warner Bros., had already showed that Hollywood could make money from iconoclasm through exploitation of the youth market itself. As David Brown, then an executive at Twentieth Century–Fox, put it in 1968, "The cinema today is for youths in every corner of the world. Pictures with either artistic creativeness or critical content are helping both the industry and the film business. . . . The world is in revolution. We are mirroring it."[1]

For older costume, makeup, and hair designers, the late 1960s and early 1970s were both bleak and energizing. In 1967, when Edith Head's contract was not renewed by Paramount's new owners—the corporate conglomerate Gulf & Western—she thought that "the studio designer . . . was suddenly a thing of the past."[2] Deborah Nadoolman Landis, a costume designer in her own right as well as a scholar in the field, describes Hollywood during the late 1960s as an "industry asleep," with studios resembling ghost towns and production at a virtual standstill.[3] In 1970, the bankruptcy-driven auctioning off of the contents of MGM's vast wardrobe warehouses signaled the end of the elaborate and fully staffed costume department. The year before, Dennis Hopper and Peter Fonda's *Easy Rider* had ridden to box office success without any costume designer at all, and in 1971 Robert Altman followed suit. For *McCabe and Mrs. Miller*, Altman instead had his actors select their own period wardrobe from pants, shirts, vests, dresses, and accessories he had gathered and that their characters would have owned. The actors then patched and repaired what they had chosen so as to blend costume with character.[4]

The paradox, of course, is that costume, makeup, and hair were crucial to both *Easy Rider* and *McCabe and Mrs. Miller* as signifying systems, even if the role of the designer was minimized, ignored, or assumed by other creative personnel. Dorothy Jeakins, who won the first Oscar for Best Costume Design (color) for *Joan of Arc* (Victor Fleming, 1948), believed, like Edith Head, that her field had become "obsolete" in the 1960s.[5] But Jeakins ultimately had no problem finding work in the new decade, even on films made by directors like Coppola, with whom she worked on *Finian's Rainbow* (1968), or Penn, for whom she designed the costumes for *Little Big Man* (1970); she stayed in the business for the next twenty years. Head moved to Universal and continued to design costumes virtually until her death in 1981, like Jeakins not only adapting but thriving in the new era.[6]

By the mid-1970s, in fact, the youth-oriented big-budget feature film had begun its rise to a prominence it has yet to relinquish in the twenty-first century. A large number of period films were also made during the decade, by young and more seasoned directors alike, representing a conflicted nostalgia for the past during a time of intense and lively social activity and turmoil and once again dependent on the careful research and labor of costume, makeup, and hair designers, even if they usually competed for their jobs in a freelance market and sometimes bought costumes from thrift stores or borrowed them from relatives.

Just as important, the tremendous box office success of the first high-concept "summer blockbusters," Steven Spielberg's *Jaws* (1975) and George Lucas's *Star*

Wars (1977), which employed very profitable exhibition strategies such as saturation booking to flood thousands of screens with the same film over a single weekend, signaled the renewal of a film industry that would be less interested in revolution or social change than in catering to filmgoers who were willing to spend a great deal of money to lose themselves in fantasy or science-fiction worlds—sometimes at least partly computer-generated—far, far away (Lucas's effects company Industrial Light & Magic was founded in 1975). This too was a part of the auteur renaissance, though individual films arguably ended up being less consequential than the profitable franchises they created and that were nourished by ever more sophisticated special effects. For designers, the most important aspect of the spectacle-driven blockbusters was that they depended, as they had in the past, on elaborate and expensive costumes, prosthetic appliances and character makeup, and complicated wigs and hairdressing, and by the end of the 1970s all three crafts were once again flourishing.[7]

New Methods

The smaller budgets of films of the late 1960s and early 1970s both limited and gave greater expressive freedom to the designer. With the organizational structures of the studio system gone, many designers, no less than directors or other creative personnel, were sometimes flying by the seat of their pants; frequently one person was hired, and given very little money, to purchase materials and perform tasks that had been the province of large staffs in well-funded departments during the studio era. As Deborah Landis puts it, costume design had "come full-circle in some respects. As in the early, primitive days of Hollywood, on low-budget independent modern films, actors might be asked to provide their own clothing as costumes if it worked for the part."[8] Unfortunately, the lack of a corporate structure and the records they tended to keep is partly why there is little archival material available to scholars interested in the costume, makeup, and hair of this era. However, some of the studies that do feature the work of designers of the 1970s, for example Landis's 2012 interview-based *FilmCraft: Costume Design* as well as her 2013 book *Hollywood Costume*, help us to elucidate the work environment of the decade through the accounts of designers themselves.[9]

In an interview with Peter Biskind included in *Hollywood Costume*, Ann Roth, who worked on several iconic films of the era—*Midnight Cowboy* (John Schlesinger, 1969), *Klute* (Alan J. Pakula, 1971), and *The Day of the Locust* (John Schlesinger, 1975), among others—discusses her career trajectory, from late-studio department employee to post-studio freelancer, and the challenges she and her colleagues faced and the way their design processes evolved as filmmakers either left the studios where they had trained or started productions on locations all over the country.[10] Often the films' production was supported by not much more than some sort of financing (occasionally by studios hoping to reap profits from the "artistic creativeness or critical content" that David Brown eulogized in 1968), a university degree in filmmaking, and a passionate desire to express oneself with film. Although what replaced the studios' methods and conventions never became as standardized or as rigid as they would have been under the hierarchized "lead designer" structure of the old wardrobe departments, Roth's account is echoed by others of the period and suggests that the initially freewheeling approaches tried out during the auteur renaissance did ultimately become somewhat systematic as well.

One such approach was to merge design—now more often shopped than fabricated, though sometimes both—with a Method-derived narrative and character analysis that was not particularly interested in fashion, beauty, the maintenance of a star image, or product tie-ins but instead in concrete support of a director's vision. Roth began her career in set and production design until her path was altered by the legendary costume designer Irene Sharaff, who took her to Hollywood to work at MGM in an apprentice role on Vincente Minnelli's fantasy musical *Brigadoon* in 1954 and then hired her for several more projects both in film and on Broadway. Sharaff had already broken with the Hollywood practice in which costume designers dressed the glamorous leading ladies of a film, leaving the rest of the cast to the wardrobe department, and Roth continued in her footsteps. She has described Sharaff's insistence on designing an entire show or film as being deeply offensive to traditional costume designers and to the unions, who supported what Roth saw as an unproductive hierarchy.[11] In the freelance era, Roth and her colleagues could more easily work beyond the union-ordained limits of each craft, and benefited both from collaboration with each other and with newer and less hidebound directors. Like many others, she often made decisions on her own that would have been out of the question as a studio-contracted employee.

Roth's work with Dustin Hoffman on *Midnight Cowboy*, in particular, is representative of these newer but now standard methods, especially on a character study. She would begin an informal conversation with an actor by having her or him try on all the clothing possibilities she had bought, found, or made until something "clicked." In turning Hoffman into Ratso Rizzo it was the "cockroach-in-the-corner shoes, cucaracha shoes, very pointed toes" that led to the "magic" she was seeking. She "had the heels built up, and . . . had one of them weighted. So when he got them on, it threw him into a different posture, and suddenly there was somebody in front of me who was nothing like Dustin Hoffman. . . . It's a very nice thing to happen in the fitting room, and that's what I enjoy doing."[12] Also important to the characterization of Ratso was a pair of white pants purchased from a table in front of the Port Authority Bus Terminal in New York. The pants were "so filthy they had yellow and black creases," and were matched with a white jacket that was found in a garbage can bearing traces of vomit. "So

FIGURE 25: Dustin Hoffman and Jon Voight in *Midnight Cowboy* (1969). Costume design by Ann Roth, makeup by Irving Buchman (makeup consultant Dick Smith), hair by Bob Grimaldi.

that was Ratso Rizzo," Roth declared. "That's how those things happen."[13]

But while Ratso's clothing was "found," it was also subtly transformed; Roth added a crest to the pocket and stripes down the legs of the pants in the Miami dream sequence, using design as well as chance to affect our notions of who a character is or wants to be. *Midnight Cowboy's* makeup and hair, by Irving Buchman and Bob Grimaldi, also appear "undesigned" but carefully chart the decline and developing relationship of the two main characters. The faces and hair of Hoffman and Jon Voight, as Joe Buck, become increasingly layered with oil and sweat as they sink deeper and deeper into abject poverty, but the moving relationship that grows between them is made manifest as they cut or comb each other's hair and wash each other's faces (figure 25).

For Alan J. Pakula's *Klute*, which starred Jane Fonda as prostitute and model Bree Daniels, Roth designed some costumes and acquired others off the rack or from thrift stores. And while Grimaldi was the film's credited hairdresser (Buchman was its makeup artist as well), it was Roth who had Fonda's hair cut into a "shag," a cut that "became a sensation. It never occurred to me to tell the director," Roth says. "It never dawned on me that this might be a rash thing. I just knew how I saw this character."[14] (In 2002, Roth devised the prosthetic nose for Nicole Kidman as Virginia Woolf in *The Hours*; in Roth's words, the "nose could've come off. But you couldn't put the hair back on Jane.")[15] Roth, like other post-studio designers, had begun to think about characters, whether "contemporary" or in period films, as having "backstories." She talked with actors about the people they were playing—how much money they had, what they did for a living, where they lived, where they put their clothes at night, and who did the laundry.[16] She continues to ask makeup and hair designers to come to costume fittings with the actors because all their work is so fully interrelated, something that did not happen much in the studio system because of its overriding interest in star images rather than character integrity or depth.[17]

FIGURE 26: Jane Fonda as Bree Daniels in *Klute* (1971). Costume design by Ann Roth, makeup by Irving Buchman, Fonda's hair stylist Paul McGregor. In the film's credits, Buchman's name is misspelled as "Buckman," and McGregor's as "Macgregor."

For *Klute*, Roth's goal was to dress the main character against her profession ("If there is such a thing as a theme in my approach," Roth states, "it is pretty much that").[18] Bree first appears in a no-nonsense, professional-looking outfit of the time—a turtleneck sweater, midi-skirt, and boots—carrying a large leather portfolio. The fact that she does not wear a bra and sports a necklace with a golf-ball-sized ornament that looks more like a weapon than a decoration indicates an alliance with feminism. When she is humiliatingly rejected for a modeling assignment and arranges a trick in response, the outfit is transformed into a highly seductive one. When she sits on the bed and crosses her legs, the skirt is revealed to be a wrap-around one that is open virtually to the waist. Yet the watch that she wears and glances at twice in the encounter makes it clear that she is a businesswoman, and that her seductive talk is her labor. The control that she seeks in her sex work is manifest in her brown, gray, or beige clothing, her high necklines and blazers, and her short haircut (figure 26). When Bree is relaxing alone at home and during her audition for the role of Joan of Arc, she wears vibrant red with a deep neckline, which gives depth to the character that Fonda builds during the film's psychiatric sessions.

The most intriguing costume, and the most glamorous, is the black, sequin-covered sheath that Bree wears during her talk-only session with a man who owns a factory that makes clothes for women. The dress evokes armor, which resonates with the earlier Joan of Arc reference and the haircut, as Bree is seen from behind the multiple sewing machines, cutting tables, and rolls of multicolored fabric, parading back and forth, spinning the tale of her client's fantasy. The relationship between the maker of objectifying clothing for women and the woman who is tormented by being an object seems benign.[19] But it is no accident that the climax of the film, in which Bree is almost murdered by a serial killer of prostitutes, happens in this factory. The film ends with Bree leaving New York, perhaps with John Klute, wearing the same outfit in which she first appeared. In a film that is in some ways about costume, Roth creates mystery with a wide-brimmed straw hat with long, apricot satin ribbons that is visible in every scene in Bree's apartment. The impossibility of imagining a scenario in which Bree Daniels might wear this hat helps create the unease with which the film leaves the viewer, but it also makes her into a complex human being with a conflicted past. She is not just a woman designed to be looked at but one who understands, and manipulates to her own ends, the patriarchal structures (like pretty clothes and "femininity") meant to keep her contained.

As Roth's story shows, not only were actors in this period working in a mode of "authenticity" through various versions of the Method—digging into their own memories and experiences to discover and feel the emotions of the characters—but costume designers, too, were finding clothing for actors in the actual places where they were imagined to live. Makeup and hair designers were also paying attention to the people around them and what they looked like rather than designing them to appear glamorous or to hew to some studio-sanctioned ideal of beauty or handsomeness. Anna Hill Johnstone and Theodora Van Runkle worked with the young Francis Ford Coppola on *The Godfather* (1972) and *The Godfather: Part II* (1974), respectively, and, like Roth, Grimaldi, and Buchman, took risks and experimented in ways that the studio system might have indulged in training and apprenticeship, but rarely at the production stage when the wrong decision could incur extreme costs in time and money.

In designing the costumes for *The Godfather*, for example, Johnstone argued with Coppola over her desire to have actors repeatedly wear a key piece of character-building clothing whether it was crucial to a given scene or not. Coppola finally agreed, and found, as Deborah Landis notes in her book *Dressed*, that Johnstone's technique of making only minimal changes in character costuming from scene to scene not only saved money but meant that Coppola had the freedom to worry less about the maintenance of continuity in the shooting and editing of scenes as well.[20] In *The Godfather: Part II*, Van Runkle learned that Coppola was unhappy that she had dressed the Corleone men in suits rather than tuxedoes for an afternoon event in the film's opening scenes. But it took him only fifteen minutes to accept her compelling point that the movie's immigrant family would adopt a WASP preference for underdressing in their desire to assimilate.[21] Although some studio-era directors certainly valued the suggestions and ideas of their designers (see the discussion of Irene's contributions to Tay Garnett's 1946 *The Postman Always Rings Twice* in the introduction to this book), such cooperation made more sense, and was of course easier to implement, in the absence of the assembly-line rules and regulations of the older quasi-corporate structures.

Aggie Guerard Rodgers was hired by George Lucas to design for *American Graffiti* (1973) when he overheard her saying that she remembered "'dragging the main' in her sister's cherry/blue '54 Ford." Lucas was interested in creating as authentic a sense of the period as possible, and had more faith in her direct connection with it than he had in a long résumé. The costume budget was two thousand dollars, and Rodgers worked alone, without a dresser, out of a small motor home that was shared with makeup, hair, and wardrobe. Everything except for a sweater that belonged to a friend of Lucas's was purchased secondhand (although Lucas himself created the roller-skating carhops with their bellboy caps and ski pants). While Rodgers cut down collars and made alterations when necessary, the clothes were used and purchased with an eye to regional style.[22]

Rodgers has stated in interviews that, like Roth, Van Runkle, Johnstone, and other designers of the era, she was interested in creating people in films who were "real" rather than fabricating an image or picture of a time period, and thus she employed some of the photographic or documentary methods of *cinéma vérité* even in period films. Her method was much the same on films set in her contemporary present, for example Francis Ford Coppola's *The Conversation* (1974). Coppola himself chose the translucent raincoat worn by Harry Caul (Gene Hackman) that is so essential to the characterization—it is as though Caul is perpetually wrapped in a membrane that he hopes will protect him from the world—and Rodgers purchased two dozen of the fragile items at an army surplus store in order to have enough to last through shooting. She did all of the rest of the costume selection and shopping, working from the notion that none of the characters would have perfectly fitting clothes or pay much attention to current

FIGURE 23: Gene Hackman as Harry Caul in *The Conversation* (1974), wearing the translucent raincoat with which the character is identified. Costumer Aggie Guerard Rodgers, no credits for makeup or hair.

fashion.[23] To her as to her colleagues, the film's low budget again became more of an inspiration than a problem (figure 27).

For designers, then, it was a welcome paradox that directors such as Schlesinger, Lucas, Pakula, Coppola, Scorsese, and Kubrick, who considered themselves the auteurs of their highly personal artworks, were also so open to collaboration with the crafts of costume, makeup, and hair, crafts on which the studios had depended but did not always seem to respect. Education and training had given the younger filmmakers an awareness of the medium and its history, and while they might not have learned much about the day-to-day or quotidian labor and techniques of costume, makeup, or hair design, they could sense its contributions to the movies they had studied, sometimes obsessively, and admired. And, as was true across many areas of art and culture during the period, the directors' involvement or at least sympathy with various youth-driven political movements also encouraged a more dialectical than authoritative creative process. Their films were born of their knowledge and love of Hollywood's films and genres, but also their desire to offer a countercultural critique of the older myths and ideologies embodied by them and to communicate it to an audience poised to accept it.[24]

The Period Film and Genre Critique

Considering the minimal resources and nonexistent wardrobe departments in this period, it seems counterintuitive that so many of the most notable directors of the first half of the 1970s chose to set their films in the past. But from *American Graffiti* to *The Godfather* saga to *Chinatown* (Roman Polanski, 1974) and *Barry Lyndon* (Stanley Kubrick, 1975), filmmakers repeatedly returned to other eras from which to consider their own. While some critics have described these period films as dominated by nostalgia or romance,[25] a film can go further in its commentary on the present when it is set in another time and opens itself to the bricolage that allows past, fantasy future, and present to interact with each other visually and conceptually. Deborah Landis believes that films set in the present are actually more difficult to design than ostensibly more lavish period pieces because, in addition to creating the characters, the costumes of contemporary films have to look and feel recognizably authentic *to the audience*, a mix of old, new, and borrowed or handed-down, sometimes purposefully ill-fitting because that's all a character might be able to afford.[26]

Setting a film in the past also facilitates genre critique. The cinephile filmmakers of this period were certainly influenced by New Wave films, such as Jean-Luc Godard's *À Bout de Souffle* (*Breathless*, 1960), which reveres the gangster films that featured the likes of Humphrey Bogart but recognizes Hollywood's oppressive cultural and commercial power. Many of the young directors working in the United States went beyond the early New Wave's approach to demythologization.

Chinatown, its director a European art-film émigré, is a biting indictment of structural inequities and corrupt forces that work at the whims of untrammeled power, as well as a beautiful and entertaining work of art. And the costumes, designed by Anthea Sylbert, are a key part of the film's success.

In a 2007 interview with Landis, Sylbert repeats a point made by many other designers throughout Hollywood's history—namely, that costume design is distinct and serves a different expressive purpose from fashion design. In Sylbert's words, one "must not leave a movie whistling the clothes."[27] She notes in particular that she used no couture fashion magazines to design *Chinatown*, instead turning to her family photograph albums and to popular news magazines and newspapers contemporaneous with the film's setting for inspiration. As a result of her research and professional knowledge of cultural specificity in relation to dress, she used the fact that while the *nouveau riche* of the 1930s dressed flamboyantly in order to display their wealth, the old-guard rich rarely did.[28]

At one moment in the film, this notion and the costumes that were born of it come into play with depth and efficiency. Sylbert dresses the imposter Mrs. Mulray (Diane Ladd) in a poor woman's fantasy of a rich one: she wears an extravagant feathered hat with a partial veil, furs draped around her neck, and glittering bracelets over her black satin evening-length gloves. It says something important about Jake Gittes, the detective played by Jack Nicholson, who is coded as being vain and attentive to clothing, that he is fooled by her. Later in the film, the real Evelyn Mulray (Faye Dunaway) arrives at a restaurant in order to divert Gittes from his investigation through a series of lies. Up until this moment, she has appeared in impeccably elegant and even severe suits of muted colors, but now wears a more subdued and perfectly tailored version of the outfit worn by the imposter, minus the feather and many of the jewels.[29] The two ensembles echo each other and suggest the corruption and deception that pervade the world that has been put into play by the all-encompassing, devouring behavior of Evelyn's father, Noah Cross (John Huston).

Sylbert's decision to dress the latter in the clothing of some sort of Central American overlord—a guayabera shirt buttoned to the neck and a woven red sash at the waist—makes him chillingly slippery and invasive in his evil. The makeup and hair, by Hank Edds, Lee Harman, Vivienne Walker, and Susan Germaine, are also central to establishing both the time period and the nature of the characters. Early in the story, Gittes impetuously launches a fight with a man in a barbershop, despite the fact that Gittes's face is covered with white shaving foam. It is no surprise, then, that his short fuse and smart mouth lead to him being disciplined by thugs who slit his nose with a knife, resulting in a large white bandage taped across a third of Gittes's face for much of the film. The bulbously bandaged nose utterly undercuts his attempts, through his sharp but overly detailed suits and his carefully pomaded hair, to look like a suave as well as successful detective (figure 28).

FIGURE 28: Jack Nicholson and Faye Dunaway in *Chinatown* (1974). Nicholson is wearing the most discreet version of the white bandage he sports for much of the film. Costume design by Anthea Sylbert and wardrobe by Richard Bruno and Jean Merrick, makeup by Hank Edds and Lee Harman, hair by Susan Germaine and Vivienne Walker.

Chinatown, like any work of art, is about its own moment even though it is mediated through another. In addition to facilitating the critique of genre and creating practical efficiencies, film and design scholar Jane Gaines suggests that period films enable directors to use costume, makeup, and hair in a manner similar to studio-era melodramas—to enrich and layer narrative meaning through textures, weights, surfaces, and embellishments that would be out of place in mid- to late twentieth-century dress.[30] An example of this tendency appears in many of the films designed by Milena Canonero, from *A Clockwork Orange* (Stanley Kubrick, 1971) to *Barry Lyndon* (co-designed with Ulla-Britt Soderland), films in which the crafts speak in ways as complex as music.

Canonero is one of the few costume designers who studied and remained interested in fashion design and history, which Kubrick took full advantage of in his work with her. However, in interviews she has stated clearly that her film work is not at all like fashion design but rather, as with the other designers of this era, a close collaboration with the director and with makeup and hair stylists.[31] In *A Clockwork Orange*, set in the future, she was inspired by the black boots of London street fashion, but the lead character, played by Malcolm McDowell, becomes a charismatic yet terrifying visual icon thanks to her pastiche of many different fashions, including the large false eyelash he wears on one lower lid, a bowler hat, and an outlandish codpiece worn on the outside of an ensemble that resembles a union suit.

Barry Lyndon, set in the eighteenth century, offers a more elaborate example of Canonero's exacting work; it is a film known for its relationship to the composition, lighting, and color of the paintings of William Hogarth and the clothing, elaborate hairstyles, and pale faces of Thomas Gainsborough.[32] Kubrick

hired a large team—ten credited makeup and hair artists, in addition to ten credited wardrobe personnel—because attire and appearance, or the sumptuousness
or lack thereof, are the heart of the film. Visually, one might say that the film
functions to investigate the people in the well-known paintings. The dominant
rhythm of its three-hour length is created by beginning a scene with a medium
shot of one or more people and then slowly and methodically tracking back to
an extreme long shot, which is held so as to recreate a painting, so to speak. The
people, scarcely visible in the landscape paintings themselves, are elaborately created and brought to intimate life through costume, makeup, and hair that ranges
from modest and subtle in the early scenes of farm life to excessively ornate as
Redmond Barry becomes Barry Lyndon (Ryan O'Neal), to unkempt and gray
with the death of Barry's child and his subsequent ruin.

Indeed, it is not too much to claim that Barry's tragedy unfolds through costume and makeup changes. Envy of the beautifully designed red soldier uniforms
launches the film (color plate 8), and ever more decorative suits and heavier and
more intensely colored makeup chart his rise and fall, and differentiate authentic emotion from grasping performativity. The devastating effects of the duel in
which Barry receives a crippling injury at the hands of his detested stepson near
the film's conclusion are expressed partly through costume color and its relation
to space. Barry wears a coat and hat that match his gray eyes and is positioned in
front of a stone wall lit in the same color. His cowering but vicious antagonist is
dressed in deep brown and disappears into the shadows behind him. While Barry
refuses to shoot the pathetic boy in the duel, the young man does no such thing,
firing on Barry even after he has lowered his weapon. The film ends with Barry,
minus one leg and on the way to financial ruin, still radiant in the color blue as he
fades into the darkness of a carriage in the frozen frames of the final image.

Turned-On Design: Gender and Androgyny

Whether working on a period film or one set contemporaneously, costume,
makeup, and hair designers of the late 1960s and 1970s were often embroiled,
offscreen as well as on, in ideological battles fomented by divides between the
World War II generation and their huge numbers of baby-boomer children. To
a degree perhaps difficult for us to imagine now, the youth movement's rejection
of culturally proper clothing and personal hygiene served as a weapon in these
skirmishes. Young people differentiated themselves from those in authority and
labeled themselves as radical by wearing vintage, eccentric, exotic, and suggestive
clothing. Young men who refused to have their hair cut appropriately were reviled
and punished, particularly in connection with the draft for the Vietnam War.

For women, the issue was especially complex, and had been since the early
1960s. As part of the social and sexual liberation of this period, young women

rejected traditional clothing and the support system of undergarments that it demanded as confining and controlling. They turned to more eclectic clothing with a looser or less predetermined fit, which signified both personal taste rather than adherence to any fashion system as well as a refusal to be objectified. Yet as Elizabeth Wilson points out in her essay on clothing and its representation during the era, while excessive or deviant clothing in men is read as rebellious, it tends to be dismissed as mere fashion-following when worn by women.[33] More important, women's attempts to subvert oppressive gender-based attitudes through the proud wearing of sexually outrageous apparel is invariably read as dressing provocatively. Thus, the only really radical dress available to women involves refusing all signifiers of femininity by dressing like men. Such issues perforce affected cinematic costume, makeup, and hair design, particularly in relation to androgyny and to notions of liberation in dress and appearance for women, but also to changing definitions of masculinity.

In a broad sense, the relation between costume design and fashion had been clear-cut for most of film history. Commercial tie-ins between film costume and fashion were not uncommon—see the famous white frilled "Letty Lynton" dress designed by Adrian and worn by Joan Crawford in the film of the same name in 1932, simplified copies of which were sold at Macy's; or the various "Holly-wood" patterns based on women's film clothing available to home seamstresses described in the previous chapters; or the retail clothing lines and hats based on Dorothy Jeakins's designs for Ingrid Bergman in *Joan of Arc* in 1948.[34] As has been discussed, Adrian and several other Hollywood designers also had retail fashion lines at various points. The relationship between film and fashion in the late 1960s and 1970s, however, evolved differently due to the political impact of clothing and personal appearance in the culture at large, and the fact that so many films were shopped rather than designed.

What complicates the usual assumptions about fashion and its distinction from film costuming and design in the late 1960s and early 1970s begins with the fact that young people were dressing to reject fashion, and costume designers then created clothing and appurtenances for their characters, in collaboration with—or sometimes functioning as—makeup and hair designers, in accordance with this cultural (or more properly countercultural) reality. However, in assem-bling wardrobes for film characters based on eclectic and transgressive street wear, costume designers also inspired fashion designers who looked to whatever was "new" and "bold" in order to appeal to this iconoclastic generation. In the end, the fashion world co-opted what it saw in film, and then sold it back to those who had created it but whose purpose was to *reject* fashion. In short, it became ever more difficult, especially in film, to use clothing subversively.

The film *Hair!* (Milos Forman, 1979) offers a vivid example of both the some-times contentious interplay among street clothing, fashion, and film costume, and how much of it was shorn of its countercultural edge by the end of the decade. Ann Roth designed the costumes for the film, saying later that while she loved doing it, she was not well suited to the project because she was a professional woman in the 1960s—a bohemian but not at all a hippie: "To this day, I don't know if I did a really good job on that movie."[35] Indeed, the costumes in the film were critically regarded as less than successful because of how trendy the formerly transgressive clothing had become since its first defiantly political deployment in the 1968 Broadway play. The rock musical *Hair!*, by Gerome Ragni and Galt MacDermot, was immediately famous, or notorious, for its scandalous attitude toward sexuality, race, and the Vietnam War, and its use of full nudity. Clive Barnes's affectionate review of the play makes note of the "junk-art setting" and Nancy Potts's "cleverly tattered and colorful, turned-on costumes."[36]

The difference between those costumes and the ones that were designed for the film eleven years later are exemplary: what had appeared as second-hand, ill-fitting, and androgynous on stage became expensively tailored, flatteringly styled, and gender-specific in the film. Radically eclectic combinations became ensembles, and ethnic fabrics and details look like haute couture rather than found thrift-shop material. Roth's costumes reflect the international bohemian style of the period, launched by Yves Saint-Laurent in the 1960s, rather than anything transgressive and carnivalesque as might have been the case if the film had been made earlier in the 1970s (color plate 9).

In fact, there is not a great deal of difference between the clothing worn by the men in *Hair!* and Warren Beatty's wardrobe in *Shampoo* (Hal Ashby, 1975), but the costuming, by Anthea Sylbert, and the makeup and hairstyling by Tom Case and Kathryn Blondell, respectively, are the brilliant center of the film. The feminization of Beatty's character, George, from his layered bouffant hairdo and mascara to his multiple necklaces, bracelets, and rings to his closely fitted tunic and leather jacket, positions him as the attractive and androgynous cipher around which the film's other characters move. The women whose hair he cuts and styles feel comfortable around him because he is at home with them, and they are not put off by his excessiveness. The men face the real challenge; they can only read George's clothing as indicating homosexuality, yet they intuit that he is not only attractive to their wives and mistresses but actually sexually involved with them.

The signs and very definition of masculinity are thus under consideration in *Shampoo*. Early in the story, a banker easily dismisses George in order to deny him the funding that would allow him to operate a business as a member of the world in which the banker himself resides. As a result of the rejection, George tears off and discards the clothing that he thought would gain him access, not understanding that his tie was too wide and bright and his shirt too dark. On the other hand, the wealthy husband in the film seeks to understand and emulate what his wife, mistress, and daughter see in George. While the husband's sartorial explorations fail—he substitutes a white turtleneck for his usual shirt and tie—it is his wealth that attracts the women in the end, leaving George baffled and brokenhearted.

FIGURE 29: Warren Beatty cutting an androgynous figure in *Shampoo* (1975). Costume design by Anthea Sylbert (women's wardrobe by Thalia Phillips, men's by Laurie Riley), makeup by Tom Case, hair by Kathryn Blondell with uncredited help from Jan Van Uchelen.

In an interview about the film, screenwriter Robert Towne makes the observation that George is "very sweet: He never seduces anybody. He's really the girl in the movie. . . . He's really the dumb-blonde in the picture."[37] Towne is sympathetic to his promiscuous but nice character, but he enforces the idea that male accomplishment demands separation from femininity (figure 29).

Unfortunately, *Shampoo*'s women are all blatantly signified as types through their clothing—the naïve girlfriend in baby-doll mini-dresses, the dowdy wife in headscarves and curlers, and the mistress in haute couture. Beautiful George in his androgynous clothes is oblivious to the way in which his blurring of gender signifiers hurts him, but he is neither rebellious nor radical. It was in the realm of music in this period that androgynous men in elaborate makeup and dress made their mark, with only David Bowie, costumed by May Routh and with makeup by Ellis Burman Jr. and Linda de Vetta and hair by Martin Samuel, making a serious foray into film in the science-fiction vehicle *The Man Who Fell to Earth* (Nicolas Roeg, 1976). The androgynous costume, makeup, and hair that Beatty sports in *Shampoo* were ahead of their time; it would be another decade at least before normative notions of masculinity and sexual behavior were challenged by commercial retail fashion rather than couture. That fashion, and the loosening of gender strictures for both men and women, had to catch up to film, so to speak, was because of the power that cinema's images were acquiring in the increasingly ubiquitous media culture of the 1970s.

The "New Natural" and/as Invisibility

A counterweight to the exploration of androgyny in this period was the rise of actors who had neither the appearance nor the attitude of the classical movie star and whose ordinary looks were associated with greater authenticity in both their performances and their relation to the cinema as professionals. The presence of actors such as Dustin Hoffman and Gene Hackman in lead roles, rather than as sidekicks or in character parts, was part of the nonconformity of the era. In discussing *Chinatown*, Robert Towne described the casting of men who were good-looking but "normal people" as one of the highlights of films of the 1970s.[38] It was of a piece with this rejection of movie star looks that Jack Nicholson was willing to spend a good part of *Chinatown* with his face absurdly obscured by a white bandage.

However, it is Hoffman's career that offers perhaps the clearest example of changes in notions of film stardom in the late 1960s and 1970s. His short stature and ordinary and somewhat ethnic looks are hardly those of even the least polished or most rebellious movie stars of earlier eras—such as James Dean or Marlon Brando—and, like Gene Hackman and even Jack Nicholson, he cultivated a career in which he became famous for his acting rather than attempting to become a movie star. Although he had earned countercultural plaudits and adoring fan mail alike for his first starring role in *The Graduate* (Mike Nichols, 1967)—which also made lots of money at the box office—his performance in Penn's 1970 film *Little Big Man*, a year after his stunning success in *Midnight Cowboy*, involved even more serious deglamorization.

As with *Midnight Cowboy*, the later film demonstrates how much perceived skill in acting, especially character acting, continued to depend, as it had during the classical era, on the skills of costume, makeup, and hair designers. As Mary Desjardins has discussed in this volume, when actor Paul Muni won an Oscar for Best Actor in 1936 for playing Louis Pasteur, he thanked only his makeup man, Perc Westmore, in his acceptance speech. Just as Ratso Rizzo's dirt, sweat, and tears were partly Hoffman but also designed and applied, so did Hoffman's performance of a man from youth to centenarian in *Little Big Man* depend not only on his acting ability or the skill and care of his director but on latex and silicone appliances.

Little Big Man begins with a close-up of Hoffman as a 120-year-old man (color plate 10). His sparse hair and wrinkled face and hands were designed by Dick Smith, who had been a makeup consultant for *Midnight Cowboy* as well. Smith began his career in television, where he became the "undisputed master," as effects historian Richard Rickitt puts it, "of old-age make-up effects."[39] Through having to age actors quickly in live television, Smith innovated the use of multiple added layers of latex appliances rather than a single large one that covered the face, which appeared more realistic and was also more comfortable for actors. Smith created straight as well as character makeups on a wide range of films across many genres, including the *Godfather* films, *The Exorcist* (William Friedkin, 1973), and *Taxi Driver* (Martin Scorsese, 1976). For Robert De Niro in *Taxi Driver*, Smith helped create one of the iconic images of the era, De Niro with his head shaved into a menacing mohawk (color plate 11).[40]

There are many reasons, of course, for the increase in graphic and sometimes literally nauseating visual realism in character makeup and hair in commercial cinema as the 1970s progressed. In films like *The Exorcist*, which was based on an equally graphic best-selling novel, prosthetic makeup and appliances were used to create gruesome imagery meant at once to convince and to shock in an era no longer regulated by the Production Code's prohibitions against showing blood, internal organs, or the effects of severe corporeal violence, and used to disturbing visual realities through television's news coverage of the Vietnam War.[41] In other cases, authenticity in relation to an actor's performance and his or her connection to the audience as a character (and as a person in the world) was crucial for political as well as artistic reasons. In *Little Big Man*, Dorothy Jeakins's costumes, along with Smith's makeup, chart the many phases of the hero's career, from Indian to adopted "child" to gunslinger to storekeeper to hermit to old man. It is the combination of the exaggerated costumes and Hoffman's slight build and willingness to appear funny-looking that give the film its particular tone—both absurdly funny and deeply critical of the behavior of the United States toward Native Americans.

For women in the 1970s, the cosmetic and hairstyling industries quickly found a way to twist the naturalness and lack of makeup and styling that feminists had used politically to signal their desire to be taken seriously as functioning people into something that had to be carefully styled or applied with products. Makeup artist Way Bandy and hairstylist Maury Hobson, among many others, created for the fashion world what was known as "the natural look" of this period. The models who came to the fore tended to be athletic, with strong features, but they appeared in magazines in remarkably heavy makeup. These young women, who emerged in *Vogue* with its claim to offer "real clothes for real people," became so well known that they were able to achieve more or less successful careers in film.

Model Lauren Hutton had a key role in *American Gigolo* (Paul Schrader, 1980), a film that is best remembered for the Giorgio Armani clothes worn by Richard Gere. Margaux Hemingway starred in *Lipstick* (Lamont Johnson, 1976), Farrah Fawcett appeared in multiple films and television shows and became an American icon in *Charlie's Angels* (ABC, 1976–1981), and Candice Bergen starred in *Carnal Knowledge* in 1971 and subsequently found success in television as the star of *Murphy Brown* (CBS, 1988–1998). In his 1977 book summarizing his work with these women, *Designing Your Face*, Bandy adopted and distorted the notions of transformation and self-determination that had been inspirational for the feminist movement. Women's power was returned to their images, deriving once again from how perfectly and beautifully, if apparently artlessly, they could be made up and styled. In fact, the amount of makeup and hairstyling that had once been limited to the production of editorial fashion and cinematic images—or confined to bordellos—was now popularly decreed to be necessary for real women who wanted to "be themselves" and to appear "natural" too.[42]

That the "natural look" became popular for women, onscreen and off, during the 1970s interacts in interesting ways with how other aspects of costume, makeup, and hair design also became associated with, if not the natural, at least the artless. Films of the period seem to be so "lived in" that the labor of designers, again most of them women, was rarely featured in promotional and publicity material. *Chinatown*, for example, was described in an interview with its screenwriter, Robert Towne, as a "collaboration between a who's-who of [1970s] film icons." He mentions the director, cinematographer, and music director in glowing terms, but the only Sylbert he names is Richard—costume designer Anthea Sylbert's brother-in-law, who did the production design. While Towne eventually does call both Sylberts "the best in the business," he waxes most nostalgic about the many evenings spent with the "men" involved in the production.[43]

As earlier chapters in this volume show, such overlooking of costume, makeup, and hair is ironic considering that in classical Hollywood they were virtually the only crafts that had a presence in promotion and publicity, although not coincidentally the most famous designers then, with one or two exceptions, were male. Hollywood's "invisible system" was predicated on the idea that all crafts, from directing down through camerawork, editing, design, and even sound, were supposed to be self-effacing, to operate to support the narrative but not exceed it; but in the case of costume, makeup, and hair, as with movie stars themselves, Hollywood wanted also to profit from their draw and appeal off the screen whenever possible. In the auteur renaissance, such invisibility was itself called into question, influenced by New Wave notions that any work of art should instead show signs of its authorship and the labor by which it is made, to foreground its status as an utterance rather than a dream or a story told from nowhere and no one. There is thus a paradox that classical Hollywood's most visible supporting crafts were the most invisible in auteur-led filmmaking of the 1960s and 1970s—indeed coming closer than they ever had, or arguably would again, to fulfilling classical Hollywood's mandates.

Deborah Landis's research efforts have drawn attention back to the work of these invisible costume designers—if not that of makeup and hair artists—many of whom are living and whose histories she has helped to preserve. Ruth Morley's methods and experience illustrate how strongly the notion of the director as auteur, largely a late 1960s development in the United States, affected not only design processes on a practical level but who should be given credit for what we see on the screen (this despite the fact that Morley is virtually the only designer of this era whose archives have been saved and made accessible to scholars).[44] The shirt and army jacket that Morley found and purchased for Robert De Niro to wear in *Taxi Driver* in 1976 were crucial to the changing identity and militarization that his character, Travis Bickle, undergoes in the film, but publicity stories focused on the fact that De Niro took his costume home every day and wore it so that the pieces aged organically and felt ordinary to him (figure 30).[45]

1: Cyd Charisse's costume in *Singin' in the Rain* (1952) demonstrates the use of Louise Brooks's "flapper" bob to suggest the era in which the film is set, as well as the relative leniency with which dancing costumes were evaluated by censors. Costumes by Walter Plunkett, makeup by William Tuttle, hair by Sydney Guilaroff.

2: Janet Gaynor being made up with an eye to "correcting" her face in the 1937 version of *A Star Is Born*. Makeup and hair uncredited.

3: Bette Davis in Perc Westmore's full character makeup and Errol Flynn in anachronistic "straight" makeup and hair in *The Private Lives of Elizabeth and Essex* (1939).

4: Margaret Hamilton, Judy Garland, and Billie Burke in *The Wizard of Oz* (1939). A wide range of straight and character makeups was a large part of the film's appeal.

5: A model in a gown by Adrian in the Technicolor fashion show in *The Women* (1939).

6: Vivien Leigh in *Gone with the Wind* (1939). In the top image, sweat has been added to her face and her hair is disheveled (and her dress is one that becomes more and more ragged as the film progresses), but the makeup plan is otherwise identical in the image below.

7: In *The Graduate* (1967), the predatory Mrs. Robinson (Anne Bancroft) is dressed, not very subtly, in a variety of animal skins and prints.

8: Color contrasts in costume and makeup chart the rise and fall of Redmond Barry/Barry Lyndon (Ryan O'Neal) in *Barry Lyndon* (1975).

10: Dick Smith's character makeup and the use of layered appliances turned Dustin Hoffman into a 102-year-old man in *Little Big Man* (1970).

11: Dick Smith's hair and makeup help chart the increasing dangerousness of Travis Bickle (Robert De Niro) in *Taxi Driver* (1976).

12: A final tableau of futuristic costumes, hair, and makeup all drawn from the past in *Star Wars* (1977).

13: Kate Winslet and Leonardo DiCaprio in sumptuous and romantic period costumes in *Titanic* (1997).

14: Tom Hulce, as Mozart, trying on wigs in *Amadeus* (1984).

15: Kim Basinger as Lynn Bracken in Ruth Myers's black velvet cape in *L.A. Confidential* (1997).

16: Performance capture, digital animation, and digital makeup in *Avatar* (2009).

17: Prosthetic makeup, digital makeup, or special effects? "Davy Jones" in the "live-action" film *Pirates of the Caribbean: Dead Man's Chest* (2006) is primarily a digitally animated character—mocapped form and voice provided by actor Bill Nighy—created by hordes of digital VFX artists rather than the traditional crafts of costume, makeup, and hair

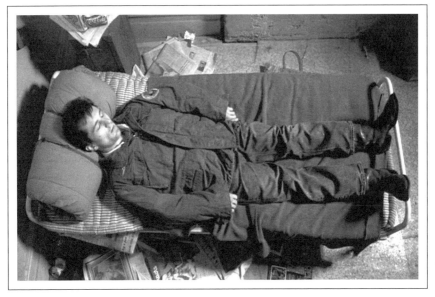

FIGURE 30: Robert De Niro as Travis Bickle in his army-surplus jacket in *Taxi Driver* (1976). Costume design by Ruth Morley (wardrobe by Al Craine), makeup by Irving Buchman and Dick Smith, hair by Mona Orr.

For Woody Allen's *Annie Hall* (1977), Morley's work was so spot-on that it looks like Diane Keaton simply wore her own clothes in the film. But since the film *did* have a credited costume designer, and Keaton's "Annie Hall look" became so popular and widely copied, Morley was asked how she came up with it. In a 1978 interview in the *New York Daily News*, Morley described how she "started her shopping at Reminiscence, that stay-loose-and-cheap compendium of antique clothes and dyed army surplus. Most of the vests and ties came from thrift shops. The 'period undershirts' and men's hats were bought at Unique Clothing Warehouse. The pleated men's pants, one of the items most copied on Seventh Avenue now, came from the Eaves Costume Co., as did Keaton's men's shoes." Morley's goal was to convey the degree to which the Annie Hall character was unformed and unsure of her path, but she ended by creating a persona and style for and with Keaton that persist to this day.[46] For *Kramer vs. Kramer* (Robert Benton, 1979), Morley shopped throughout New York in vintage and high-end department stores to create a facsimile of the wardrobe of an actual Upper East Side family. Indeed, in his review in the *New Yorker*, Roger Angell wrote that the film "achieved near perfect attention to detail on every level, including costume design."[47]

An attention to details that support characterization and narrative and that are so appealing that they are adopted by audience members as their own styles as well—with the knock-off looks quickly becoming the background against which the designers' work is now evaluated—led Landis to the conclusion that costume designers had become "victims of their own virtuosity" by the end of the 1970s.

Their costumes appeared to be so natural that they could not have been designed. Even directors sometimes "forgot" the talent and the labor with whom they had collaborated; Woody Allen mentioned "that costume lady, Ruth Morley," in some early interviews, but claimed that he told her to "let Keaton do her own thing."[48] Later, Allen stopped mentioning Morley altogether, referring only to Keaton's talent for "creating her own style through dress."[49]

Venerable fashion guru Diana Vreeland responded to the era's film designers by lamenting the "demise" of cinema costume design in her Met Costume Institute show of 1976, "Romantic and Glamorous Hollywood Design." But "romantic and glamorous" design had not disappeared, either from films or from what was becoming increasingly important during the era, the culture of celebrity.[50] Landis details the transition that occurred in Hollywood from full awareness of the complex art of costume design to simple fascination with the glamour of the red carpet, finding the apotheosis of the shift at the 1987 Academy Awards. When Cher was awarded the Oscar for Best Actress for her work as a dowdy, love-lorn bookkeeper in *Moonstruck*, directed by Norman Jewison and with costumes by Theoni V. Aldredge, she accepted her statuette in an outrageous semi-nude showgirl outfit designed by Bob Mackie.[51] While Mackie is surely good at his job and designed the costumes for Barbra Streisand in *Funny Lady* (Herbert Ross, 1975), he is less a builder of character through design than a creator of glamour, and does so far more frequently off the screen than on.

The "Return" of Design

The significant changes in the crafts of costume, makeup, and hair design that accompanied the end of the studio era remain with us still. Design budgets for "contemporary" films of the late 1970s—*Taxi Driver*, *Annie Hall*, and *Kramer vs. Kramer*, for example—were more substantial than they had been earlier in the decade, but their craftspeople continued to employ a combination of manufactured and "shopped" costumes, with "straight" makeup and hair products also often purchased from drug- or department-store shelves. The blockbuster success in 1975 of *Jaws*, which had three uncredited makeup artists and hairstylists combined and three uncredited wardrobe personnel in contrast to fifteen or so special effects men (who were all male, though not all of them were credited), pointed the direction toward the "New Hollywood" to come, in which effects became the stars of films that were nevertheless made by many well-known auteurs like George Lucas or Francis Ford Coppola. While Coppola's *Apocalypse Now* (1979) was an expensive failure at the time, its large cast was at least supported by a crew of credited costumers and makeup and hair stylists as well as a large number of effects artists.

Landis writes that the blockbuster films of the second half of the decade revived the film industry, though it was only one kind of blockbuster that truly did the reviving, what she calls the "optimistic genre films" of this period beginning with Spielberg's *Jaws* and moving to his *Close Encounters of the Third Kind* and Lucas's *Star Wars* in 1977.[52] It was really the popularity of the fantasy films, especially but not exclusively science fiction, that made costume, makeup, and hair designers popular again too—particularly makeup artists, like Dick Smith, who could turn humans into aliens, monsters, or any other being in addition to aging them. Characters created through animatronics also needed designed wardrobe, hair, and makeup, and the ability to create and alter images on computers (though as yet only occasionally used) would come to depend more and more on such designers in the decades to come.

The techniques that Smith employed on a challenging film like *Little Big Man* and the more conventional horror of *The Exorcist* in the early 1970s showed that the crafts could be used to create ever more believable images of humans transformed by time, illness, or the supernatural, as well as creatures of the imagination, both of which science fiction depended upon and which were enabled by the technical sophistication the crafts had achieved by mid-decade. Strategically, as costume designer and historian Elois Jenssen puts it in her essay "Visions of the Future: Costume in Science Fiction Films," costume, makeup, and hair designers tend either to "make a conscientious effort to predict how styles may change, or they may simply let their imaginations run wild." But, Jenssen notes, Hollywood designs of the future "almost always reflect historic influences. . . . The heroes and heroines may be on other planets, millions of years into the future, but the [designs] in the film often recall . . . Ancient Greeks and Romans, harem girls and sheiks, samurai and geisha, or medieval knights and maidens."[53]

This was certainly the case with probably the best-known film of the 1970s, *Star Wars* (now known as *Episode IV: A New Hope*). Lucas's first choice for costume designer for *Star Wars* was Milena Canonero, who was unable to take the job but recommended John Mollo, her historical consultant on *Barry Lyndon*. Mollo was an expert in military history and hardware and had consulted on the period films *The Charge of the Light Brigade* (1968) and *Nicholas and Alexandra* (1971), due to his expertise in creating apparently authentic rather than "little theater" uniforms. Mollo met Lucas in 1975 to discuss the drawings that illustrator Ralph McQuarrie had made for the film. Lucas wanted costumes that would be unobtrusive and that would appear both familiar and strange at the same time. Before Mollo began, Lucas had decided that the bad guys would have a "fascist" look and the hero would have the aura of the American Wild West, yet he apparently did not look to any particular films as references (color plate 12).[54]

The process of creating Darth Vader reveals much about the playful, collaborative approach that prevailed on a film with a relatively low budget (especially compared with later entries in the franchise).[55] With McQuarrie's drawings, paper dolls, and reference books at hand, Mollo began by pulling things from stock, such as a black motorcycle suit, a Nazi-era helmet, a gas mask, and a

FIGURE 31: Above, the robots C-3PO and R2-D2, in *Star Wars* (1977); below, the well-known mask of Darth Vader. All three were collaboratively designed by George Lucas, the costume designer John Mollo, and a large number of effects specialists.

medieval-looking monk's cloak. Using his imagination rather than detailed drawings, Lucas selected the elements that resonated for him, which Mollo used to create the actual costumes (figure 31). The masks were modeled with clay so as to be adjustable according to Lucas's vision. For the robot C-3PO, Mollo shopped and built with the drawing as a guide, spending only $1,175. The face was created with Liz Moore, who made nine versions that were presented for approval. (Moore had previously created the Star Child for Kubrick's *2001: A Space Odyssey* in 1968 and created sculpture and paintings for *A Clockwork Orange*.) With the shape of the C-3PO head settled, Lucas poked two coins into the clay for eyes, to get the fastidious robot's slightly humorous, silly look, and adjusted the mouth to suit. The loose process through which the film was created is reflected more concretely in the fact that the tight budget delayed the formation of the makeup department six weeks past the scheduled start date.[56]

Mollo worked on another well-known science fiction film of the 1970s, Ridley Scott's *Alien* (1979), which, like *Star Wars*, created a profitable franchise and for which he created equally quirky costumes and characters. Mollo has noted that Scott wanted to avoid any suggestions of utilitarian "space suits" for his film, and looked for inspiration to the samurai silhouette.[57] The costumes that he designed are meant to look like clothing that people would wear to be comfortable while working hard in trying circumstances, far from home. The individual costumes that include everyday elements such as baseball caps, sweat bands, and a Hawaiian shirt both define characters and create a sense of unity among groups of characters. Through his unusually neat costume, the android Ash (Ian Holm) stands out, as does Ripley (Sigourney Weaver), who wears what appear to be regulation overalls to signify her authority. In a pattern that is not unusual in the 1970s, H. R. Giger's "xenomorph designs" for the monster in *Alien* received multiple awards and much attention, but virtually no notice was taken of the perfectly designed costumes of the human characters.[58]

While the 1970s appears to be divided, then, between the auteur renaissance of the first half, with its complicated and sophisticated stories and smaller-scale production processes, and the blockbuster second half, with its interest in adventure genres and technology and a corresponding increase in special effects, the examples of *Star Wars* and *Alien* reveal more similarities than differences in working methods and design requirements. For costume, makeup, and hair designers, the 1970s was a decade of adaptation to an entirely new mode of work, which was driven by the demise of the studio system. Necessity was indeed the mother of invention at this time, as designers learned to work with vastly smaller sums of money as well as quotidian materials that often already existed in the world rather than being dreams of glamour created by staffs of hundreds working around the clock in wardrobe departments and workrooms.

With their creativity spurred on by brilliant young directors who considered film the equal of any art form, designers collaborated, often without credit, on films that are everywhere regarded as works of art. But designers who worked on the era's blockbusters were no less inspired, and their directors—sometimes the same ones—were equally adventurous and knowledgeable. While technological innovation would take the place of sophisticated design and character-building to an ever greater degree in the highly successful franchises that dominate later decades, the film industry owes a great deal to the enterprising and inventive costume, makeup, and hair designers of the 1970s who managed the transition out of, and in some sense back into, the studio system with skill, persistence, and brilliance.

5

THE NEW HOLLYWOOD, 1981-1999 Tamar Jeffers McDonald

The most financially successful movies of the 1980s and 1990s, some of which were entries in franchises begun the previous decade, were blockbusters that emphasized action, special effects, and, increasingly, computer-generated images but that overall did not represent a break with established practices in the crafts of costuming, makeup, and hair. Steven Spielberg's *E.T. The Extra-Terrestrial* (1982) and his trilogy *Raiders of the Lost Ark* (1981), *Indiana Jones and the Temple of Doom* (1984), and *Indiana Jones and the Last Crusade* (1989), for example, as well as his *Jurassic Park* (1993) and *The Lost World: Jurassic Park* (1997); James Cameron's *Terminator* (1984) and *Terminator 2: Judgment Day* (1991); or George Lucas's *Star Wars, Episode I: The Phantom Menace* (1999), in spite of more and more sophisticated digital effects, relied mainly on practical or physical techniques in makeup and hair design that were well in place already. In 1992, Robert Zemeckis's *Death Becomes Her,* with digital effects created by Industrial Light & Magic, was called a "glimpse of things to come" in its combining of "physical make-up and animatronic effects" with CGI to put the "first CG body part on a living human," Meryl Streep's backward-facing head.[1]

The biggest box-office success of the era, Cameron's *Titanic* (1997), certainly used costume, makeup, and hair as Hollywood always had: to highlight and reveal personality traits, to help actors develop a character, and to provide visual pleasure (color plate 13). Its costumes, by Deborah L. Scott, were designed with attention to these as much as to historical accuracy, and the romantic sumptuousness of the clothing, makeup, and hair styling also provided one of the key delights to viewers, as the popularity of copycat outfits and accessories subsequently demonstrated.[2]

Oscars for costuming, as for makeup (which was finally given its own Academy Award category in 1981, functionally but not explicitly including hairdressing), continued to celebrate efforts, like *Titanic*'s, in historical reconstruction, but there is yet more continuation from the previous post-studio decades in the opposition, onscreen and off, between the designed and the "shopped." While actors may appear to wear "ordinary dress" in *Working Girl* (Mike Nichols, 1988), *Rain Man* (Barry Levinson, 1988), and *Basic Instinct* (Paul Verhoeven, 1992), their costumes are no less crafted and carefully chosen than the more elaborate apparel designed for pictures set in the past.

Even those films that did attempt to re-create a historical period were not always devoted to producing bonnets and bustles but found fruitful material in more recent history. Regardless of whether the time shown represents centuries or merely decades ago, meticulous re-creation of or impressionistic reference to historical designs can both evoke a period and draw out character points and clashes. The painstaking re-creation, in *Amadeus* (Milos Forman, 1984), of the eighteenth-century costumes, hairdressing and wigs, and makeup worn by—and distinguishing among—royalty, court, professionals, the bourgeoisie, and servant classes; or the styling of a more fantastic film set in the same era, *Sleepy Hollow* (Tim Burton, 1999), creates and underlines personality no less and no more than do the 1970s shag haircuts, frosted eyeshadow, flared jeans, and pointy-collared nylon shirts of *Boogie Nights* (Paul Thomas Anderson, 1997).

Films of the 1990s, especially, increasingly used costuming, makeup, and hair self-reflexively, employing earlier movies as well as other historical mass-media texts as sources of design and styling, a trend that continues in the present.[3] In the 1990s, copying not just earlier styles "realistically" but as they appeared in other movies and modes—such as the costuming that marked out the femme fatale in 1940s films noirs—permits design personnel to pay homage to classic entries in the film canon while also serving more basic narrative ends. In *Basic Instinct*, the central female character is outfitted in contemporary fashions that also speak to earlier femme fatale predecessors. In *L.A. Confidential* (Curtis Hanson, 1997), character Lynn Bracken consciously adopts the styles of an actress partially known for her femme fatale roles, Veronica Lake. *Boogie Nights* brings the 1970s to life via costumes and accessories for both its male and female stars and through allusions to well-known films from the era, including *Saturday Night Fever* (1977).

All these films employ highly developed and refined techniques in costume, makeup, and hair design and execution; if there is comparatively little practical "innovation" discussed here, this is because it was not required given the quality and reliability of methods that were already in place—although CGI, as yet sparingly used in cinema, would alter certain practices profoundly in later decades. Instead, these films demonstrate the polish and confidence with which the crafts were being practiced across a variety of genres, and the ongoing importance of trained professionals, working in careful collaboration with the actors they were designing, in supporting commercial cinema's ability to convey story information, delineate character, and provide visual gratification and pleasure.

"Contemporary" Styling: *Working Girl, Rain Man,* and *Basic Instinct*

Screen costumes for films set in the time of their production inevitably reflect changes in contemporary offscreen fashions. Since 1981–1999 was a period of continuing social and cultural change in America, it is not surprising to find films reflecting such changes too, moving from the power-dressing of the 1980s to the more casual or anti-fashion ("grunge") of the 1990s. There is a close relationship between trends and fads in clothing being worn by real people and by those onscreen depicting them, and films can be revisited for snapshots of "the way we wore." It sometimes requires effort to get beyond the superficially exotic elements of a recent period's fashion—giant shoulder-pads, gelled hair—to understand what the film's designers were trying to achieve. Even if a production has been shopped, its wardrobe bought off-the-rack rather than designed, the costumes are still chosen to express character qualities.

Working Girl, with costume design by Ann Roth and makeup and hair design by Joseph Campayno, Alan D'Angerio, and J. Roy Helland, foregrounds the importance of clothing, makeup, and hair in two ways: by having characters able to read the meaning of each other's outfits, and by showing that people judge one, at least initially, entirely on appearances. For Tess McGill (Melanie Griffith) to achieve her goal of rising from the secretarial pool to the ranks of financial dealmakers she has thus only to change her clothes and her styling. At the start of the film she is found on the Staten Island ferry en route to Manhattan with many other secretaries all dressed like her: in an ensemble seemingly designed to take up as much space as possible, with a giant shoulder-padded jacket, miniskirt revealing lots of leg, big coat, and huge crimped and teased hairdo, accented with large pieces of jewelry and maximum makeup. Tess yearns to use her evident financial skills on her own behalf, rather than making forecasts that her male colleagues appropriate, but she has not yet learned the film's message about fitting in. To become a boss she will have to look like a boss.

She learns this lesson slowly, as she first believes that having a new female superior, Katharine Parker (Sigourney Weaver), will make the difference to her fortunes. Katharine tells her on their first day together that they are a team, they will work together and share ideas, but also that they have "a uniform: simple, elegant, impeccable." Tess perceives anxiously that Katharine is judging her appearance, but when she asks, tremulously, "How do I look?" the somewhat patronizing answer is "Terrific . . . but you might want to rethink the jewelry." Katharine tells Tess this while herself employing a carefully understated look in accessories: discreet jewelry, soft, neatly arranged hair, and minimal makeup. The next scene has Tess in the ladies' room removing her clunky earrings and bangles and wiping off some of her eye makeup.

Until this point Tess has been wearing separates as work-wear, but studying Katharine teaches her the added smartness that a suit can lend, and she begins also to copy her supposed mentor's outfits directly. After betrayal by her boss, who has tried to steal her idea, Tess decides to fight back and steal, or at least borrow, some of her clothing. Tess and best friend Cyn (Joan Cusack) explore the treasures of Katharine's wardrobe, looking for the perfect garment to represent the new persona Tess is determined to adopt. Tess pulls out a dress—black, modestly cut, but enlivened with sparkles—and pronounces it perfect since "it says confident, a risk-taker." Cyn, however, balks at the garment when she finds the price tag still affixed to it: "Six thousand dollars? It's not even *leather*!" The film neatly juxtaposes the old and new versions of Tess here, as she correctly identifies the value of the expensive item before knowing its cost and appreciates what it will do for her image; while Cyn, representing the old Tess and her former priorities, repines at its ostensible lack of glitz. In a final move away from her old self, Tess enlists Cyn's help to cut off her huge halo of hair, opting instead for a shorter, more professional crop. As Tess tells Cyn, the cut is essential for her progress in business: "If you want to be taken seriously, you need serious hair."

Working Girl enables the viewer to enjoy seeing Tess in her new persona of successful business executive at the event for which she has transformed herself: wearing Katharine's black dress and high heels, and sporting her new hairdo, she ventures into a work party at a bar and picks up executive Jack Trainer (Harrison Ford). Purged of the visual excesses of her typing-pool persona, Tess now teams her expensive gown with softly curled coiffure, glossy amber lips, and smoky gray eye, an understated look that emulates Katharine's but, through her own warmth, transcends mere copying. Interestingly, Tess's former boyfriend Mick (Alec Baldwin) can read the difference in her appearance when he sees her again, noting that "you look different, good, classy," but also associating her improvement with an attempt at impressing social superiors: "You have to go to traffic court?" He lacks the imagination to see that she wants to move into a higher class herself. With so many of the characters being able to read the importance of the right—and wrong—look to self-presentation, the film inevitably encourages its audiences to read clothes and hair that way too, to think about their own wardrobes for what their suits, separates, hair, and accessories are implying about them (figure 32).

FIGURE 32: Tess (Melanie Griffith), Katharine (Sigourney Weaver), and Nick (Harrison Ford) in *Working Girl* (1988). Above, Tess in the "wrong" hair and makeup; below, now executive-caliber because of her "serious" hair, subdued makeup, and discreet clothing. Costume design by Ann Roth, with wardrobe for women by Melissa Stanton and for men by David Dumais; makeup by Joseph A. Campayno and J. Roy Helland; hair by Alan D'Angerio and J. Roy Helland (and Francesca Paris, uncredited). There are also two credited "wardrobe shoppers" on the film.

It is important for the story that Tess is back in her jeans and a simple black sweater when she makes the final speeches convincing businessman Oren Trask (Philip Bosco) to believe in her. Through this the narrative underlines that not everyone can elevate herself from the secretarial pool by masquerading as an executive: in the end it is ideas that count, and jean-clad Tess beats out power-dressed Katharine. This is perhaps the film's last-reel attempt to soften its rather stark advice to women seeking advancement at work. Like the social elevation films of the 1930s, which often starred Joan Crawford, a simple upscaling of wardrobe enables the heroine to pass as one of her social superiors. *The Bride Wore Red* (1937) has a storyline similar to *Working Girl*'s, although the job left behind by Anni (Crawford) is that of a singer in a dive, and she mimics not professionals but the leisure class. Both films have been identified as versions of the Cinderella story, but the later film's emphasis on the importance of its heroine's work life marks it as part of the corporate 1980s.[4] While the 1937 film ultimately punishes Anni for her temerity in aping her betters, *Working Girl* at its conclusion rewards Tess for her tenacity by giving her both her own office with secretary and a man who will be a fitting partner in business as well as romance.

Like other transformation movies, *Working Girl* appears to make rather worrying assumptions about the fluidity and impermanence of female identity, given the ease with which Tess becomes another person just by donning Katharine's clothes; this is why the narrative strives to underscore her intelligence and commitment *before* her sartorial alteration.[5] Nevertheless, the implication, via the film's address to viewers over the necessity for "serious hair" and the right clothes and accessories, remains that women are changed by their outward trappings. An anxiety about shallowness or mutability lies underneath the consumerist promise that purchasing the power suit, the smart leather briefcase, the understated pearls will enable young women to assimilate themselves to the professional milieu.

Rain Man also uses its costumes, designed by Bernie Pollack, to indicate character change, but its narrative's project, in simple terms, is to get Charlie Babbitt (Tom Cruise) to *be* better by *dressing* worse. This is consonant with a well-established trend in Hollywood films toward messing up and dressing down their heroes as a form of interior revelation. Although there have been many leading men identified with sartorial elegance—William Powell, Fred Astaire, Cary Grant, any of the versions of James Bond, for example—films as different, and as chronologically distant, as *Aggie Appleby, Maker of Men* (1933), *I Love You, Alice B. Toklas!* (1968), and *American Gigolo* (1980) attest to a competing desire to return men to the "real" business of ignoring their appearance.[6] So whereas *Working Girl* suggests Tess is right to try on different identities with different outfits, what *Rain Man* wants Charlie to do is forget about his flashy clothes and concentrate instead on the *inner* him. The film uses costume progression to show Charlie's successful journey toward becoming a better person, one who cares about other people, neatly mapping this onto an actual journey as he and his newly discovered "autistic savant" brother, Raymond (Dustin Hoffman), take an eccentric road trip from Ohio to California.

While *Rain Man* and *Working Girl* were both in movie theaters in December 1988, and thus both record some version of contemporary fashions, the styles each espouses seem worlds, or one might say *states*, apart: the outfits worn by Tess, Katharine, and Jack suggest grown-up New York business suits, but Charlie's clothes chime much more with the accent on youth and glamour of California. As a luxury car salesman, Charlie relies on flash to sell his own image along with his vehicles; he starts the film in a gray suit with pleated pants and wide shoulders in the jacket and a dark blue shirt buttoned all the way to his throat. Two gold rings and a gold Rolex adorn his hands and wrist. His outfits take up space, present his persona—brash, confident, a little obnoxious—to the audience, and hint that he enjoys an ample wardrobe, since the film shows him rapidly exchanging his suit jacket for another, darker one, for no ostensible reason.

The film works to break down the flashy exterior Charlie projects in order to put him in touch with his own emotions as he learns to look after the brother he has removed from an Ohio mental hospital; his traveling garments, pulled repeatedly from his weekend bag, become more crumpled and travel-worn as the journey continues, and Charlie himself seems to be coming apart. Although he tries to maintain his usual dominance over events by wearing his power suits, when he is stranded in a motel due to Raymond's refusal to travel in the rain Charlie's habitual persuasive charm on the telephone fails him suddenly, and his clothes testify to his lack of control over his situation, their increasing dishevelment over the scene signaling his unraveling.

The narrative also uses costume and styling straightforwardly to establish character differences. In contrast to Charlie's capacious wardrobe and artfully tousled hair, Raymond wears the same outfit every day: pale jeans, white tee under pale shirt, pale zip-up jacket, hair neatly parted. Raymond's preference for the same clothes works well as a plot point, fitting with his obsessive personality, but also breaks down the easy oppositions that might seem to obtain between the pair, situating Raymond on the "wrong" or undesirable side of the dyads: Charlie cocky, sexual, a flashy dresser, and skittish; Raymond insecure, innocent, a quiet dresser, and steady. The obvious contrasts between the two brothers are also broken down via small narrative details that reveal instead their similarities, as in the moments where they both reel off car facts. This contrast underlines that the compulsive absorption and repetition of trivia is not only part of Raymond's illness, but also a socially sanctioned aspect of masculinity.

Charlie's overuse of sunglasses also works on two levels. Partly the wearing of Ray-Bans is due to the star persona of Tom Cruise himself, since he has been associated with the brand since *Risky Business* (1983); partly also, however, they act as a literalization of his blindness to others' feelings and needs.[7] In one of the film's most blatant uses of this device, Charlie, wearing his sunglasses when no other character is similarly attired, looks straight at Raymond and utters the line "I don't have a brother." The film's project is then to make Charlie remove his metaphoric blinkers and accept and value their relationship.

Seeking to capitalize on his brother's extraordinary memory, Charlie takes Raymond to Las Vegas, checks into Caesar's Palace, and pawns his Rolex for money to outfit them both as high rollers. The subsequent shopping montage, focusing on Raymond's sartorial transformation more than Charlie's, could be imagined shot from the former's perspective, so swift are the tracking shots over racks of pants and jackets and shelves of footwear. Ray retreats into his usual self-comforting rituals, rocking and muttering; while having a suit made to measure, his fragmented image in half a dozen mirrors reflects his confusion about the sudden activity around his clothes.

A trip to a ladies' beauty parlor accomplishes a haircut; then the transformed brothers, for once outfitted in near-matching clothes, descend the escalator onto the casino floor. Although they seem at first to be wearing matching outfits—gray suits, white shirts buttoned up to the chin, no tie, leather loafers—their clothes are still subtly different: Raymond's suit has a double-breasted jacket and fuller trousers, as accords his conservative character, while both jacket and pants for Charlie are more slim-line, showing off his leaner figure. Raymond also commits the solecism of wearing brown shoes with his gray suit, unlike Charlie, whose shoes are black. The two thus seem most in harmony and for the first time dressed in complementary style, yet Charlie still manages to stand out as fashionably dressed while Raymond remains uncomfortable in his new clothes, the fact that his jacket is too long in the sleeve despite being made-to-measure showing that he is never at ease with himself.

Yet it is this Vegas suit that Raymond is wearing when Charlie, having realized Raymond will be happiest in his old hospital environment, hands him back

FIGURE 33: Dustin Hoffman and Tom Cruise, costumed by Bernie Pollack, made up by Edwin Butterworth and Rick Sharp, and with hair by Joy Zapata, descending a Las Vegas escalator in *Rain Man* (1988).

to the doctor to escort him home. The significance of the brothers' clothes in this final scene seems to be that despite the seemingly impenetrable emotional barrier created by his condition, Raymond has been changed by his time with Charlie. Charlie, however, is wearing the same clothes as when he first met Raymond; the nubby blue-checked jacket, dark blue shirt, and lighter pants thus seem to bracket his sustained time with his brother. As the train carrying Raymond pulls away from the station, Charlie puts his sunglasses back on, hiding the vulnerable part of himself once more. The film's downbeat ending, with the brothers parted, is thus reinforced by the costume plot, which shows Raymond's improvement but hints at Charlie's imminent return to his former solipsism. It is debatable, then, whether *Rain Man* fully buys into the makeover—or make*under*—subgenre, since the effects of Charlie's sartorial transformation are not definitely forecast as permanent. Nevertheless, the film does employ some of the standard tropes of the makeover movie, including, in the brothers' spectacular descent on the casino escalator in their new outfits, a witty take on the familiar moment in which a woman, in her new finery, descends a staircase like a model coming down a ramp (figure 33).[8]

Basic Instinct, released some four years later, uses a similar, ostensibly realist approach to the clothing of its male characters, adapted to its own historical moment. Just as the clothes worn by real cops and executives would have moved away in the intervening years from the super-confident extroversion of the 1980s yuppie suit, so film costumes by 1992 reflected a new sobriety. A comparison of two roles played by Michael Douglas and designed by costumer Ellen Mirojnick neatly reflects this change across a five-year period: as Manhattan financier Gordon Gecko in 1987's *Wall Street*, Douglas wore "custom-tailored suits, colored shirts with crisp white collars and cuffs, wide suspenders and woven-silk ties."[9] Now, as San Francisco police detective Nick Curran, he is outfitted predominantly in just one suit-shirt-and-tie combination. Gone are items like the red suspenders and the trademark shirts with contrasting white collar and cuffs, both seen on so many cinematic corporate traders across the decade in films such as *Trading Places* (1983), *St. Elmo's Fire* (1985), *The Secret of My Success* (1987), and *sex, lies, and videotape* (1989).

Now, playing the insecure Nick, Douglas's vulnerability is made visible through his dressed-down wardrobe of leaner pants, casual jeans, and sweater combinations. Most symbolically of all, his character's standard suit and shirt are of nebulous, uncertain colors, pale gray and beige in some lights, blue and gray in others. This vague and shifting coloring aptly captures the character's morality: although he is initially set up as the hero of the movie, Nick is soon revealed to have a disreputable past, a history of addiction and violence. Conversely, his police partner Gus (George Dzundza), a stockier man, wears double-breasted jackets with contrasting pants in clearly defined colors, indicating the relative simplicity of his moral universe.

The costumes worn by Douglas's character in *Basic Instinct* did not attract notice in the fashion media; by contrast, the tailor responsible for the suits in *Wall Street*, Alan Flusser, had claimed at that time that "the clothes in the film are what's happening now," and designer Mirojnick also noted that after the film's release, "People from money men to boxing promoters have phoned to ask where they can get 'that Wall St. look.'"[10] The only item of Nick's wardrobe that attracted sustained attention was the V-neck sweater he wore to a hip nightclub, although this seemed more to suggest a style for men *not* to emulate. Instead, costume attention toward *Basic Instinct* was much more for what Sharon Stone was wearing—or not wearing—as Catherine Trammell. While Catherine is first shown in a soft knitted taupe sweater over a similarly colored tee and loose shorts, the scene is not long and the character seems mysterious rather than alluring. It is the all-white outfit she next puts on that confirms her femme fatale status, since this was the color that most classic noirs chose to dress such characters in, at least for their first appearance.[11] Nick spies on her as she slips into the white dress and thus sees that she does not put on underwear beneath it.

Trammell's white dress, worn for the police interview scene, seems to have taken on an afterlife of its own, being referenced in other media products, including movies *Hot Shots Part Deux* (1993) and *Scary Movie* (2000), episodes of television shows *The Simpsons* and *Seinfeld*, and the video game *Grand Theft Auto: San Andreas* (2004). The dress thus can claim iconic status, since it has held a place within popular awareness for over a decade. It also shows that onscreen contemporary costume can have a further impact on clothing choices outside the movie theater: all Stone has to do to recall her moment of greatest fame is to wear a short white dress.[12] This self-reflexive turn is similar to the use of

Cruise-associated costume items in *Rain Man*, but here the use is extradiegetic. Both quote from an earlier film to remind the viewer of a star persona, but Stone's use is personal since she is the star in question. This adds an interesting layer of self-reflexivity to the *Basic Instinct* costumes, which already consciously evoke earlier movie clothes.

In contrast, the film's other main female character, Beth Garner (Jeanne Tripplehorn), is predominantly outfitted in rich brown tones complementing the actor's hair and eyes, her silhouette tending toward the broad-shouldered and mannish. Although the male characters have left that style behind, she seems to persist in wearing the 1980s yuppie power suit, her jackets more reminiscent of the style of Gecko than female executives such as J. C. Wiatt in *Baby Boom* (1987), where Diane Keaton's shoulder-padded jackets are contrasted and softened by the tight cinching of the waist to produce an exaggeratedly feminine outline. Beth tends to wear tight dresses or tops with pencil skirts under the flowing expanse of the jackets, the latter garments hiding the curves of her body and perhaps acting as both armor and camouflage, as she is a female professional in a male-dominated and demonstrably sexist milieu. Beth hides her shape to conform to the masculine work place, but Catherine's supreme self-confidence can be read in her fondness for clothes that reveal her body's form to the viewer, as well as for soft fabrics that will feel good against her own skin: while she is acutely aware of and manipulates the effects her appearance has on others, she dresses not only to influence their opinions of her but also with a narcissistic imperative toward the sensual.

The jacket Catherine wears at first over the white dress conforms most nearly to the silhouette that Beth tends to wear, the big-shouldered look. On Catherine, however, this looks less mannish, and less like camouflage: her body's performance in wearing the jacket highlights its width, but with its soft lines it flows to give her a sort of swagger that is perfectly in tune with her confidence. When she removes the jacket in the interrogation scene she reveals that the sleeveless dress is cut away at the arms to draw attention to them and her shoulders, thus using her outfit, the physique it reveals, and her behavior to manipulate and confuse her interrogators. She wears a dress colored to suggest purity and innocence, but with no underwear. She denies stabbing her lover, yet emphasizes her strong arms. Her subdued makeup and artfully arranged blonde hair, entirely pulled back from her face, focuses attention there as if to assert that she has nothing to hide, yet her arch and knowing answers to their questions cause the detectives to doubt her. It is as if she is daring the policemen to look beyond the physical perfection of her beauty and judge her on what she says, all the while confidently knowing that they will privilege the visual over the auditory.

Her hairdo, which features a neat tucked curl at the back, is just one of a variety Catherine employs (the film credits four hair stylists); while the rather vortex-like curl may seem a reference to another San Francisco film, Alfred

FIGURE 34: The rapidly changing hair arrangements of Catherine Trammell (Sharon Stone), by Audrey L. Anzures and others, highlight her unstable personality in *Basic Instinct* (1992). Costume design by Nino Cerruti and Ellen Mirojnick, makeup and hair by David Forrest and others (the film has eight-plus credits for makeup and hair alone).

Hitchcock's *Vertigo* (1958), and its similarly blonde, mysterious central female, the actual impossibility of such styling in the time given onscreen—mere seconds for what required brushing, pins, and hairspray—also creates a sense of Trammell existing as a fantasy. Her changing hair arrangements across the film, even more than her outfits, which are generally either white or various shades of cream and caramel colors to set off her honey-blonde looks, underline the potentially fragmented nature of her psyche (figure 34). Hair has this role to play for Beth too; although her standard style for work is reminiscent of the "serious hair" Tess adopts for business in *Working Girl*, the narrative revelation here that Beth was once as blond as Catherine sends a jolt through the plot and underlines that she too may have a dangerously fluid nature.

Nick's persistent wearing of his work suit, then, takes on a further meaning: while its colors may be uncertain and hard to pin down, the frequency with which he wears the jacket and pants at least indicates a solid personality within the clothes. Catherine's numerous shifts in styles and looks echo her pathology, a worrying notion since frequent costume changes are so routinely used in film in outfitting the women characters. This is another point where the consumerist impulse that Hollywood cinema fosters collides with the suspense narrative; having the clothing transformations affect the internal as well as external woman indicates her instability.

Thus, while costume, makeup, and hair in films set in the time of their making can provide moments of audience pleasure as well as character and narrative information, the similarity of the items and fashions shown onscreen to the audience's own might also create feelings of discomfort, for example if notions about getting ahead through better dressing or grooming conflict with styles or clothing we ourselves affect or wear. Similarly, the transformation motif in these films underlines the importance of clothes as indices of character but is also disquieting in its insistence on the permeability of the self. This conundrum sets up a potential problem with the proximity of contemporary styles in film, and it is also easy to overlook the care with which they are prepared and schematized by invisible craftspeople. The costumes, makeup, and hair of films set in the past may not affect viewers so personally, but their designers face issues of their own.

Styling the Distant Past: *Amadeus* and *Sleepy Hollow*

The primary dilemma facing "costume films," as those set in the historical past are significantly often called, is the need to ensure that their outfits do not seem just empty spectacle. The filmmakers may risk alienating audiences from the immediacy of the action if the costumes make their characters seem too distant from contemporary mores. Designers thus work to ensure their creations are not too pristine, too stiff, lest they make the people inhabiting them seem like posing mannequins rather than real folk, but their clothes, hair, and makeup also need to be relied upon to provide uncomplicated pleasures for viewers through their sumptuousness and spectacle.

Certainly the filmic re-creation of past times through period costumes is often rewarded with industry recognition. Morgan Fairchild's scripted introduction to the Best Costume nominations at the 1982 Academy Awards noted that "all the designers nominated *this* year had to research the clothing of years gone by." Fairchild's delivery emphasized "this," but she could have been talking about any year in the period under consideration, or indeed most subsequent ones.[13] From 1981 to 1999 just one Academy Award for Best Costume went to a designer who had produced contemporary clothing, Lizzy Gardiner for *The Adventures of Priscilla, Queen of the Desert* (1994), although the fact that the film's characters spend much of their time in outrageously spectacular and extravagant drag show numbers lessens the idea that this award is, finally, a triumph for contemporary clothing. Outside of genres reliant on special effects and fantasy or extreme character makeup, the Oscar for Best Makeup was also given primarily to period films in the 1980s and 1990s.

While they are much more likely to be singled out for attention at award ceremonies, then, films with period costumes, makeup, and hair inherit distinct challenges around accuracy versus impressionism, while also respecting the usual Hollywood imperative to create and delineate character. *Amadeus* is the first film to have won Academy Awards both for Best Costume and Best Makeup (and hairstyling), plaudits that were entirely deserved. The impact of the costumes commences with the first scenes between the elderly Antonio Salieri (F. Murray Abraham), a new inmate in an insane asylum, and the young Catholic priest Father Vogler (Richard Frank). Salieri is wearing a once-sumptuous dark red brocade dressing gown over a wilted shirt. The faded clothes and the soiled lace parallel the now vastly diminished glory of his former musical career, which Salieri's recollections detail, but the color of his dressing gown also links him to the priest via the rich burgundy of the latter's clerical stole. The color matching thus establishes a surprising bond, which Salieri confirms at the end of the film. Pointing out that Vogler is powerless to absolve him, Salieri, in a neat reversal of the usual relationship between priest and supplicant, assures Vogler he will intercede for him since he "speak[s] for all mediocrities."

While the film uses costume to establish a parallel between the priest and the supposed lunatic, the static outfits of the pair also provide a useful point of stability across the film's extensive running time and multiple flashbacks. As Salieri confesses his jealousy of Mozart and the priest unwillingly listens to the old man reveal his plan for ruining his rival, their long dark night of the soul is enacted through one literal night, during which they remain in the same garments. The point of fixity inherent in their clothes creates a backdrop against which the constantly changing dress of the flashbacks is heightened, an effect exacerbated when we see the opera singers in their colorful and cartoon-like stage costumes and makeup, all exaggerated versions of those worn by nobles of the Viennese court. Caterina Cavalieri (Christine Ebersole) plays the heroine of *Die Entführung aus dem Serail* (1781) in an oversized curly blonde wig and a gown seemingly constructed solely of frills, bows, and profound cleavage.

The opposition between Salieri and Mozart (Tom Hulce), the film's main topic, is also maintained throughout by their styles of dress. Salieri's sober clothes, his preference for dark hues and restrained ornament, is set against Mozart's peacock array of colors in the scene where they are first introduced, for example. Salieri wears black hose and breeches, a matching jacket, a dark waistcoat, and a white shirt trimmed with an elegant fall of snowy lace at throat and cuffs that provides the main relief from the otherwise somber effect. Mozart forms a complete contrast through his lighter and more varied color palette: his lilac watered silk coat is worn over darker purple breeches and a richly embroidered peach waistcoat. A peachy velvet tricorn hat is sometimes perched on his pure white wig, sometimes waved for emphasis, and matches his high-heeled shoes.

While it therefore looks as if Salieri, the older, more experienced musician, has not been led astray as the younger Mozart has by the fashions of the day, a closer look at their contrasting outfits tells us a little more. Although he is dressed in black, Salieri's clothes are of sumptuous fabrics, the very depth and luster of his black jacket drawing the eye and sucking in the light. His cuffs are no less wide than the other man's, his buttons no less numerous: he only appears less frivolous because of his carefully restricted color scheme. Indeed, his waistcoat, of a dark gray fabric with silver chased designs, seems much more luxurious than Mozart's simpler embroidered garment.

A similar contrast is maintained in their hairdressing. Mozart conforms to fashion with his high, white, elaborately curled and powdered wig; Salieri—alone of all the emperor's musical advisers—wears an approximation of his own hair in natural color, unpowdered, brushed back, and secured in a tail with a neat black bow (figure 35). While this eschewing of the powder of the court seems ostensibly like a lack of fuss prompted by modesty, his unique position as the only person with a wig resembling natural hair actually signals Salieri's arrogance, a faux humility entirely in accord with the towering ego now narrating the story. He looks restrained, but is actually as self-indulgent as Mozart.

By contrast, Mozart's bright profusion of colors seems not so much undisciplined as generous, an indication of his pleasure in life and beauty. Just before the scene where the emperor and his chief music advisers receive the young composer, we see Mozart buying new wigs for the occasion. Presented with three different styles, he is at a loss to choose just one: "They're all so beautiful! Why don't I have three heads?" (color plate 14). His ample spirit contrasts very much with Salieri's pinched and careful front of modesty. Mozart's bright color palette also indicates his self-confidence, and is in opposition again to the humility Salieri pretends: while he wishes to appear as if he wants to blend modestly into the background, he actually broods and bridles if he is overlooked. Salieri pretends to be Mozart's friend but is secretly working against him, just as he appears to be restrained in his clothes but is as arrogant and self-obsessed as the younger composer and, crucially, as the film demonstrates, with less reason.

FIGURE 35: Salieri (F. Murray Abraham), with back to the camera, and Mozart (Tom Hulce, right) in *Amadeus* (1984). Costume design by Theodor Pistek (and Christian Thuri, uncredited). Typical of most period productions, there is a large number of credited and uncredited makeup, hair, and wig designers as well as costumers on the film.

The scene thus visually establishes the terms of the core differences between the two men while building on the most significant contrast between them: Salieri's inadequacy compared to Mozart's genius. While narratively this is economically achieved through the device of a little march Salieri has composed in Mozart's honor, which Mozart immediately improvises into what will later become "Non più andrai" from *Le Nozze di Figaro*, the costumes have already crystallized their dissimilarity. The film maintains this differentiation, and audience pleasure is invoked through the spectacularization of Mozart's pleasure in reveling in colors, fabrics, wigs, and dressing up. When he, his wife, and his father go to choose fancy dress costumes for a masquerade ball, his infectious laugh rings out across the shop and the succeeding scenes of the party. The adroit use of styling also tells the opposite story: while his enjoyment of fashion's vagaries illustrates Mozart's rise within the court, his decline, both financial and physical, is represented by the unkempt natural hair and dirty dressing gown in the scenes that speak to the composer's developing illness.

Makeup is also a crucial part of the film's success, not only the powdered faces and painted-on beauty spots of the courtiers, but also the realistic old-age makeup, by Dick Smith, that Abraham wears in the framing scenes.[14] The beady eyes of the older Salieri peer out of their wrinkled sockets like a sly turtle's, deep grooves set into his face, while his hair, once cropped short beneath his understated wigs, hangs in lank sidelocks and his bald pate shows age spots. Now that he can confess openly to his arrogance and malice, his former fastidiousness in appearance has been abandoned.

Press material surrounding *Amadeus* suggests its design was also ruled by a desire for historical accuracy.[15] The *Washington Post* interviewed costume designer Theodor Pistek about his methods after he won the Oscar for Best Costume: "His work on 'Amadeus' began with a year of study in Vienna and Salzburg. 'You must start with the information—the rest of the job is one's own imagination.' About 100 of the costumes were created from scratch, and more than 600 others borrowed from costume houses in Europe, the sizes and styles adjusted under his supervision."[16] Besides using his research in designing the costumes and headwear for the film, and finding inspiration in paintings by Watteau and Fragonard, Pistek also took his pursuit of accuracy to greater lengths, sourcing and using in the film some of Salieri's own clothes for Abraham to wear. His aim with all these different methods was to create costumes that looked as if they were real garments: "It should look like something the actor has lived in his whole life."[17] The historical accuracy thus becomes meaningful because it is matched by the creative use of the costume to convey character information.

The framing confession sections of *Amadeus* are set in 1823, with flashbacks to 1791, the year of Mozart's death, and earlier. *Sleepy Hollow* is set in 1799; so the main diegesis in both films is roughly contemporaneous, despite differences in setting (the emperor's court in Vienna versus a Dutch settlement in upstate

New York). But the costumes in Tim Burton's film seem immediately to be trying to achieve something very different from historical accuracy. Designer Colleen Atwood, Burton's frequent collaborator, gives a more impressionistic version of costume at the end of the eighteenth and the dawn of the nineteenth centuries. In Burton's adaptation of the Washington Irving short story, Ichabod Crane (Johnny Depp) is a police constable in New York City, seemingly alone in his awareness that his city's police force lacks analytic rigor and the employment of scientific innovations. Crane wants America to keep pace with the exciting discoveries being piloted in Europe, not to remain a backward country ruled by superstition. Despite his belief in the importance of objective facts, Crane is also tempted to believe in spiritual or supernatural phenomena: his adherence to evidence, detection, and facts will be tested in his visit to Sleepy Hollow where he confronts otherworldly forces, first in the shape of the Headless Horseman (Christopher Walken).

Because of this germ of "scientific" modernity in the characterization of Crane, his costume is the most contemporary-seeming of all the film's characters: he wears a black frock coat over a black waistcoat and breeches, his white shirt and stock the only relief from the gloomy palette. While his clothes are lacking in ornament compared to the embroidered finery of the wealthy bourgeois merchants and professional men he meets in Sleepy Hollow, his hair is also worn naturally rather than being elaborately dressed like the women's or covered by the large wigs some of the gentlemen affect. This stripped-down look is also appropriate because it is worn by Johnny Depp the star: his trademark black hair and beautiful face are seen unmediated by overly historical costume or wigs.

Crane provides a point not only of modernity, however, but also of stability, since he wears the same outfit throughout the film, with very minor variations.[18] In contrast, the other characters, especially the two main women, Katrina Van Tassel (Christina Ricci) and her stepmother, change their clothes with each successive scene. But while they are the only characters dressed predominantly in black, Crane and the Headless Horseman are not associated with each other by their similar styles of clothing. Instead, the film pursues an alternative schema of association via the costume plot, repeatedly providing clues to the identity of the person controlling the Horseman that are in opposition to the drive of the main narrative to keep the viewer in suspense.

The first clue is offered during an account of the horseman's legend, told to Crane by his host, Baltus Van Tassel (Michael Gambon). He relates how the Horseman— originally a Hessian mercenary—met his death; while his voiceover continues, the scene opens up and the viewer can see the events he is describing and, crucially, ones he is not. Pursued by soldiers, the Hessian had fled into a wood where he encountered twin little girls gathering firewood. Although he enjoined them to silence, one of the girls snapped a branch so the sound would direct his pursuers to him; she watched as the soldier was then surrounded and killed, his head cut off with his own sword. Although Baltus does not mention the girl or the way in which she betrayed the mercenary, she grows up to be Lady Van Tassel (Miranda Richardson), and it is she who uses the Horseman to destroy her enemies.

While the Hessian in his richly tooled black leather armor and the little girl in her sweet pink gown seem greatly contrasted by age, height, and ferocity, she proves to be the more dangerous. The costume similarity between them is the carapace-like item each wears, the soldier's breastplate echoing the little girl's stiff stomacher. This costume link is established in the visualization of the legend and then continued throughout the film: only Lady Van Tassel is consistently seen wearing a pronounced stomacher, a triangle of material that conceals the front opening of a gown. Interestingly, however, her stepdaughter Katrina wears a dress with this feature prominently shown in the one scene where Crane suspects she may be the sorceress. For the rest of her scenes, Katrina has been outfitted in softer and looser gowns with large draped bustles at the back; her dresses do not have the stiffened fabric, like armor, which marks Lady Van Tassel's front sections. Their colors, too, are more fitting for a young woman, being in shades of peach, primrose, or robin's-egg blue. A dramatic hooded riding cape with embroidered flowers masks her identity in one scene, but her benevolent intentions toward Crane are borne out by the stitched poppies and leaves. By contrast, her stepmother's dresses are generally opulent, frequently feature black, and are often in shiny fabrics, which speaks to her husband's wealth. On Crane's arrival at the Van Tassels', the lady of the house is wearing a yellow-and-black striped dress and a stiff, carapace-like stomacher that, aptly, make her resemble a poisonous insect.

Catherine Spooner, writing about costume in Burton films, suggests that the final dress Lady Van Tassel wears, when the main narrative finally catches up with the costume plot and reveals her as the villain, is a copy of a gown in a painting by Edward Burne-Jones of a supposed sorceress from the sixteenth century, and indeed the dress is very reminiscent of the one in *Sidonia Von Bork 1560*, with its black knot-work encasing a paler under-gown.[19] Spooner takes this reference to Burne-Jones and his enchantress as a sign of the film's gleeful plundering of history for elements it deems attractive, regardless of notions of periodicity or historical accuracy. The knot-work dress should probably be recognized as a quotation meant to be appreciated by a very few, however; much more accessible is the fact that the gown's large black whorls and loops are made of ribbon suspended, like a cage, over the pale fabric of the gown underneath. One does not have to be an art historian to perceive that this looks like a spider's web, with Lady Van Tassel the smug spider within. The black knot gown is the only one she wears that lacks the stiffened stomacher. Since she appears in the gown once she has acknowledged that she is the mastermind of the murders, she no longer needs the stomacher as a literal false front (figure 36).

Sleepy Hollow concludes with a short scene with Crane back in New York City, accompanied by Katrina: they dismount from their carriage and walk into the

FIGURE 36: Detail from *Sleepy Hollow* (1999) showing the spider web dress designed by Colleen Atwood. There were many credited and uncredited makeup and hair artists and even more in costuming and wardrobe, but their numbers are dwarfed by the film's enormous numbers of personnel devoted to art direction and special and visual effects.

city as snow begins to fall. Crane is still in his customary monochrome garb, and Katrina has now adopted his color scheme, wearing a striking black-and-white striped dress. The permanence of Crane's clothing style seems to suggest that he is fundamentally unchanged by his trip to Sleepy Hollow and its supernatural occurrences. Katrina's garb may not simply be representative of her new status as Crane's betrothed, however; black-and-white striped clothing has been a Tim Burton fixture since his short film *Vincent* (1982).[20] These striped outfits—which appear in *Beetlejuice* (1988), *Big Fish* (2003), *Sweeney Todd* (2007), *Alice in Wonderland* (2010), and others—are recognized within popular discourse as a sign of his authorial presence. Indeed, the 2009–2010 exhibition dedicated to Burton at New York's Metropolitan Museum of Art not only foregrounded this motif by creating a striped entrance to the gallery, but also used the colors on the website advertising the exhibition.[21] Given the long-term creative relationship between Colleen Atwood and Burton—nine films so far—the appearance of a black-and-white striped garment in *Sleepy Hollow* could also be a symbol of her authorial signature.

Styling the "Remembered" Past: *Boogie Nights* and *L.A. Confidential*

Movies set in the more recent past are no less historical than so-called costume pictures, but because their pasts have been lived through by some portion of the audience or, equally significant, been visualized in a huge number of earlier Hollywood movies, the films are in greater danger of being perceived as parodic or superficial. *L.A. Confidential* is set at a very precise time, Christmas 1952. Its dating to this moment is overdetermined, since it is established by the opening voiceover referring to actual incidents, such as mobster Mickey Cohen's arrest and imprisonment; by narrative events, such as the Christmas party that introduces key characters Ed Exley (Guy Pearce) and Bud White (Russell Crowe) and sets them against each other; and by its set-dressing. The film works hard to ensure that every detail of the mise-en-scène should announce the period; there is even an old issue of *Look* magazine lying around the abandoned Victory Motel where the main protagonists have their shootout at the film's climax, dated December 4, 1951, and featuring Doris Day on its cover, among other celebrities.

It is thus interesting that a film that goes to such extreme lengths to establish its periodicity should have been so frequently criticized for not doing so with regard to its costume, hair, and makeup; but several writers have argued that *L.A. Confidential* aims more at a self-reflexive and vague "retro" feeling than faithful historical re-creation. In a chapter on neo-noirs in the book *Fashion in Film*, Ula Lukszo finds the film's costuming of prostitute and Veronica Lake lookalike Lynn Bracken (Kim Basinger) to be based not so much on Lake's film clothing but on generic femme fatale style from classic films noirs. She states that the audience for the 1997 film would have little precise knowledge of the original Lake and thus its costumes do not need to be re-creations of her garments to be successful: "Though Basinger may not physically resemble Lake, she sports Lake's signature hairdo, the platinum blonde color and retro gowns that, even if nothing similar was ever worn by Lake, code Lynn as of her time period."[22]

Lukszo calls this loose mode of quotation "noir for noir's sake," noting that, in the film, "fashion is most certainly in charge, and the plot and characters become secondary to [its] self-conscious channelling of noir fashions."[23] She cites two other critics, Jans Wager and James Naremore, who also comment on the film's clothing; the former opines that Lynn Bracken "dresses the part" of a femme fatale, while Naremore's condemnation of the entire film is summed up in his line that *L.A. Confidential* "turns history into a fashion show."[24]

However, not only is character revelation through costume primary in this film, as is traditional in Hollywood, but costumier Ruth Myers did carry out much careful research to ensure her costumes evoked the correct period. Contrary to Lukszo's suggestion, at least one of the gowns worn by Basinger seems to be a direct copy of one worn by Lake; the black satin sheath dress, with a black organza overskirt and transparent sleeves, seen briefly on Bracken at a party, is similar to a dress Lake wore in *I Married a Witch* (1942) and that was heavily featured in publicity for the René Clair comic fantasy (figure 37).

The outfits for the men are also period-appropriate. While Exley tends to wear suits and White favors separates, what unites them is the accuracy of their attire. Exley may look superficially smarter in his gray suit, white shirt, and dark tie striped in gray, but his outfit conforms very much to one featured in a Christmas

FIGURE 37: Veronica Lake (left) in a publicity photo for *I Married a Witch* (1942), costume design by Edith Head, makeup by Wally Westmore, hair by Leonora Sabine (uncredited). Kim Basinger (right) as Lynn Bracken in *L.A. Confidential* (1997), costume design by Ruth Myers. Basinger's costumer was Donna O'Neal, her makeup was by Francesca Tolot, and her hair by Peter Savic. The film employed many more costume and wardrobe, makeup, and hair personnel as well.

advertisement for soft drink 7-Up in the December 24 issue of *Life* magazine for 1951; the comparable ad in the following year's issue features a Bud lookalike instead, in close but contrasting slacks and jacket of nubby tweed.[25] The two men in the ads even have the same haircuts as their *L.A. Confidential* counterparts. White's less formal attire can therefore be seen as more up-to-date for the film's actual period, while Exley's slightly fussy appearance chimes with his adherence to rules and regulations rather than new fashions.

Regardless of whether these precise images were inspiration for the styling and costuming of the two men—as well, homicide detectives in 1940s Los Angeles were notorious clotheshorses—the presence of similar outfits and hair treatments in contemporaneous lifestyle sources indicates how carefully period details were applied in the film, despite critics' comments to the contrary. It should be noted, however, that most of this specific historical re-creation and sourcing will pass audience members by; they will simply see Bracken, White, and Exley in costumes that complement their characters, as always the preeminent task of film costume, makeup, and hairstyling. But it is endowed with an extra emphasis in *L.A. Confidential* given how much of the narrative centers on the importance of costume and appearances.

In Bracken's case, it is her job to look like Veronica Lake; we are told this explicitly in the film's dialogue, which largely removes the need to wonder whether her bright red mouth and pale makeup is period- or character-appropriate. We simply note that she is striking, and styled in a particular way to remind her clients of a famous woman. The obvious point with Bracken's clothes is that she wears 1940s styles in a story set in the 1950s: Lake's short period of fame was in the early to mid-1940s, mainly during World War II, so Lynn copies her bias-cut satin gowns rather than wearing 1950s fashions that would have been influenced by the postwar New Look of Dior. Postwar hairdos were also substantially shorter than those worn during the early 1940s. A 1941 *Life* article on the famous Lake hairdo of "peek-a-boo bangs" asserted that her waist-length hair was "a cinema property of world influence," but Lake was soon enjoined by the government to eschew her trademark style so that her many copiers would not endanger themselves or the products they were making in factories.[26] A filmed *U.S. News Review* from 1943, put out by the Office of War Information, shows the actor taming her locks by setting them in a neat V-roll on her head, while the male voiceover notes that her "witch-lock" is "out of place in a war production plant."[27] With film actresses such as Lana Turner, Rita Hayworth, Doris Day, Elizabeth Taylor, and Ava Gardner adopting shorter styles in the early 1950s, Bracken's long flowing hair is an intended anachronism explained by her adherence to the most famous look of the woman she is imitating.

Thus, the viewer does not need to be a costume historian in order to read Lynn Bracken's clothes as indices of her personality. Her hairstyle, for example, partly frames, partly hides her face: it underscores her attractiveness but also hints at her actual shyness when not hiding behind her Lake performance. In comparison with her usual reticence, the final scene of the film shows Bracken more forthcoming to Exley about her future plans, more optimistic and outgoing. Paralleling this character shift, her hair is shorter and styled in a softer curly fashion, mostly brushed back away from her face and therefore more revealing of it; her face appears less mask-like, too, because she has swapped the pale foundation and very red lipstick for more "natural" colored cosmetics. Similarly, the 1940s clothes Bracken wears in her work role all have marked qualities of sensuousness and tactility, due to the silk and satin from which they are made; at the end in her cheery yellow she has given up her shiny stuff for matte, moved out of her bedroomy fabrics and into plain cotton. Bracken's story is thus told through her wardrobe progression; as she moves from being a lookalike prostitute to, presumably, a housewife, her clothes lose their sumptuous, sensuous, and spectacular edge, but she herself is happy to be less theatrical, less displayed for consumption.

Ruth Myers has talked about her pride in her design for the first outfit Bracken wears: the black velvet cape trimmed with white satin (color plate 15).[28] It is easy to understand her satisfaction, since the dramatic garment accomplishes many things at once: it is show-stopping, both for the audience and, diegetically, for Bud White, as he encounters the woman and cannot at first see her face. Symbolically it echoes the cloak of Little Red Riding Hood: like her, Bracken is alone in a metaphorical forest and definitely surrounded by wolves. That her cape and hood are black underlines the serious and deadly milieu in which she seems trapped. The cloak also makes for a grand entrance for Bracken and for Basinger playing her, but two other factors are also at work. First, the same type of garment appears on the cover of a November 1941 issue of *Life*; though there it is transparent and worn by Gene Tierney rather than Veronica Lake, the presence of such a striking garment in a middle-brow, high-circulation periodical does indicate that Myers has done her research.[29] Second, it also establishes, for those familiar with classic film noir, that Bracken is not a femme fatale: while we might expect the spider women of classic noir to be dressed in black to match their dark desires and motives (as noted with regard to *Basic Instinct*), actual noir femmes usually appear at first in white, in denial of their fatal qualities. As events in *L.A. Confidential* go on to prove, Bracken is copying the hairdo and clothing styles of Veronica Lake the actor, rather than those of the ambiguous characters Lake plays in noirs such as *The Glass Key* (1942) and *The Blue Dahlia* (1946). Although *L.A. Confidential*'s suspense plot flirts with the idea that she might be treacherous, this fear is dispelled by the end.

L.A. Confidential employs the costume, hairstyling, and makeup of the 1940s and 1950s (as well as in 1940s and 1950s films) in a meticulous fashion that echoes *Amadeus*'s attention to period detail of a much earlier time. And like *Amadeus*, the 1997 film also foregrounds the importance of appearances within its story; if any of the outfits feels too stagey, too much worn by actors rather than by people, this actually fits a narrative in which characters are constantly having to dress to assume a deceptive identity or character trait.

Another 1997 film, *Boogie Nights*, also returns to a historical period closer than that found in many costume pictures, here the 1970s. It uses the extravagant styles and clothes of that period not only to signal the narrative's chronological setting but also to create a frisson for the audience at the spectacular garments. This frisson may not be pleasure, exactly, since so many of the items and looks now connote bad taste, but is certainly based on recognition and amusement. *Boogie Nights*, like *L.A. Confidential*, also openly emphasizes the importance of clothes for creating an image by which characters are judged and assumed known; somewhat ironically for people whose job as porn stars is to spend a lot of time without any clothes on, they are acutely aware of the significance of dressing, not only in certain items to prove they are successful ("Are [those shoes] lizard?" "No, they're Italian") but also in ways to express their own identities. Buck Swope (Don Cheadle) attracts negative comment for dressing as a cowboy, but the film shows that his first makeover, which leaves him resembling a kind of space-age Egyptian pharaoh, is also a disaster, and it is not until he gives up any definitive style that his fortunes improve.

The first scenes of *Boogie Nights* are set in 1977, and the film employs all the expected costume signifiers: flared and bell-bottom pants, tank tops, maxi skirts, safari shirts, halter-neck trouser-suits, and platform heels. Versions of classic contemporaneous hairstyles are employed to match the period costume too: "Amber Waves" (Julianne Moore) channels Farrah Fawcett Majors's famous "bouncy, glamorous, sexy tresses," as a how-to article from *Woman's Day* that year called the style (it noted the feathered flip was difficult to achieve).[30] "Roll-ergirl" (Heather Graham) moves from pigtails to a crimped shag, and the men sport mullets, short in front and long in back, although the hair is never as extreme as was actually worn at the time. It is as if the film is content to let the costumes be accurate but the hair more impressionistic. With makeup, too, the 1970s use of shimmery eye powder and super-glossy lips is employed—comically, during the porn scenes especially. Costumes, makeup, and hairstyle are all also used to signal the passing of time as well as the rise and fall in the protagonists' fortunes, so the 1980s are heralded by the arrival of halter-neck dresses, acid-washed denim shorts, and sportswear as casual wear, and the hero moves from his simple tousled crop through bouffant hair to a mullet and then gelled slick-ness at the film's end.

Another method of showing the passage of time is using repeated shots of characters performing the same actions but with different styling. Eddie Adams/"Dirk Diggler" (Mark Wahlberg) is frequently seen appraising himself before his mirror, but two key scenes bookend his porn career. In the first of these moments, before his first time on camera, Adams sits in a dressing room nervously preparing, muttering his lines. He is dressed for the porn movie in a burgundy suit and a patterned shirt with a very sharply pointed collar. The way the suit—too big for him, too long in the sleeve—overpowers him and makes him look slight and undersized indicates his nervousness, and hints at how "ill-suited" he is to this industry. When he removes these clothes, however, revealing his very large penis to his work colleagues and the diegetic camera—but not to the *Boogie Nights* audience—he gains in confidence and proves he does have the talent to "perform" in pornographic films.

At the other end of the movie, after drug use has impaired his potency and he has been sacked from his job, he is forgiven and taken back into his dysfunc-tional porn family. In seemingly the same dressing room again, contemplating his reflection in the mirror before a scene, "Diggler" now appears in a 1980s ensemble: a white suit with the jacket sleeves pushed up his forearms over a pale pink shirt, and with his hair slicked back with gel. He seems to be copying Don Johnson from the then-popular television show *Miami Vice* (1984–1989), effec-tively confirming the date of this final segment. Beyond this reference, the white suit might be hinting that Eddie has cleaned up his lifestyle and stopped doing the drugs that previously damaged his ability to gain an erection; certainly he seems "innocent," lacking self-knowledge. He still repeats his karate moves and intones "I'm a star, I'm a star," now directly to his penis, unzipping his pants and producing the member—to the film's audience for the first time—that has been his ticket to fame. With the penis flaccid, it seems vulnerable and pathetic, add-ing to the downbeat nature of the film's ending.

Because the 1970s are relatively recent and its popular culture artifacts, including clothing and stylings, still visible and familiar, *Boogie Nights*'s costume designer Mark Bridges had to find a way to evoke the period without sinking into parody. This was achieved by mostly using actual garments from the time so as to avoid exaggeration. As a consequence of this, almost every item of film costume was shopped, sourced from existing stock, rather than designed and then made to measure.[31] Rooting the production in actual garments helped Bridges avoid cliché or pastiche, no matter how implausible they appear now. The pale blue denim evening suit that "Diggler" wears to the Adult Film Awards is one of the most eye-catching items, consisting of a tuxedo and pants in pale brushed denim, with satin lapels to the jacket; it is also one of the few actually made for the production, but even with this outlandish garment, Bridges drew on his research of actual clothing from the period.[32]

Boogie Nights employs costume, then, for two purposes. The first is the traditional mode, whereby the costumes provide clues to character, draw parallels or links between them, and sometimes forecast action. These uses are all engaged when Dirk and fellow actor "Reed Rothchild" (John C. Reilly) go shopping and buy identical shirts (figure 38). The duplication of the item mocks the men's attempts at using clothes to show their uniqueness; it confirms the rivalry/friendship of Reed and Dirk in the porn business; and it shows how desperately the sound man Scotty J. (Philip Seymour Hoffman), who also buys one, wants to be both "one of the boys" and more to Dirk than just a crew member. The ill-fitting nature of Scotty's shirt foretells how doomed his attempts at fostering intimacy with Dirk will be.

FIGURE 38: One shirt, three looks. Mark Wahlberg as Eddie Adams/Dirk Diggler, John C. Reilly as Reed Rothchild, Philip Seymour Hoffman as Scotty J. in Boogie Nights (1997). Buying the same garment undermines the actors' attempts at unique personal style, while showing how much Scotty wants to fit in. Costume design by Mark Bridges. IMDb.com lists twenty-plus credited makeup and hair personnel, including several for special effects and prosthetic makeup, as well as many others in costume and wardrobe.

The second way in which the film uses costume is as part of a larger interest in movie self-referentiality. *Boogie Nights* is linked to other films in ways both verbal and visual; Buck Swope, for example, borrows his surname from the counter-culture classic *Putney Swope* (1969), about a black advertising man who tries to subvert the industry from within. *Putney Swope*'s director, Robert Downey Sr., also appears in *Boogie Nights* as a music studio owner, the cameo role underlining that Swope's name is no coincidence. Buck is not modeled on Putney and does not share his career, character, or fate; the allusion to the counterculture film seems more the result of cinephilia than any specific point. More obvious is the film's use of *Saturday Night Fever* (John Badham, 1977). In his bedroom Eddie has Bruce Lee and Al Pacino posters on his wall and the same picture of Farrah Fawcett Majors as in Tony Manero's room in the earlier film. Adams contemplates his image in the mirror, throws some karate punches, and adjusts his genitals in a similar way to Manero, and while Wahlberg as Eddie is not entirely styled to look the same as John Travolta as Tony, they both sport bouffant hair and very tight briefs.

The prompt to evoke *Saturday Night Fever* presumably comes from the historical moment the two films share, although they both tell a story about the fortunes of a young man endowed with a special gift. *Boogie Nights* takes its narrative arc further, however, giving "Diggler" a rise and then fall, whereas the Travolta film finishes with its hero on the cusp of decisions that will perhaps lead to a different life. *Boogie Nights*, too, despite its title, does not concentrate on the disco dancing that is the center of the earlier film; while there is one disco scene, it seems significant that it is intercut with, and acts as the climax of, a shopping montage that has "Diggler" and his porn star pals indicating their film success through consumption. The dancing here is a way to show off the new shirt of "imported Italian nylon," rather than the clothes being fashioned to show off the body while dancing, as in *Saturday Night Fever*.

Finally, the casting of Burt Reynolds as porn impresario Jack Horner inevitably gestures to the 1970s as a period, since Reynolds was the most popular star across the time span re-created in the film.[33] His film persona at this point arose from such movies as *Semi-Tough* and *Smokey and the Bandit* (both 1977) and *Starting Over* (1979), which are tacitly referenced through this casting choice and add to Horner's character the overtones of macho, sexualized good humor these films fostered. The porn director is not good-humored, however, but exploitative of his porn "family," perhaps indicating a criticism of the institutionalized sexism of the 1970s as well as of the alienating effects of the porn industry. *Boogie Nights* can thus use its casting strategy both to reference the time of its setting and to comment tacitly on popular culture assumptions in a way that serves its narrative.

Films that make use of historical costume, makeup, and hair, then, whether of the remote or nearer past, inherit a series of dilemmas: whether to aim for historical accuracy, which risks creating empty spectacle, or to use historical elements more impressionistically, which risks visual anachronism. But the crafts are and have never been innocent or transparent; there are no fewer predicaments for a designer tasked with producing screen clothing and styling for a production based in contemporary times than for one researching the past. The tensions traced here illustrate the quandaries all designers must solve, and although the primary one may at first sight seem like a simple binary—historical/current—these then break down, subdivide, and multiply themselves to reveal the variety of choices to be made. With the historical costume picture, is the remote or recent past being referenced? Will the method necessitate meticulous research in the pursuit of accuracy, or is a more impressionistic approach permissible? Although they can share some of the problems of historical pictures, films set at the time of their making also need to resolve whether their narratives will dictate choices that may seem fiats to the audience, suggesting that viewers should learn a lesson from the fact that a character's fortunes seem to be linked to her or his sartorial decisions. In the films discussed here women and men are taught to succeed somewhat differently in regard to clothing, makeup, and hair, but the fact that both need to be schooled in these different areas suggests contemporary societal assumptions and anxieties about the appropriate spheres of influence for different genders.

As noted above and throughout this volume, the standard job of Hollywood costume, makeup, and hair, whenever a film is set, is to assist in the delineation of character and the furtherance of the narrative. Occasionally, as with *Sleepy Hollow*, the costume plot can work in opposition to the dominant story line and give away secrets before the big reveal. It is not just historical films that play with their suspense plots, however; M. Night Shyamalan's *The Sixth Sense*, from the same year (1999), also betrays its finale's famous "gotcha" moment from very early on, if one is aware of the costume changes of the central character, Malcolm Crowe (Bruce Willis). The film's notoriety comes from the fact that Crowe, seen taking a lead role in events throughout the narrative, actually died at the start of the story. He interacts with a young boy whose particular type of clairvoyance means that he can interact with the dead.

While this fact is hidden until an end-reel revelation by the narrative proper, the costume plot reveals it swiftly: Crowe wears the same garments throughout the film, those he had on the night he was killed. It seems that, in whatever purgatory he finds himself, he can use any of the items he was wearing that last evening—tee, shirt and tie, jacket and pants, waistcoat, coat and scarf—in any combination. Thus, he is seen outside his house in coat and scarf, or inside in sweatshirt and tee, but the clothes amount to nothing other than what he wore on his last night, notwithstanding that the film's lighting makes his suit seem at times gray and at others brown. The fact that Crowe is seen in the same garb, as well as makeup and hair, throughout the film undermines the suspense plot that would trick viewers into thinking he survived the shooting in the opening scenes.

This last instance indicates one final way that film costume, makeup, and hair can be employed, regardless of historic or contemporary setting: to give pleasure not just through spectacle or vicarious sensuality, but through setting up an intellectual puzzle with which viewers can wrestle. All the films discussed here foreground, in their various ways, the importance of all three crafts in our own lives as well: as the means to present a different, or improved, identity, or to be like someone else; to secure respect; to appear modest or successful. They all similarly reveal that if viewers become more accustomed to reading them, costume, makeup, and hair can be fully recognized as the source of narrative as well as of character information, and always of a variety of pleasures.

6

THE MODERN ENTERTAINMENT MARKETPLACE, 2000-PRESENT

James Castonguay

The sheer scale and ubiquity of a largely digital twenty-first-century media culture make it more difficult to think about film as film, and its component crafts have likewise been affected in myriad ways. As in the last decades of the twentieth century, costume, makeup, and hair designers working with traditional techniques continue to find work, but are also being supplanted by digital technologies that shape film content aesthetically as well as commercially. "'We'll fix it in post!' has become the mantra," according to Christien Tinsley, who designed the old-age makeup worn by Leonardo DiCaprio in *J. Edgar* (2011).[1] Often augmenting if not outright replacing the practical work of craftspeople, the ubiquity of CGI blurs the line, arguably more forcefully than in the past, separating the three areas from the realm of special effects and animation.

In addition, the intersection of films with other media technologies has altered film's use of prevailing fashions and how those fashions are marketed to or adopted by audiences. The relationship between stars and changing conceptions of celebrity on and off the screen, as well as media and new media discussions involving the value and/as cultural capital of films, stars, and fashion, have meant that the ways in which we might choose to analyze costume, makeup, and hair in films have also changed.

In fact, while the definition of the words "film" or "films" has been somewhat pliable since the advent of television, in the digital era the meaning of the terms has become even more elastic. No longer need a spectator sit in a "four-wall" in a multiplex, or even in his or her own elaborately outfitted home theater, to watch a movie. Instead, audiences are as likely to experience film as just another of the many forms of "content" available through an array of delivery systems, such as broadband networks, social media, and mobile apps. *Variety*'s 2014 annual entertainment industry marketing summit challenged its participants to address the following overarching question: "With the entertainment marketplace splitting up across screens and platforms, how can brands break through the clutter to connect with their target audiences?"[2] The "strategies" adopted are now familiar to most of us, for better or for worse. To "traditional" and digital product placement, cross-promotion, and licensed merchandising and tie-ins have been added highly customized and targeted marketing (a.k.a. "personalization"), branded videos, blogs, and online publications, and "real-time marketing" that exploits social media and mobile apps to synchronize the consumption of entertainment content—including films—with shopping and purchasing.[3]

In addition to thinking about costume, makeup, and hair in films themselves, then, the crafts must increasingly be understood in the context of contemporary marketing methods. These include retail apparel and fashion and beauty products "inspired by" and explicitly licensed from films and television shows as well as the participatory communities that comprise "cosplay" (costume-play) film fan culture. Trade journals, industry union publications, and interviews with industry professionals also help provide the voices and perspectives of the costume designers, makeup artists, and hair stylists who have been affected by changes in the film and television industry since 2000.

Consolidation, Convergence, and Costume Culture

The merger of Time, Inc., and Warner Bros. in 1989 is symptomatic of the consolidation of media industries that intensified in the 1980s and 1990s and continued into the twenty-first century. Facilitated by several decades of deregulatory policies, large U.S.-based global media companies like the Walt Disney Company, News Corporation and 21st Century Fox, TimeWarner, General Electric, Viacom, the CBS Corporation, Sony, Comcast, and DirectTV have joined with each other in various combinations to increase profits and enable the creation and distribution of their own content. Vertical and horizontal integration across different types of media and multiple distribution outlets have effectively reduced competition and increased market share by using economies of scale, acquiring competitors and other media outlets, and franchising films and television programs.[4]

Within this context, Disney has become the world's largest entertainment conglomerate through the acquisition in 2009 of Marvel Entertainment and Marvel Studios in addition to ESPN, ABC, Pixar, LucasFilm, and theme parks around the world. Disney franchises include Mickey Mouse, Winnie the Pooh, "Disney Princess" (a line of products based mainly on animated princesses from roughly thirteen Disney films), and the characters from Marvel comics and their associated films (including Spider-Man, Captain America, Iron Man, Thor, the Fantastic Four, the X-Men, and Ant-Man). The films *Cars* (2006) and *Cars 2* (2011) and *Frozen* (2013) are franchised across Disney's movie studios, theme parks, and consumer products. The *New York Times* reported in August 2014 that Disney's profits were "soaring" as the conglomerate earned $2.25 billion, or 22 percent more than the previous fiscal year, "helped in large part by the success of its Marvel franchise [films]" and television syndication sales that "helped lift operating income at Disney's broadcast division by 66 percent."[5]

These record profits came on the heels of the economic success of the animated "princess" musical *Frozen*, which according to trade publications was "poised to outstrip other successful franchises such as *Harry Potter, Hunger Games, Lion King*, and even *Star Wars*."[6] Each year Disney-owned characters are among the

FIGURE 39: The character Anna in Disney's digitally animated film *Frozen* (2013) and the dress, designed and copyrighted by Alfred Angelo, "inspired by" *Frozen* and part of his 2014 "Disney Fairy Tale Weddings" collection. Despite the importance of the characters' clothing and "visual looks" in the film, *Frozen* has no credited costume, makeup, or hair designers as such, but hundreds of art department, animation, and visual effects personnel.

top-selling Halloween costumes, and the corporation consistently tops *License! Global*'s list of the world's largest and most profitable licensors. Disney's apparel and accessory licensing partnerships range from its many film-inspired collections sold through the Hot Topic retail chain to more specialized items such as Alfred Angelo's 2015 "Disney Fairy-Tale Weddings" bridal collection, which includes a "*Frozen*-inspired Elsa wedding gown" (figure 39).[7]

Disney also benefits financially from the fact that costume purchases now extend beyond holidays and parties to include a year-round multibillion-dollar "cosplay" industry and fan culture that support hundreds of major conventions and meetings along with websites and articles dedicated to cosplay communities, fashion, and criticism. Cosplayers epitomize the kinds of creative fan communities and participatory cultures in an age of media convergence celebrated by some media scholars.[8] Moreover, entertainment conglomerates like Disney and Marvel—as well as costume designers and the apparel industry—have increasingly engaged these most committed and passionate of fans by integrating their participatory communities into their websites, marketing, and production processes, and by orchestrating social events and panels for them at conventions. Marvel's corporate media universe comprises film, television, and an official social media presence that includes a Facebook page with over 18 million "likes," a Twitter account with over 2.2 million followers, and an official YouTube channel with over 1.8 million subscribers.[9] Marvel maintains its own blog and web gallery devoted to cosplayers, and the Costume Designers Guild forms a Comic-Con committee each year to attend the convention and to cosplay alongside fans.[10]

In 2014, attendees were invited to enter a fashion competition for the opportunity to design actual costume clothing lines for retail outlets like Hot Topic in partnership with the Her Universe online store. Other online vendors like Cosplay House sell tailor-made and made-to-order cosplay costumes, wigs, props, and shoes, and websites like CosTrader.com and eBay.com provide online venues for buying and selling cosplay costumes. Cosplayers have posted millions of costume and makeup tutorials on YouTube and, according to a 2013 study, the majority of cosplayers attend three or more conventions each year and spend at least forty hours and $100 or more preparing each costume.[11]

With the release of the "superhero" film *Avengers: Age of Ultron* (Joss Whedon, 2015), Disney and Marvel extended their collaboration with fans beyond the more marginal cosplay community to include a mainstream menswear line inspired by the film in partnership with the Five Four Club subscription fashion service. The Five Four Club's website offers men "the easiest way to never have to shop again," promising "effortless style created just for you, delivered right to your doorstep." As the male voiceover in the Five Four Club ads elaborates, the paid subscription-based service assigns each subscriber a "personal stylist who hand picks a package [that] matches the man, [because] men don't have the time to or want to put in the effort to shop." While the discourses surrounding the male user and consumer of makeup construct a feminized masculinity framed in the context of "men being like women," the marketing of the Marvel menswear and fashion reinforces the gendered difference that "men buy, women shop."[12] The online subscription service avoids the word "shopping" by focusing on the "effortless" acquisition and convenience made possible by technology to the point where purchasing Marvel menswear online is not shopping at all.

Marvel is thus extending its place within the entertainment marketplace from the highly participatory and creative communities of Comic-Con goers to include the male consumer more broadly. Unlike previous trend-setting films that have had an effect on fashion and style, these Marvel collections are more deliberate and directly accessible examples of commodifying the costumes, clothes, and looks from the screen and selling them not only to serious fans but also to more casual consumers who do not identify themselves as cosplayers or Comic-Con "geeks."

Alongside its first-ever Marvel menswear line, Disney Consumer Products partnered with the online retail site Her Universe and the Hot Topic retail chain to sell a fashion collection for women inspired by Marvel's Avengers. Created by Her Universe founder Ashley Eckstein and the winners of the "Geek Couture" fashion design contest held at the 2014 San Diego Comic-Con, the Marvel By Her Universe collection reflects what feminist scholars and critics have described as some women's "self-objectification" within the cosplay community. Some cosplay "appeals to heterosexual male fantasies, participates in the objectification of the cosplayer, and (purposefully or not) positions the cosplayer as an object for consumption by male geeks."[13] But the "sexy geek" aesthetic can be problematic in its own way—indeed, as Derek Johnson has argued about "pink franchising" and the Her Universe website more generally, although *Her Universe* [has] opened up a feminized space of fan subjectivity, . . . the transgression of normative consumer ideals by girls [is] re-inscribed within postfeminist and heteronormative gender roles . . . in relation to beauty, princesses, romance, and other postfeminist (but traditionally feminine) ideological frames."[14]

The many accounts documenting the sexual harassment of women at Comic-Con events further demonstrate that cosplay culture does not provide a utopian social space free of regressive societal realities like sexism (which has led to the implementation of a "Cosplay Is Not Consent" public relations and educational campaign). This is not to suggest that consumers of these texts, or fans who participate in conventions and cosplay, are simply passive ideological dupes who uncritically embrace the messages and products being marketed and sold to them. Rather, the participatory engagement of these fans and consumers within media culture has become increasingly complicit with that culture's dominant meanings and desires rather than actively resisting or subverting its profit-driven goals and exploitative messages. At the very least, these participatory fan communities should not be celebrated uncritically as examples of politically progressive or egalitarian inclusion.

It is worth noting in this context that it is precisely the popular and some-what frivolous connotation of the term "costume" that Deborah Nadoolman Landis feels has done a disservice to the profession and craft of film costume design. For Landis, "costume is such a horrible word" due to its association with "Halloween, Mardi Gras, fancy dress, all superficial because it has to do with sur-face."[15] Speaking from her professional perspective as a costume designer as well as costume historian, Landis elaborates: "The word 'costume' works against us. The word is vulgar when what we do is incredibly refined."[16] In the end, Landis reminds us that "the role of the costume designer is really quite simple: costume designers design the people in the movie," thus emphasizing the central and pro-found importance of the costume designer to the narrative filmmaking process.[17]

During the 2014 Academy Awards, the Marvel franchise bore the brunt of several jokes facilitated in part by the nomination of the eventual winner *Bird-man: Or the Unexpected Virtue of Ignorance* (Alejandro González Iñárritu, 2014), whose main character tries to exorcise the ghosts of his commercial superhero movie past through the live "authenticity" of Broadway theater. Long before this somewhat elitist and certainly hypocritical condescension against Marvel, superhero films had been consistently overlooked by members of the Academy of Motion Picture Arts Sciences in the category of costume design despite—or per-haps due in part to—the centrality of costume to the genre. An overdetermined signifier fetishized by fans of the comic superhero film genre, the "first glimpse" of an actor in his or her superhero costume is often used for the initial publicity and promotional campaign for a film and sets the aesthetic tone for the mise-en-scène and the character's psychology.

According to comics historian Peter Coogan, "The costume . . . as an element of identity, marked the superhero off from previous hero types and helped to establish the genre [by] remov[ing] the specific details of a character's ordinary appearance [and] leaving only a simplified idea that is represented in the colors and design of the costume."[18] (As the *New Yorker*'s Anthony Lane put it in his 2015 review of *Ant-Man*, "When fans talk about the Marvel universe, what they really mean is the Marvel wardrobe. You could hang all the characters on one costume rack.")[19] Consequently, a costume designer must engage with the legacy of the superhero costume in all its various intermedial manifestations, arguably making the costume itself, not the character or star, the culturally privileged sig-nifier. In 2013, the "cheerlessly dark" and "scaly" colors of "Superman's new look" in *Man of Steel*, for example, was named one of the "10 big pop culture moments" in film and television costume by *Entertainment Weekly*, the "Dark Knightiza-tion of Superman" attributed to the influence of Christopher Nolan's successful *Batman* franchise (*Batman Begins* [2005], *The Dark Knight* [2008], and *The Dark Knight Rises* [2012]) (figure 40).[20]

Superhero films have been overlooked even when the critical response to a film's reception has been overwhelmingly positive or laudatory and even

FIGURE 40: Left, Batman's costume in *The Dark Knight Rises* (2012), costume design by Lindy Hemming and Roberto Craciunica. Right, Superman's "scaly" costume in *Man of Steel* (2013), costume design by James Acheson, Michael Wilkinson, and Roberto Craciunica (uncredited). Both films have huge numbers of credited makeup and hair artists as well as other costume and wardrobe personnel.

though other science-fiction and fantasy genre films, like director Peter Jackson's *Lord of the Rings* trilogy (2001–2003), have been routinely recognized by awards for costume design (in addition to other categories). Indeed, the most critically acclaimed film in the Batman film cycle, Nolan's *The Dark Knight*—which received eight Oscar nominations, including Best Makeup, in part on the strength of Heath Ledger's Oscar-winning performance as The Joker—was not acknowledged with a nomination for its costume designer Lindy Hemming, who had received an Oscar in 1999 for Mike Leigh's British period film about Gilbert and Sullivan, *Topsy-Turvy*. Similarly, although costume designer Alexandra Byrne has been nominated for four Academy Awards for her non-superhero genre work and received an Oscar for *Elizabeth: The Golden Age* (Shekhar Kapur, 2007), she has not been recognized by her Academy peers for her work on the Marvel films *Thor* (Kenneth Branagh, 2011), *The Avengers* (Joss Whedon, 2012), or *Guardians of the Galaxy* (James Gunn, 2014).

This lack of critical acclaim is arguably an indication of the low cultural status assigned to the costumed superhero genre within the film industry. While its box office potential is undeniable, the genre is associated with comics and a younger or "geeky" audience in opposition to high-culture or more "serious" contemporary dramas and period pieces (like *Topsy-Turvy* or historical dramas about Queen Elizabeth I). The costume design process for superhero franchise films has been described by Alexandra Byrne as "massively collaborative" and involving several departments; it consequently does not lend itself to recognizing a single artist or designer.

This lack of critical and peer acknowledgment does "not [go] unnoticed by costume designers," notes Lisa Tomczeszyn, assistant costume designer for *Spider-Man* (Sam Raimi, 2002) and three of the four *Hunger Games* films (2012, 2014, 2015) and co-costume designer for *X-Men: The Last Stand* (Brett Ratner, 2006). "Even when we honor our own . . . the made-to-order costumes for the superhero projects are largely ignored, which is a shame as the creation of the superhero, comic and sci-fi characters are where the great technological breakthroughs happen in costume design and costume production."[21] Tomczeszyn's emphasis on the technological over the artistic and creative may also point to another reason for the lack of official recognition of the genre. While established designers routinely acknowledge technical challenges that creative teams must overcome when designing a superhero costume, there is an implicit assumption that the practical requirements and limitations of technology-driven work are anathema to the artistic process.[22]

CGI, Motion Capture, and "Digital Makeup"

Along with some kinds of costume designers, a significant percentage of makeup artists and hairdressers have also historically been associated with "special effects" through the use of prosthetics and appliances to "age" actors or transform them into monsters or some other type of fantasy being as well as devices like the blood-spurting squib. In this context, debates over the relative merits of traditional character makeup techniques—additive processes involving the use of materials such as rubber, latex foam, silicone, padding, wigs, and the like—versus computer-generated images (CGI) have been constant since the newer technology's fledgling forays into interacting with actors' bodies in the 1990s.[23] Whether CGI and digital effects (often referred to by the shorthand FX, or VFX for "visual effects") would replace practical or "physical" makeup and prosthetics became a renewed focus of discussion with the blockbuster success of James Cameron's *Avatar* in 2009.

Director Cameron and British actor Andy Serkis (one of whose earliest roles was in *Topsy-Turvy*) began to argue that motion capture (mocap), in which a human substrate provides the shape and movements for a digitized character, should instead be called "performance capture" and qualify the subsequently digitized human for Oscar nomination in the acting category along with "live" actors. Steven Spielberg amplified the controversy in 2010 when the *Los Angeles Times* and other articles quoted him as saying, "I like to think of [the performance capture process] as digital makeup, not augmented animation [because] it's basically the actual performance of the actual actor, and what you're simply experiencing is makeup. . . . In the case of *Avatar*, the digital makeup is so thin you actually see everything that [the actor] is doing."[24]

Although often attributed to Spielberg, Serkis, and Cameron, the overarching metaphor of the performance capture process as being akin to "digital makeup" most likely originated with executives at New Zealand's Weta Digital VFX company, describing their own artistic and technical production and postproduction processes.[25] As facial capture technology was developed for *Avatar*, the *Lord of the Ring* films, and *Rise of the Planet of the Apes* (2011) and *Dawn of the Planet of the Apes* (2014), the final rendering of the performance on the screen has become less additive and more closely aligned with and dependent on actors' performances by capturing the details of their full-body and facial movements, gestures, and expressions (color plate 16). The term "digital makeup" is thus intended to describe a less transformative process of animation that is thinly layered over an actor's performance rather than building the majority of the performance primarily through the postproduction process of animation. Far from intending to minimize the actor's role in the process, then, the description was meant to emphasize that real actors and their performances are necessary to the process and that the animation is built on top of "real" physical performances.[26]

Spielberg's, Cameron's, and Serkis's description of the postproduction or animation component of the motion capture process as "digital makeup" is instructive for the negative responses it elicited from different sectors of the film industry. Mocap animators were convinced that Serkis, whose actions, facial expressions, and gestures were also used as the basis for the digitally animated character Gollum/Sméagol in the *Lord of the Rings* films (figure 41), was "dead set on diminishing the animators in the filmmaking process" when he claimed that "the only thing that the digital artists at Weta do is paint 'digital makeup' over his immaculate acting." This prompted the director of animation for *The Lord of the Rings: The Two Towers* (2002), Joe Letteri, to insist that "the animators on *The Lord of the Rings* [films] were most certainly not 'digital makeup artists,' and nobody has any business saying that they were." For Letteri, who was also the visual effects supervisor on the *Planet of the Apes* films—in both of which Serkis starred as the ape Caesar—"the difference is that makeup is passive. And the more makeup you put on, the more it actually deadens the performance, [and] we sometimes need to enhance the performance. So yes, we do make those sorts of translations all the time. Sometimes we have to exaggerate it so it reads in camera."[27]

This distinction between "passive" traditional makeup and "active" motion capture technology is not only dubious on theoretical and practical grounds, it makes a problematically gendered distinction between the passively "feminine" and less valued makeup artist and the actively "masculine" and more usefully productive motion capture professional. At the same time, as Stephen Prince rightly points out, despite the development of performance capture

FIGURE 41: Digital makeup in *The Lord of the Rings: The Two Towers* (2002). Frame enlargement from the "Andy Serkis Animation Reference" on the film's "Special Extended DVD Edition" showing Serkis's expressions as the basis for those of digitally animated character Gollum/Sméagol.

technologies and increasingly realistic CGI techniques, "costuming, makeup, and masks [will] continue as essential components of acting in cinema."[28] *Avatar* also employed over eighty "traditional" costume, makeup, and hair artists, further supporting Prince's claim that "CGI happily coexists . . . with the traditional techniques of cinema" and that "few of cinema's traditional expressive formats have been undermined by digital tools."[29] *The Curious Case of Benjamin Button* (David Fincher, 2008), released a year before *Avatar*, is significant in this context. The expensive adaptation of an F. Scott Fitzgerald story about a man (played by Brad Pitt) who is born old and "reverse-ages" to babyhood is notable for the way in which it combined digital enhancements and CGI with prosthetic age makeup (in addition to normal straight makeup) and was recognized with Academy Awards in both the makeup and visual effects categories (figure 42).

At the same time, *The Curious Case of Benjamin Button* also illustrates the curious economic crisis then facing the VFX industry; the company Digital Domain, whose effects team won the Academy Award for *Benjamin Button*, declared bankruptcy four years later in 2012—despite its continued status as an industry leader working on high-profile blockbusters. Founded by James Cameron in 1993, Digital Domain remained the highest profile visual effects studio closure until the company Rhythm & Hues filed for bankruptcy in 2013 just two weeks before its team of VFX artists won the Academy Award for their work on the spectacular adventure *Life of Pi* (Ang Lee, 2011), which featured a fully digitized tiger and other animals.

Among the artists picketing outside the Academy Awards event that day was Daniel Lay, who lost his job at Digital Domain after having been the hair and technical director for films like *I Am Legend* (2007) and *TRON: Legacy* (2010). Lay has since become an activist whose widely read blog "VFX Soldier" documented the crisis facing his profession as a result of outsourcing not only to countries with cheaper labor costs but also to those that offered attractive subsidies to studios such as the United Kingdom and Canada.

Although a significant percentage of makeup artists and hair designers have always from time to time ventured into or straddled the border between makeup and hairdressing and special effects, Lay represents the newer breed of digital makeup artist who specializes in animating and simulating hair and cloth effects. He would thus seem to epitomize the supposed technological threat posed from the outside and feared by the leadership of the industry's guilds of makeup artists and hair stylists. And yet, as a member of a non-unionized profession, Lay and his VFX colleagues are even more vulnerable to financial

FIGURE 42: Digital makeup and animation of Brad Pitt as the title character in *The Curious Case of Benjamin Button* (2008). Costume design by Jacqueline West, supported by sixty-plus costumers and wardrobe personnel. Of the more than fifty makeup and hair artists, the majority are listed under "makeup effects" and "special makeup effects," but this does not include the many others in the special and visual effects and digital animation categories such as "hair technical director" or "CG hair stylist."

instability than many of his practical makeup and hair colleagues. Indeed, despite this supposed shift from practical makeup to computer-generated or digital makeup techniques, in 2013 it was widely reported that the VFX industry remained in "deep financial trouble."[30]

It is thus understandable why members of the VFX industry, reeling from bankruptcies and layoffs and feeling slighted by the lack of recognition of their financial plight at the Academy Awards, would respond defensively to comments that they perceived as diminishing their role in the creative process—by making them equivalent to makeup artists or hairdressers, for example. At the same time, actual makeup artists and hair designers could also take issue with the overriding assumption that equating an animator with a digital makeup artist or hair designer was an insult in the first place, since it assumed that they were not a valued or significant part of the production process. Like their VFX colleagues, makeup artists and hair stylists have experienced their own economic crises and professional challenges as the Hollywood production model has shifted geographically. As Susan Cabral-Ebert, president of the Make-Up Artists and Hair Stylists Guild (IATSE Local 706), wrote in a 2014 letter to the guild's membership, "The excitement of learning that 88 Make-Up Artist and Hair Stylist Guild members earned nominations for their outstanding artistry also made it even clearer how much runaway production has affected the lives of our families and friends. Of all the nominated productions, approximately half were shot in states with large tax incentives or are right-to-work states."[31]

The Burbank-based Make-Up Artists and Hairstylists Guild joined with other unions to successfully lobby the California state legislature to raise the state tax incentives in order to bring more work back to California, which in 2014, for the first time, saw fewer television pilots (which had helped replace already-lost film production) shot in Los Angeles than in New York. According to Cabral-Ebert, "What we are asking is for a fighting chance, to be competitive with other states whose productions have doubled while our talented artisans and their families have suffered and been torn apart." While she focuses on the negative effects of domestic tax legislation on her membership, in his 2014 message to the membership of the East Coast Makeup Artists and Hair Stylists Guild (IATSE Local 798), President Todd Kleitsch added an international dimension to the current challenges faced by the profession:

> The industry [in which] we make our living and support our families has changed. . . . We can no longer operate in an entertainment vacuum. Film and Television shows are produced in every corner of the world. Budgets and profit lines are calculated on over-seas sales. . . . How can we protect and insure employment in a global economy? . . . Now we must become international business people with strong Collective Bargaining Agreements and an informed membership that moves forward.[32]

In addition to the geographical decentralization of film and television production, like other U.S. unions the makeup and hairstylist guilds have seen declining
memberships as more states have adopted right-to-work laws.

Given this economic context, it is not at all surprising that guild leadership
would be quick to criticize what it perceived as the potentially negative effects
of newer technologies on the lives and work of makeup artists and hair stylists.
One response from the guilds has been to dismiss or diminish digital makeup on
the grounds that it is a purely technical skill devoid of any creativity. As Cabral-
Ebert has claimed, "When you put dots on a frame or a grid and then capture it
[sic], and then someone in a lab changes everything, that's not makeup artistry."[33]
While it is certainly understandable that makeup artists already experiencing
runaway production might react negatively to the perceived additional threat of
digital makeup, Local 706 member and accomplished makeup artist Tegan Taylor also points out, "With the growing technologies co-mingling with traditional
makeup techniques of the past, we [should not] minimize our importance on
each production. Whether it's traditional makeup, special effects, or 'powdering
a face' to minimize shine for the DP—or whatever else we are required to do to
participate—we [remain] an integral part of the overall whole production."[34]

According to Taylor, whose credits include *Avatar, Dawn of the Planet of
the Apes, The Adventures of Tintin* (Steven Spielberg, 2011), and the video game
series *Halo*, "As makeup supervisor on big budget motion capture films and
cutting-edge gaming projects, I work closely in tandem with the visual effects
supervisor in layout and placement of the facial grid, and how it best reflects
the individual movement and nuances of an actor's face."[35] Similar to Max Factor's development of "flexible greasepaint," "color harmony" face powder, and
Panchromatic makeup in the early decades of the twentieth century,[36] Taylor's
company MoCapFX develops motion capture face paints and employs a team of
makeup artists to apply her company's MoCapInk paints to actors' faces. "We
employ chemists to help formulate our products and have patents on our products as well," Taylor explains. "Our products must perform well in the evolving
world of motion capture, so we are always reformulating and adjusting our formulas to accommodate the needs of each production."[37] For Taylor, "the work is
very detail-oriented and requires the precise application skills and steady hand
of a seasoned makeup artist," and she insists that "only an artist who has actually
experienced this first hand will understand the skill required, as well as the VFX
producers who bring us on board to participate."[38]

Costume designers have also increasingly had to contend with shifts in the
definition of their work in response both to the digitization of the film image
and what many perceive as an overreliance on fantasy and superhero films.
Hollywood films have always employed special effects—matte painting, double exposure, rear and front projection, and animation, among many examples.
But generally, no less than makeup and hair designers and technicians, costume

designers created and oversaw the manufacture of the costumes that actors wore, even if the actors were really stuffed dummies filling in crowd scenes. But for Stephen Prince, "the costumes worn by actors are visual effects, and, in light of cinema's composited nature, it makes no sense to differ with the logic that motion capture provides actors with the means of wearing digital costuming and makeup."[39] While this is true enough on a conceptual and theoretical level, as with earlier technological shifts there are real differences for and effects on professionals in the industry. And although actors, especially stars, are still on (somewhat) firm ground, costume designers, makeup artists, and hairstylists would seem to be less secure (color plate 17).

As *Avatar* producer and former executive vice president at Fox Jon Landau enthusiastically put it, "What CGI technology does is it replaces prosthetics. Actors can now play any character that is designed in the computer without going through hours and hours of makeup. Gone is the need for camera and lighting set-ups, makeup retouches, and costume fittings."[40] Although Landau and Cameron appear to be championing the significance of human actors, or at least stars—and a Hollywood producer might be reluctant to exhibit public enthusiasm about the prospect of eliminating stars from the filmmaking process given their cultural capital—interviews and behind-the-scenes extras shown on cable TV or included with DVDs routinely feature producers expressing their giddy enthusiasm at the possibility of eliminating the traditional processes of makeup and costume changes in the name of cost-effectiveness and efficiency,[41] which are also a major motivation behind the industry's broader trend of mergers and acquisitions.

By increasing efficiency through the use of new technologies and the concentration of media ownership, companies can decrease payroll by firing employees who are viewed as unnecessary or redundant. Consequently, the new political economy of conglomerate franchising often means more revenue and profits for the conglomerate but fewer jobs for artists and entertainment industry professionals. At the same time, however, the current reliance on sophisticated and "realistic" computer-generated and mocap characters means that animators, who had been the de facto costume, makeup, and hair designers of their "cartoon" characters for decades, now require the services of professional designers once again.[42]

The Old in the New: Digital Media and Fashion

Rather than marking a radical break with the past, then, some changes within the media industry and entertainment marketplace retain significant characteristics of established practices in the newer forms. For example, although Max Factor's infamous mechanical "beauty calibrator" (or "beauty micrometer") from the 1930s has since been described as an antiquated and bizarre mechanical "torture device" from a distant sexist and patriarchal past,[43] it has its digital and contemporary counterpart in the popular "facial beauty analysis" website AnaFace.com (which stands for "analyze face") and its complementary AnaFace mobile app. Just as the beauty calibrator was described in 1935 as a "one-of-a-kind" instrument "designed to aid [Hollywood] makeup men" and help them "accurately analyze facial flaws . . . invisible to the ordinary eye,"[44] the digital AnaFace app invites "users [to] upload a photo of their face and get an instant rating of their beauty—so they can emphasize their most positive features and downplay the negative ones."[45] The CEO of AnaFace elaborated in a press release that users "can accentuate certain features through cosmetics, different types of glasses, and in the more extreme case plastic surgery, [all of which] can have a direct impact on your love life, job performance, promotions and interviews."[46] Similar to earlier marketing strategies for cosmetics, this new device provides women with "hope in an app" that promises personal and social transformation through the ubiquitous "makeover" first popularized by the marketing premise that "a woman could not only change her looks but remake herself and her life chances" (figure 43).[47]

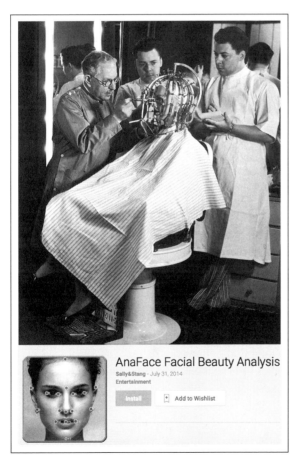

AnaFace Facial Beauty Analysis

Sally&Stang - July 31, 2014
Entertainment

Install   Add to Wishlist

In addition to using the beauty calibrator in his role as the "makeup man to the stars," Max Factor's promotional methods and advertising also took a leadership role in "promising an individual beauty diagnosis to each consumer, then instruct[ing] retailers how to make 'personal' recommendations based on hair and skin-types."[48] Complementary beauty columns in fan magazines would use Hollywood actresses' different complexions and coloring "types" to "offer . . . female

FIGURE 43: Above, a 1935 publicity photo of Max Factor, with Perc and Ern Westmore, and Factor's "beauty micrometer" used to measure the proportions of women's faces in order to correct them with makeup. Below, a frame grab advertising the AnaFace app (the face shown is Natalie Portman's), which promises to do much the same thing digitally.

viewers the opportunity to find their own 'color harmony,'"[49] and "encouraged [women] to play with their looks" including, in Kathy Peiss's words, "ethnicity defined as style, [which] could, like makeup, be easily applied and washed off."[50] The January 1935 issue of the fan magazine *New Movie* ran a feature asking women readers "Which Type Are You?" and offering a menu of movie star choices accompanied by "a new service from Hollywood for our readers" in the form of "advice and suggestions regarding make-up, dress, coiffure, etc., most appropriate to the type to which you belong." Selected fans who had sent in their "height, weight, hair and eye coloring, . . . the name of the star or featured player whom [they thought they] most resemble[d], and an inexpensive photograph or snapshot" were later featured in an article entitled "Hitch Yourself to a Star" that included professional before-and-after photographs of readers re-creating the "looks" of actresses alongside similar portraits of stars.[51]

This genre of fan article also has its contemporary digital counterpart in InStyle.com's "Hollywood Makeover virtual hair and makeup tool," which invites consumers and fans to "try on your favorite celebrity hairstyles, hair color, eye make up and cosmetics." Replete with personalized style and beauty advice, users can upload personal photos and "try on" and "clear" different celebrity "looks" in separate sections devoted to emulating the hair, eyes, lips, and skin of actress Mindy Kaling of *The Mindy Project* (Fox, 2012–2015) ("See yourself in Mindy's ombré waves!") and over fifty other female entertainment, television, and film celebrities, including actress Kerry Washington from the television show *Scandal* (ABC, 2012–present), for whom the tool offers thirteen "complete looks."[52] The Hollywood Makeover tool is synchronized with the opportunity to purchase the precise cosmetic and beauty products required to "achieve that celebrity look," and is supplemented with beauty and fashion advice along with the celebrity gossip and entertainment news ubiquitous throughout the InStyle.com website.

On the one hand, InStyle.com's seamless and virtual selling of beauty products through the digital emulation of stars' on- and offscreen makeup and hair styles is part of a broader increase in retail partnerships and merchandising agreements (InStyle.com, along with the print magazine *InStyle*, is owned by Time, Inc., now merged, as mentioned, with Warner Bros.), and facilitated by the growth of the Internet and mobile technologies in the twenty-first-century entertainment marketplace. On the other hand, however, we can trace this business strategy back to the marketing and promotional strategies begun in the 1920s and 1930s when, as Charles Eckert states in his classic essay "The Carole Lombard in Macy's Window,"

> Hollywood seemed to dominate the cosmetics industry because its stars appeared in the thousands of ads that saturated the media. . . . The cycle of influence made up of films, fashion articles, "beauty hints," columns featuring stars, ads that dutifully mentioned the star's current film, and

tie-in advertising in stores, made cosmetics synonymous with Hollywood. . . . No more potent endorsements were possible than those of the
women who manifestly possessed the most "radiant" and "scintillant"
eyes, teeth, complexions, and hair.[53]

Eckert's observations and the above comparisons point to Hollywood's consistent
targeting of women consumers in relation to beauty products and cosmetics, which
is symptomatic, as Peiss puts it, of the "self-conscious identification of women with
consumerism after 1890 [that can be] linked to the growing sense that consumption involved not only the purchase of goods but an entire way of life."[54]

As other essays in this volume have shown, this gendered marketing strategy
remained firmly in place across ensuing decades. Nevertheless, the merchandising and marketing of *Memoirs of a Geisha* (Rob Marshall, 2005) and *Bridget Jones:
The Edge of Reason* (Beeban Kidron, 2004) were deemed newsworthy by trade
journals and the business press for the ways in which the film studios, cosmetics companies, and retail outlets partnered to reach new or broader segments of
women consumers. The *Wall Street Journal* described Sony's marketing of *Memoirs*, an adaptation of a historical novel by American writer Arthur Golden, as an
"ambitious effort to sell the movie using the same marketing tie-ins long associated with cartoons and comic-book blockbusters."[55] As another business reporter
put it shortly before the film's release, "*Harry Potter* wristwatches. *Batman* action
figures. *Memoirs of a Geisha* face wash. What? A movie tie-in geared toward
adults?"[56] To which the *Los Angeles Times* added, "'Geisha' shoes? Only if they're
classy . . . 'Memoirs' [is] lux all the way."[57] The *Wall Street Journal* boiled down the
marketing challenge to whether or not a "highbrow film with Oscar aspirations
[could] help sell silky kimono-inspired dresses and sake-infused oils" the same
way that "cereal boxes and action figures can help sell animated films to kids."[58]

The advertising rhetoric and representations that Sony and the cosmetics
company Fresh used to overcome the supposed challenge to appeal to an upscale
demographic with upper-class tastes were replete with exoticized images and
claims that the makeup line would allow Western women to "emulate the sensual
allure of the Geisha" by offering "everything you need, in a convenient package,
to transform yourself" into the book's and film's orientalist fantasy of the mysterious female Asian "other." This explicit example of the cultural appropriation
and "emulation" of the image of the sexualized Asian woman through makeup
use extended to other aspects of the film's marketing and merchandising such
as a "limited-edition, Asian-inspired" line from Banana Republic (named "East
meets West") that included "purses, kimono-like shirts, and dresses," as well as
other licensing deals for "luxury candles," perfume, and tea.[59]

While the merchandising and licensing of *Memoirs of a Geisha* were notable
for their targeting of an upscale audience through a "highbrow" aesthetic, the
2004 sequel to the 2001 film *Bridget Jones's Diary* provided the cosmetics industry

and its marketers with an unprecedented opportunity to exploit the "average woman" with "everyday problems." As *Brandweek* summed it up, the cosmetics companies were "jonesing for tie-ins": "While Renee Zellweger was busy repacking on the pounds to play Bridget Jones, Universal [was] bulking up on partners including Max Factor, Clairol, Noxzema, TRESemmé, and French Connection," which the trade journal describes as "unusual in that all of the cosmetic brands are rivals."[60] As part of their makeup line tie-in, Max Factor ran a sweepstakes to win a trip to the Los Angeles premiere for a makeover by a Max Factor makeup artist. Clairol's ads for their hair coloring product tie-in were described as "a departure" because they did not feature the usual shots of models with "flawlessly hued hair." Finally, Noxema's ad campaign focused on "getting the guy, getting the job and still not getting up to wash your face,"[61] suggesting the degree to which the marketing strategies resonated with the "archetypal postfeminist heroine Bridget Jones,"[62] whose model of female identity and "empowerment" was ideally suited to the advertising techniques used to sell cosmetics as well as dieting and food products.

In addition to the *Bridget Jones* franchise's marketing of a postfeminist ethos of what film scholar Angela McRobbie calls "infectious girlishness" to predominantly adult women,[63] advertisers have increasingly attempted to reach women through newer media, including the targeting of "mom bloggers" and their children. Indeed, in 2009 *Adweek* devoted a feature story to "Why Brands Love Mommy Bloggers,"[64] and in 2012 *Forbes* reported that "remarkably, the top 15 mom bloggers influence more people than the *New York Times*."[65] To exploit this marketing and public relations potential, the retail giant Target orchestrated a promotional campaign for its first-ever tie-in clothing collection for young girls for Will Gluck's 2014 remake of the musical *Annie*. The retailer invited mom bloggers to Target Studios to preview the "Annie for Target" collection through a special "meet and greet" with the film's costume designer Renee Ehrlich Kalfus, as well as an exclusive dance party with the film's choreographer.[66] One of the moms who attended the event later posted a glowing endorsement to her popular "Stroller in the City" blog, with photos of her daughter wearing items from the collection and posing with Kalfus. This highly targeted (in all senses of the word) content marketing and promotional campaign was later countered by an online petition circulated through social media that criticized Target for using white models to promote the collection despite the fact that the role of Annie was played by the African American actress Quvenzhané Wallis.[67]

Along with these continued attempts to market to a nominally broader demographic range of women and girls, in the early 1990s cosmetics industry analysts also began to identify "gender-neutral skin care and hair products aimed at men" as a "high-growth opportunity."[68] These products coincided with the emergence of a new image-conscious "metrosexual" masculinity that, in the words of Matthew Hall, "pos[ed] a challenge to traditional notions of gender since men and women are presumed to do appearance differently, or, put simply, women are presumed to be concerned with beautification, whilst most men aren't."[69]

By the early 2000s, the cosmetics and beauty care industry had experienced steady revenue growth in the "male grooming" market and began to expand their male-focused products to include "anti-aging" skin care creams and cosmetics. *Forbes* magazine observed in 2007: "It's only natural that men would turn to makeup to look their best. Grooming, after all, has never been more acceptable. Last year, $4.8 million was spent on male grooming products in the U.S., . . . a whopping 42% increase from 2001. . . . And while still not the norm, makeup— including products from Clinique, Clarins and Jean Paul Gaultier—has become a more common part of the male beauty routine."[70]

In 2009, *Chicago Tribune* reporter Colleen Mastony attributed the increased mainstream acceptance of eye makeup by men to the leading man Johnny Depp—or rather the makeup artists of the *Pirates of the Caribbean* franchise that began in 2003 (figure 44):

Eye makeup never looked so good on a man. In the latest installment of *Pirates of the Caribbean* [2007], Johnny Depp trowels on more black eyeliner than a Kabuki dancer. Yet, even with his heavily shadowed eyes and industrial-strength mascara, Depp manages to exude masculine sex-appeal as he swaggers woozily across the big screen as the campy, over-the-top, drunken pirate Capt. Jack Sparrow. . . . Depp looks

FIGURE 44: Johnny Depp as Captain Jack Sparrow in *Pirates of the Caribbean: Dead Man's Chest* (2006). Costume design by Penny Rose, with several hundred individuals credited for costuming and wardrobe and traditional makeup and hair, as well as prosthetics and appliances, contact lens coordination, and tattoo design, among other specializations. This is again in addition to the hundreds involved in digitally created visual effects and animation.

surprisingly seductive in eye makeup, and he is not the only man calling for more kohl. Lately, eyeliner . . . has acquired a new, more-masculine and more-marketable name: "Guyliner."[71]

Mastony also cites the onscreen use of eyeliner by actor Tobey Maguire in *Spider-Man 3* (Sam Raimi, 2007), and entertainment celebrities and movie stars like Russell Brand and Jared Leto routinely included eyeliner as part of their offscreen personas and looks.[72] As one research firm put it in 2010, "Long gone are the days when lipstick and eyeliner were reserved for women, as . . . metrosexual men, with their manscara and guyliner, are here to stay."[73] Television cable network CNBC noted in 2014 that "since 2012, beauty and personal care launches specifically targeted at men have increased globally by more than 70 percent [with] U.S. sales for the men's personal care market [reaching] $4.1 billion, . . . making it one of the fastest-growing segments of the beauty industry."[74]

The official product licensing for the *Pirates of the Caribbean* franchise—a series "based on" a Disney theme park ride, marking another type of commercial and media synergy growing more common in the new century—reflected and contributed to this increased mainstream acceptance of male makeup through its merchandising motto "Real men wear eyeliner," which was printed on T-shirts, mugs, and hats.[75] Film and television star Rob Lowe launched his own cosmetics line in 2014, which, although not yet offering eyeliner, does include "under-eye serum" along with other "anti-aging products" and will soon "expand . . . to include fragrances and hair products."[76] The entertainment industry has thus extended what Charles Eckert and others call Hollywood's "cycle of influence" to men as well as women, although it is part of a broader increase in the popularity of men's grooming products and cosmetics that occurred after World War II.

It is important to note, however, that while sales to men have grown significantly since 2000, makeup is still not "readily reconciled with a heterosexual masculine identity," as Kathy Peiss has argued about earlier historical contexts.[77] Industry executives are quick to emphasize that they "don't say the M-word"; yet, as the men's magazine *GQ* explains, "Of course it's makeup," which makes the denial "a clever—and potentially lucrative—way of expanding the grooming category into bold new territory, which is why you will never hear the word makeup cross the lips of any brand manager affiliated with these products."[78] Mainstream articles and news coverage of this trend are consistently framed or explained in the context of "men being just as vain as women" or "men caring about their looks as much as women," suggesting that makeup use is still stereotypically gendered as feminine. And although the inclusion of male celebrity endorsements and the targeting of men consumers has increased, the profit-driven attempt to expand the market has hardly replaced the continued relentless targeting of women consumers through gendered advertising and marketing.

Interactive Self-Objectification: *The Hunger Games*

An instructive example of cross-gendered movie marketing is the promotion of the *Hunger Games* films (2012–2015), a franchise based on a series of books, written by Suzanne Collins, aimed at a young-adult female audience and featuring strong, intelligent, and resourceful female heroine Katniss Everdeen (played by Jennifer Lawrence). Trade journals lauded the films' marketing as a stunningly successful attempt to broaden the franchise's original demographic of girls and young women readers to include boys and men (as opposed to the more "female skewed" audience for the *Twilight* vampire film saga, also based on young-adult fiction). In addition, trade journals and industry commentators have placed the marketing and promotional campaigns for the *Hunger Games* films alongside the 1999 *Blair Witch Project* as a paradigmatic model that was successfully "rewriting the rules" for the modern entertainment marketplace through its use of cross-platform content marketing and fan engagement.[79]

The many marketing and promotional strategies for the *Hunger Games* franchise included the use of Twitter puzzle hunts and contests, Facebook games, and "a lavish Tumblr [website] called Capitol Couture dedicated to the movie's unique fashions." This promotional website and intertextual centerpiece combines fantasy and fiction by featuring actual products and real world designers through stories set in the film's post-apocalyptic fictional nation of Panem (the main site's URL is capitolcouture.pn [Panem]). A section of the website devoted to Capitol TV includes user-generated videos and a "Citizens Activity" section where fans—after providing personal information in order to claim their free Panem identification pass and citizen number—can upload and sell their own *Hunger Games* art work, crafts, and clothing creations through Cafepress.com, alongside the official Panem Office of the Ministry of Propaganda's store and other "shops" selling officially licensed *Hunger Games* products like "Down with the Capitol" T-shirts.[80]

Shortly after the first *Hunger Games* film's release in 2012, the *New York Times* announced that the "movie franchise [had become] a full-fledged cultural phenomenon [by] broadening its appeal by age and by gender," including what *Forbes* identified as a "sleeper fan base of men" attracted to a "post-apocalyptic society [with] a massive explosion, fight-to-the-death hand-to-hand combat, all kinds of weapons and . . . torture and guerilla warfare."[81] These stereotypically masculine generic traits are also what some fans and critics have identified as the potentially subversive, progressive, or feminist meanings of the *Hunger Game* books and films.[82] As *Slate* columnist Katy Waldman elaborates, "Not only are most of the characters who occupy explicit positions of power female, the issues that preoccupy Panem's inhabitants have a subtle second-sex slant. What allows the themes of revolution, individuality, and authenticity to converge so resonantly in *The Hunger Games* is something (obvious) that women have been saying for a while:

The obsession with appearance objectifies people—literally, it turns humans into symbolic objects."[83]

While these themes and potential meanings are offered within the films' narratives and the sometimes gritty appearance and physical strength of Jennifer Lawrence, the massive intertextual marketing presence orchestrated by production company Lionsgate invited users to participate in an obsessive process of interactive self-objectification through creative yet complicit consumption that mitigates or contains these progressive meanings. The fictional online magazine and website "Capitol Couture" promoted a real clothing line through an article published by fashion writer Monica Corcoran Harel about the sixteen looks inspired by *Hunger Games*'s characters and designed by the film's costume designer. As the article explains, "For our very first fashion collection, Capitol Couture turned to costume designer Trish Summerville to create a line of ready-to-wear looks inspired by our city's most stylish notables [and] available on Net-a-porter.com."

In these and other ancillary marketing materials, the *Hunger Games* films' violent, empowering, and revolutionary elements—along with their potentially progressive meanings—have been structured out due to what Lionsgate's chief marketing officer Tim Palen calls the film's "tricky subject matter . . . [of] kids killing kids, [which presents] a potential perception problem in marketing." Consequently, the elements that scholars, critics, and fans have identified as empowering, including the gender role reversals present in the *Hunger Games* narratives, are minimized in favor of a familiar emphasis on empowerment through fashion, consumption, and the creation of artifacts in ways that buttress the film's Capitol-ist oppression. In this case, then, the marketing and advertising divisions within the entertainment industry have effectively contained the libratory potential of digital and networked media by providing an outlet for creative yet complicit engagement with these online and mobile marketing materials. This is not intended to suggest an oversimplified or reductive generalization that "everything old is new again," but to demonstrate how new technological "advances" or changes are often put to regressive and historically familiar social and political uses in relation to gender, race, and class in the modern entertainment marketplace.

Cinema Fashion Redux: "Cool Stuff"

In 2000, fashion scholars Stella Bruzzi and Pamela Church Gibson summed up the discomforts of examining the subject of fashion, and/as costume especially, in film: "Fashion's fundamental dilemma is that it has inevitably been predicated upon change, obsolescence, adornment, and in the so-called First World, it has been inextricably bound up with the commercial; this has led to the assumption that it is therefore superficial, narcissistic and wasteful."[84] In 2011, however, Drake Stutesman observed, in relation to these remarks, that although "fashion as a focus has evolved prodigiously in the last ten years (with or without the true homage its creativity deserves) . . . film fashion, or what is actually *costume design*, has not. It is marginalized, if not ignored, in the way that fashion, as Bruzzi and Church Gibson defined its dismissal, was written off long ago."[85] Deborah Landis would reiterate this in 2014 when she argued to an interviewer that "costumers don't get the respect they deserve": "Costume designers are invisible. We don't have publicists, we work for hire so we don't own anything, not even our sketches or our designs nor when they're replicated on dolls or in fashion. We are not mentioned in fashion magazines but we help create the story and the people who inhabit the clothes."[86] Landis rarely refers to makeup and hair artists when she discusses costuming, but if she did, the same claims would apply.

The paradox is that, as has been shown throughout this volume, the aesthetic goal of costume, makeup, and hair designers is often, if not always, for their work to go unnoticed in their films; as with other (and also often unnoticed) elements of Hollywood's narrative style—"invisible" editing, lighting, cinematography, sound, and sometimes even acting—their labors occur in the service of story and character. Yet Landis has also emphasized that the specific working conditions for costume designers are historically gendered as feminine, which has also contributed to the field's neglect; there is a "longstanding . . . [and] nefarious gender bias" against the profession of costume design that has kept salaries far below other key collaborators. "Our minimum is tied to a union contract hidebound by long-standing precedent with the studios . . . [in which] the base salary for the costume designer is nearly one third less than an entering production designer."[87] This extends to the working conditions of the costume design profession, according to Landis: "Whether practiced by women or by men, costume design has always been considered 'women's work' and is paid (and valued) commensurately less."[88] Again, the same, if not worse, can also be said of artists working in makeup and hair design.

There is obviously nothing new about tie-ins, product placement, or other partnerships among film and television studios, department stores, and magazines and newspapers. What is new today, though, is the speed of this process in relation to how quickly products can "arrive at retail," as the trade journal *License! Global* noted in August 2014: "With increased efficiency in production capabilities and the rapid movement of trends thanks to social media and new content platforms, these collaborations are happening more quickly and more often than ever before."[89] The reverse is also true; today designers can load up film characters like James Bond (Daniel Craig) in *Skyfall* (2012) with "cool stuff" such as "designer staples and luxury gadgets" (Omega watches, and Tom Ford cufflinks, sunglasses, and suits; only Bond's underwear, which consists of both boxers *and* briefs, is "not a specific brand," according to costumer Jany Temime)—all items

:: SPY STYLE

Bond's Cool Stuff

Costumer Jany Temime highlights the tweaks she made to 007's classic look for *Skyfall* (out Nov. 9) by outfitting **Daniel Craig** with designer staples and luxury gadgets. BY SOLVEJ SCHOU

WATCH
007 alternates between two styles of wristwear—from Swiss watchmaker Omega—as the action unfolds. Both are "very masculine" yet "fine enough to sit under his cuff," explains Temime.

CUFF LINKS
"I thought it would be elegant to have the Bond family crest on his cuff links," Temime says of these custom fasteners. "We gave Tom Ford the crest design and chose the shape, and he made them for us in silver."

SMARTPHONE
What would James Bond be without a high-tech gadget or two? British fans can now buy the Sony Xperia T Android smartphone carried by the spy. A U.S. version will arrive in time for the holidays.

SUNGLASSES
"They are extremely sexy and at the same time very classy in a cool way," Temime says of the ruthenium aviator-style Marko sunglasses from Tom Ford's accessories collection. "They're very manly."

UNDERWEAR
Does Bond wear briefs or boxers? Both, says Temime. "They are tight boxer briefs in white, and they went perfectly under his trousers. They're not a specific brand—you can get [the style] anywhere."

SUITS
From his bespoke tuxes to his shirts, ties, and shoes, Bond is dressed head to toe in Tom Ford. The designer provided 60 copies of a suit used in *Skyfall*'s opening sequence, 30 for Craig and 30 for his double.

FIGURE 45: A page from *Entertainment Weekly* (October 26, 2012), showing some of the commercial design products worn by Daniel Craig as James Bond in *Skyfall* (2012) that readers can purchase for themselves, with only the underwear "not a specific brand."

that the film and character advertise and that, in doing so, make the "cool stuff" even "cooler" (figure 45).[90]

There are examples in the past—several are described in this volume—of established fashion designers collaborating on films, too, but the increasing number of television costume designers who are also creating ready-to-wear tie-in collections for retail outlets suggests a merchandising and cross-promotional shift within the industry intended to exploit new modes of screen-to-retail commerce and consumption in an era of social media and mobile apps. Through a partnership with program production teams who provide the product information in advance, the "Get This" iPad app synchronizes with program audio to allow viewers to purchase clothes, accessories, and music in real time through what has been dubbed "social purchasing." Websites ShopYourTV.com and WornOnTV.com also provide images and links for viewers to purchase clothes from television programs and films, while the "Pradux" app (there is also a Pradux website) provides incentives for users to share links through social media. *Variety* argued that the appearance of Pradux was "inevitable, as fashion bloggers have long chronicled what characters on shows like *Gossip Girl* and *Scandal* were wearing and costume designers like *Mad Men*'s Janie Bryant and [*Pretty Little*] *Liars*' own Mandi Line have become as famous as the actors they dress. Add this to the fact that the purchasing component of second-screen viewing is a staple for teen programming—particularly for music, as networks like ABC Family, MTV and the CW will tease their alternative music soundtracks onscreen during broadcasts—and it could be a retail windfall."[91]

The primary difference between past and present, then, is one of access, marketing speed or synchronization, and deliberate and instantaneous consumption. The established merchandising paradigm outlined by Charles Eckert through which a movie fan could purchase "the Carole Lombard [dress] in Macy's window" in the 1930s has been extended and intensified in the Internet and mobile era to facilitate second-screen shopping for clothes and accessories using apps and websites as the television and film programming unfolds. Digitized content allows mobile apps to sample audio tracks and then connect that content to specific products, other media content, and online retail outlets for immediate purchasing.

Despite the impact of television costume design, as well as makeup and hairdressing, on retail fashion and consumption, many of the issues designers face with television are similar to film, in particular the assumption that "present day" shows are easier to design, or require no designing at all. What is different now is arguably the status of the designer off the screen, both in his or her association with celebrities and their stylists and in relation to retail markets. In his introductory letter to the membership in the summer 2014 issue of *Costume Designer* magazine, Costume Designers Guild president Salvador Perez, who was the costume designer for *The Mindy Project*, expressed his "dismay . . . that again, no contemporary Costume Design has been recognized" with an Emmy Award, pointing out that, like the Academy Awards' privileging of period and fantasy genres, it is his own colleagues within the profession who repeatedly chose not to acknowledge contemporary work.[92] "If Costume Designers don't acknowledge contemporary work as outstanding and worthy of awards, the public certainly does. Contemporary Costume Design is being valued by the fashion industry and there are more Costume Designers designing for the retail market than ever before."[93]

Perez also makes the important points that "in period TV, most of the clothing is rented" and that "some period programs don't have the budget to build [the costumes] at all."[94] Perez designed and made approximately 20 percent of what was worn on *The Mindy Project*, a significantly higher percentage than for period programs like Masterpiece Theatre's *Downton Abbey* (2010–2016), which has received numerous Emmy nominations and in 2012 entered into a sponsorship agreement with Ralph Lauren to create a *Downton Abbey*–inspired collection.

As Stutesman points out, "Film costume design started at the lowest end of the taste scale, Hollywood, and was pitted ultimately against the highest end, Parisian couture," but by the 1930s and 1940s, Hollywood "costume design . . . [had become] a great force in twentieth-century *haute couture*."[95] It remains to be seen whether television costume design will follow a similar cultural trajectory from "lowly" commerce to respectable art, but articles about the authenticity of actors' underwear in the HBO series *Boardwalk Empire* (2010–2014) are reminiscent of similar promotion and publicity stories attending many of the prestige films of classical Hollywood such as *Gone with the Wind* in 1939 (producer David O. Selznick insisting that the lace on the female stars' undergarments be authentically hand-made, for example). Their publicized attention to every kind of visual detail perhaps places the "complex narrative" serial cable drama on the higher end of the "taste scale" along with period pieces and non-superhero fantasy dramas. In the film industry, "prestige" designers were often perceived as being closer to the high-fashion couturier or couturière and thus could gain aesthetic recognition and cultural capital. But television designers, even on well-regarded "classy" shows like *Downton Abbey*, tend still to be evaluated by commercial value more than aesthetic or design quality in a manner that echoes a familiar distinction between art and popular culture.

That said, as television has consistently become more culturally "legitimized" through "high quality" programming and the concomitant involvement of established film auteurs, so, too, have television costume designers begun to benefit, even though high/low cultural and aesthetic distinctions persist in relation to networks and channels, production values, genres, periods, and star power, as well as the producers and directors involved. As with the film industry and its aesthetic valorizing of some genres—historical dramas, literary adaptations, and the like—over others that are equally or more commercially profitable, so we see in television a familiar assumption that the widely popular contemporary genres that fill commercial broadcast networks, especially, are not as deserving of the cultural capital or aesthetic recognition given to certain serialized genres or cable programs.

But the complex political economy of the twenty-first century media industry and the realities of the modern entertainment marketplace mean that we can no longer bracket off film and television from the Internet or from one another. Regardless of venue, it is clear that costume, makeup, and hair design, whether created for actors in the flesh, digitized avatars, or a composite of both, will continue to disappear into the fictional worlds of art and entertainment they are so instrumental in creating, but also transcend and escape those worlds to leap into our own to arouse in us admiration, emulation, and desire.

ACADEMY AWARDS FOR COSTUME DESIGN

All information is from Oscars.org, the Academy's website.

1948   BLACK AND WHITE, Roger K. Furse   *Hamlet*
       COLOR, Dorothy Jeakins, Karinska   *Joan of Arc*

1949   BLACK AND WHITE, Edith Head, Gile Steele   *The Heiress*
       COLOR, Leah Rhodes, Travilla, Marjorie Best   *The Adventures of Don Juan*

1950   BLACK AND WHITE, Edith Head, Charles LeMaire   *All About Eve*
       COLOR, Edith Head, Dorothy Jeakins, Elois Jenssen,
       Gile Steele, Gwen Wakeling   *Samson and Delilah*

1951   BLACK AND WHITE, Edith Head   *A Place in the Sun*
       COLOR, Orry-Kelly, Walter Plunkett, Irene Sharaff   *An American in Paris*

1952   BLACK AND WHITE, Helen Rose   *The Bad and the Beautiful*
       COLOR, Marcel Vertes   *Moulin Rouge*

1953   BLACK AND WHITE, Edith Head   *Roman Holiday*
       COLOR, Charles LeMaire, Emile Santiago   *The Robe*

1954   BLACK AND WHITE, Edith Head   *Sabrina*
       COLOR, Sanzo Wada   *Gate of Hell*

1955   BLACK AND WHITE, Helen Rose   *I'll Cry Tomorrow*
       COLOR, Charles LeMaire   *Love Is a Many-Splendored Thing*

1956   BLACK AND WHITE, Jean Louis   *The Solid Gold Cadillac*
       COLOR, Irene Sharaff   *The King and I*

1957   Orry-Kelly   *Les Girls*

1958   Cecil Beaton   *Gigi*

1959   BLACK AND WHITE, Orry-Kelly   *Some Like It Hot*
       COLOR, Elizabeth Haffenden   *Ben-Hur*

1960   BLACK AND WHITE, Edith Head, Edward Stevenson   *The Facts of Life*
       COLOR, Vales, Bill Thomas   *Spartacus*

1961   BLACK AND WHITE, Piero Gherardi   *La Dolce Vita*
       COLOR, Irene Sharaff   *West Side Story*

1962   BLACK AND WHITE, Norma Koch   *What Ever Happened to Baby Jane?*
       COLOR, Mary Wills   *The Wonderful World of the
                                                                                      Brothers Grimm*

1963   BLACK AND WHITE, Piero Gherardi   *Federico Fellini's 8½*
       COLOR, Irene Sharaff, Vittorio Nino Novarese, Renie   *Cleopatra*

1964   BLACK AND WHITE, Dorothy Jeakins   *The Night of the Iguana*
       COLOR, Cecil Beaton   *My Fair Lady*

1965   BLACK AND WHITE, Julie Harris   *Darling*
       COLOR, Phyllis Dalton   *Doctor Zhivago*

1966   BLACK AND WHITE, Irene Sharaff   *Who's Afraid of Virginia Woolf?*
       COLOR, Elizabeth Haffenden, Joan Bridge   *A Man for All Seasons*

1967   John Truscott   *Camelot*

1968   Danilo Donati   *Romeo and Juliet*

1969   Margaret Furse   *Anne of the Thousand Days*

1970	Nino Novarese	*Cromwell*
1971	Yvonne Blake, Antonio Castillo	*Nicholas and Alexandra*
1972	Anthony Powell	*Travels with My Aunt*
1973	Edith Head	*The Sting*
1974	Theoni V. Aldredge	*The Great Gatsby*
1975	Ulla-Britt Soderlund, Milena Canonero	*Barry Lyndon*
1976	Danilo Donati	*Fellini's Casanova*
1977	John Mollo	*Star Wars*
1978	Anthony Powell	*Death on the Nile*
1979	Albert Wolsky	*All That Jazz*
1980	Anthony Powell	*Tess*
1981	Milena Canonero	*Chariots of Fire*
1982	John Mollo, Bhanu Athaiya	*Gandhi*
1983	Marik Vos	*Fanny & Alexander*
1984	Theodor Pistek	*Amadeus*
1985	Emi Wada	*Ran*
1986	Jenny Beavan, John Bright	*A Room with a View*
1987	James Acheson	*The Last Emperor*
1988	James Acheson	*Dangerous Liaisons*
1989	Phyllis Dalton	*Henry V*
1990	Franca Squarciapino	*Cyrano de Bergerac*
1991	Albert Wolsky	*Bugsy*
1992	Eiko Ishioka	*Bram Stoker's Dracula*
1993	Gabriella Pescucci	*The Age of Innocence*

1994	Lizzy Gardiner, Tim Chappel	*The Adventures of Priscilla, Queen of the Desert*
1995	James Acheson	*Restoration*
1996	Ann Roth	*The English Patient*
1997	Deborah L. Scott	*Titanic*
1998	Sandy Powell	*Shakespeare in Love*
1999	Lindy Hemming	*Topsy-Turvy*
2000	Janty Yates	*Gladiator*
2001	Catherine Martin, Angus Strathie	*Moulin Rouge!*
2002	Colleen Atwood	*Chicago*
2003	Ngila Dickson, Richard Taylor	*The Lord of the Rings: The Return of the King*
2004	Sandy Powell	*The Aviator*
2005	Colleen Atwood	*Memoirs of a Geisha*
2006	Milena Canonero	*Marie Antoinette*
2007	Alexandra Byrne	*Elizabeth: The Golden Age*
2008	Michael O'Connor	*The Duchess*
2009	Sandy Powell	*The Young Victoria*
2010	Colleen Atwood	*Alice in Wonderland*
2011	Mark Bridges	*The Artist*
2012	Jacqueline Durran	*Anna Karenina*
2013	Catherine Martin	*The Great Gatsby*
2014	Milena Canonero	*The Grand Budapest Hotel*
2015	Jenny Beavan	*Mad Max: Fury Road*

ACADEMY AWARDS FOR MAKEUP AND HAIRSTYLING

Hairstyling was included but not named in this category until 2012.
All information is from Oscars.org, the Academy's website.

1964   HONORARY AWARD to William Tuttle for his outstanding makeup achievement for *7 Faces of Dr. Lao*

1968   HONORARY AWARD to John Chambers for his outstanding makeup achievement for *Planet of the Apes*

1981   Rick Baker   *An American Werewolf in London*

1982   Sarah Monzani, Michèle Burke   *Quest for Fire*

1983   No award

1984   Paul LeBlanc, Dick Smith   *Amadeus*

1985   Michael Westmore, Zoltan Elek   *Mask*

1986   Chris Walas, Stephan Dupuis   *The Fly*

1987	Rick Baker	*Harry and the Hendersons*
1988	Ve Neill, Steve La Porte, Robert Short	*Beetlejuice*
1989	Manlio Rocchetti, Lynn Barber, Kevin Haney	*Driving Miss Daisy*
1990	John Caglione Jr., Doug Drexler	*Dick Tracy*
1991	Stan Winston, Jeff Dawn	*Terminator 2: Judgment Day*
1992	Greg Cannom, Michèle Burke, Matthew W. Mungle	*Bram Stoker's Dracula*
1993	Greg Cannom, Ve Neill, Yolanda Toussieng	*Mrs. Doubtfire*
1994	Rick Baker, Ve Neill, Yolanda Toussieng	*Ed Wood*
1995	Peter Frampton, Paul Pattison, Lois Burwell	*Braveheart*
1996	Rick Baker, David LeRoy Anderson	*The Nutty Professor*
1997	Rick Baker, David LeRoy Anderson	*Men in Black*
1998	Jenny Shircore	*Elizabeth*
1999	Christine Blundell, Trefor Proud	*Topsy-Turvy*
2000	Rick Baker, Gail Ryan	*Dr. Seuss' How the Grinch Stole Christmas*
2001	Peter Owen, Richard Taylor	*The Lord of the Rings: The Fellowship of the Ring*
2002	John Jackson, Beatrice De Alba	*Frida*
2003	Richard Taylor, Peter King	*The Lord of the Rings: The Return of the King*
2004	Valli O'Reilly, Bill Corso	*Lemony Snicket's A Series of Unfortunate Events*
2005	Howard Berger, Tami Lane	*The Chronicles of Narnia: The Lion, the Witch, and the Wardrobe*
2006	David Martí, Montse Ribé	*Pan's Labyrinth*

2007	Didier Lavergne, Jan Archibald	*La Vie en Rose*
2008	Greg Cannom	*The Curious Case of Benjamin Button*
2009	Barney Burman, Mindy Hall, Joel Harlow	*Star Trek*
2010	Rick Baker, Dave Elsey	*The Wolfman*
2011	Mark Coulier, J. Roy Helland	*The Iron Lady*
2012	Lisa Westcott, Julie Dartnell	*Les Misérables*
2013	Adruitha Lee, Robin Mathews	*Dallas Buyers Club*
2014	Frances Hannon, Mark Coulier	*The Grand Budapest Hotel*
2015	Lesley Vanderwalt, Elka Wardega, Damian Martin	*Mad Max: Fury Road*

NOTES

Introduction

1 All quotations here from Patricia Goldstone, "Academy Snub Miffs Makeup Artists," *Los Angeles Times*, March 20, 1981, VI:6. See also "Makeup Artists, Hair Stylists Step Closer in Oscar Drive," *Variety*, March 19, 1981, n.p., clipping file, Margaret Herrick Library (hereafter MHL), Academy of Motion Picture Arts and Sciences Douglas Fairbanks Study Center, Beverly Hills, California. Regarding the terms "make-up" and "makeup," Max Factor, who popularized "make-up" over "cosmetics," refused to give up the hyphen; in this volume, we will quote all source material verbatim, but drop the hyphen otherwise.

2 See the Appendix for Academy Award winners in all of this volume's categories. Over the years the Make-Up Artists and Hair Stylists Guild (Local 706; www.local706. org) and the Motion Picture Costumers Guild (Local 705; www.motionpicturecos-tumers.org), both founded in 1937, and the Costume Designers Guild (Local 892; costumedesignersguild.com), founded in 1953, have also given out awards of their own. It should be noted, however, that while there are published accounts that Max Factor and Ern Westmore won Oscars early in the award's history (in 1928 and 1931, respectively), the stories are apocryphal. Fred E. Basten, in *Max Factor: The Man Who Changed the Faces of the World* (New York: Arcade Publishing, 2008), 62, claims that Factor was given a "special certificate" by the Academy on April 30, 1928, "in recognition of his contribution to the success of 'Incandescent Illumination Research'"; and the Max Factor Beauty Museum, now the Hollywood History Museum, claims actually to have displayed the "gleaming Oscar

(which Max received himself in 1929 for his unique make-up)" in its foyer for years (www. seeing-stars.com/Museums/MaxFactor.shtml). Requests for a photograph of the base of Factor's Oscar at the Hollywood History Museum have gone unanswered. Regarding Ern Westmore, the online version of the *Encyclopedia Britannica* states that he won "the first award ever given to a makeup artist by the Academy of Motion Picture Arts and Sciences, for his work on the film *Cimarron*" (www.britannica.com/biography/Ern-Westmore), but none of the original Westmore brothers received Oscars. In both cases, it is likely that awards from other organizations were transmuted over time into Academy Awards. Many thanks to the Academy History Archive, digitalcollections.oscars.org, and Academy librarian Libby Wertin for her research assistance.

3 Academy press release dated December 16, 1981, Academy History Archive, digitalcollections.oscars.org.

4 Alicia Annas, "The Photogenic Formula: Hairstyles and Makeup in Historical Films," in *Hollywood and History: Costume Design in Film*, ed. Edward Maeder (Los Angeles: Thames and Hudson/Los Angeles County Museum of Art, 1987), 54.

5 Michaela Krützen, *The Most Beautiful Woman on the Screen: The Fabrication of the Star Greta Garbo* (Frankfurt: Peter Lang, 1992), 17.

6 Annas, "The Photogenic Formula," 55.

7 See the section "Make-Up and Color Values," in "Incandescent Illumination," Academy Reports no. 1 (July 1928): 22–29, available in the Academy History Archive, digitalcollections.oscars.org. The report lists Factor's son, incorrectly, as "David," and also includes a report by Lon Chaney.

8 Howard Greer, *Designing Male: A Nebraska Farm Boy's Adventures in Hollywood and with the International Set* (New York: G. P. Putnam's Sons, 1951), 219.

9 The terms "costume designer" and "costumer" were, and are, often used interchangeably, but there can be subtle differences depending on era and context. Theoretically if not always practically, the title "designer" implied that one had little to do with the fabrication of the clothing but instead imagined the required garments from the words of the script, drew illustrations of them (or had them drawn), and oversaw their production and fitting, usually on female stars or featured players. In the studio era, designers, such as Adrian, were heads of wardrobe as well. Costumers also designed and created garments, however, for the films' other actors, though sometimes—especially after the demise of the studio system—there was an assumption that such costumes were purchased or "shopped." The Motion Picture Costumers union now represents all positions—tailors, seamstresses, "agers," dyers, and others who work on the creation, application, and care of costumes—but not so-named "costume designers," who have a separate guild. See www.motionpicturecostumers.org/about-us/ and costumedesignersguild.com/about-cdg/overview-history/, and Desjardins and Black and De Perthuis in this volume.

10 Michelle Tolini Finamore, *Hollywood before Glamour: Fashion in American Silent Film* (London: Palgrave Macmillan, 2013), 7. Finamore does not make any explicit reference to the contributions of makeup artists, like Max Factor, or hairdressers to Hollywood's glamour during the silent era.

11 See "Costume Designers to Get Awards Recognition," in "For Your Information," 3, no. 7 (Winter 1949): Academy History Archive, digitalcollections.oscars.org.

12 Adrian, especially, at MGM from 1928 to 1941, was one of the first, if not the first, of a "Hollywood hybrid known as the costume designer/couturier." Howard Gutner, *Gowns by Adrian: The MGM Years 1928–1941* (New York: Abrams, 2001), 7. See also Margaret J. Bailey, *Those Glorious Glamour Years: Classic Hollywood Costume Design of the 1930s* (Secaucus, NJ: Citadel Press, 1982); David Chierichetti, *Hollywood Costume Design* (New York: Harmony Books, 1976).

13 Ironically, now most studies of costume design focus only on costuming and ignore makeup and hairdressing, and vice versa. However, an important scholarly resource that covers all

three topics is Maeder, *Hollywood and History: Costume Design in Film*, which by accident or on purpose returns to the studios' traditional use of the term.

14 All Westmore quotations from Wally Westmore and Pete Martin, "I Make Up Hollywood," Part I, *Saturday Evening Post*, August 4, 1956, 78–81. On the dynasty itself, which began with émigré British wigmaker and barber George Westmore's work in Hollywood and continued through sons Bud, Ern, Frank, Mont (sometimes written Monte), Perc, and Wally, see Frank Westmore and Muriel Davidson, *The Westmores of Hollywood* (Philadelphia: J. B. Lippincott, 1976), as well as Stutesman in this volume. Mont's three sons—Michael, Marvin, and Monty—also stayed in the business, with Michael sharing an Oscar with Zoltan Elek for *Mask* (1985). Two of Marvin's children, Kevin and Kandace, work as makeup artists in film and television (IMDb.com). Jack Dawn's sons Robert and Wes also followed in their father's footsteps, and grandson Jeff shared an Oscar with Stan Winston in 1991 for makeup on *Terminator 2: Judgment Day*.

15 See Richard Rickitt, *Special Effects: The History and Technique* (New York: Billboard Books, 2007), 320–321.

16 Edith Head quoted in Deborah Nadoolman Landis, *Dressed: A Century of Hollywood Costume Design* (New York: HarperCollins, 2007), 264. Head was the costume designer most honored by the Academy, with eight Oscars overall; Irene Sharaff won five.

17 Dogs, especially, often wore makeup, usually for reasons of comedy or continuity or to disguise the substitution of one animal for another. See Adrienne L. McLean, ed., *Cinematic Canines: Dogs and Their Work in the Fiction Film* (New Brunswick, NJ: Rutgers University Press, 2014). See also the "horse of a different color" in *The Wizard of Oz*, the hues created with tinted gelatin.

18 See Frederick C. Othman, "War in the World of Make-Believe," *Saturday Evening Post*, October 17, 1942, 28–29, 110–111.

19 Self-reflexive films, such as the two Hollywood-set versions of *A Star Is Born* (1937 and 1954); or the makeover scenes in *Cover Girl* (1944), Hitchcock's *Vertigo* (1958), and even the Robin Williams comedy *Mrs. Doubtfire* (1993), have always, usually with montage sequences, engaged audience fascination with the processes behind the transformative power of costume, makeup, and hair, although they never demystify the processes completely.

20 See S. G. Hall, "Make-Up for Color," *The Complete Photographer*, September 30, 1942, 2448–2453.

21 Perc Westmore, "Make-up for Black and White," *The Complete Photographer*, September 30, 1942, 2436.

22 Annas, "The Photogenic Formula," 52; for more on Westmore's "seven facial types" see Perc Westmore, "Make-up for Black and White," 2439–2443.

23 Perc Westmore, "Make-up for Black and White," 2440.

24 Mel Archer, "The Make-Up Artist in Hollywood," *National Board of Review Magazine* (October 1939): 4–6.

25 Anthony Lane, capsule review of *Mad Max: Fury Road*, *New Yorker*, June 8 and 15, 2015, 14. The film has more than forty credited makeup artists and hairdressers, with one named costume designer, Jenny Beavan, supervising thirty-plus people in the costume and wardrobe department. Information on credited and uncredited designers throughout this volume is taken from the films' entries on IMDb.com.

26 In 1942, Orson Welles called Seiderman "the only make-up man in the world!" and said that without him *Citizen Kane* "could not have been made." Quoted in Henry A. Reese, "Merlin of the Movies," *Saturday Evening Post*, February 28, 1942, 22–23, 37–38.

27 There is a useful illustrated website devoted to "actresses in character and prosthetic makeup" in a number of categories in film and television; see www.themakeupgallery.info/index.htm.

28 Perc Westmore, "Make-up for Black and White," 2443.

29 Most hair used in wigs during the studio era was imported human hair. George Westmore had pioneered the "hair-lace wig," whose edges and joins were also made of human hair rather than thread. "Crepe hair," as opposed to fuzzy "crepe wool" from sheep, is human hair that has been tied into a roll and "creped" (crimped) with string at regular intervals, then boiled; it appears wavy. See Wally Westmore, "I Make Up Hollywood," Part II, 86. During World War II, with the loss of overseas sources of human hair, Jack Dawn developed synthetic wigs, also sewn into hair-lace foundations. See Othman, "War in the World of Make-Believe," 29, 110.

30 See Frank Taylor, "Jack Pierce: Forgotten Make-up Genius," *American Cinematographer* (January 1985): 33–41. See also Michael F. Blake, *Lon Chaney: The Man behind the Thousand Faces* (Lanham, MD: Rowman and Littlefield, 1993).

31 Rickitt, *Special Effects*, 269–270; chapter 6 of the book is called "Make-up." For a list of the uncredited makeup and hair personnel on *The Wizard of Oz*, which reads like a who's who of the professions at the time, see its entry at IMDb.com.

32 Rickitt, *Special Effects*, chapter 6; the quotation is from 278–279.

33 "Makeups' [*sic*] Prestige Up," *Variety*, October 24, 1948, n.p., clipping file, MHL. Technicolor could not employ the shinier greasepaint-based makeups developed for panchromatic black-and-white stock because their sheen, so lovely in black and white, made them reflect colors from costumes and even elements of the set or other actors. Max Factor's Pan-Cake was developed in the mid-1930s to provide a matte surface to the face and became a best-seller off the screen as well. See Max Factor, "Co-ordinating Makeup with Film," *American Cinematographer* (July 1935): 286, 297–298; Max Factor, "Make-up for the New Technicolor Process," *American Cinematographer* (August 1936): 331, 334.

34 Taylor, "Jack Pierce."

35 See Sarah Berry, *Screen Style: Fashion and Femininity in 1930s Hollywood* (Minneapolis: University of Minnesota Press, 2000), 19–22. See also Bailey, *Those Glorious Glamour Years*; Chierichetti, *Hollywood Costume Design*.

36 Body makeup artists were strictly segregated by gender and race in the classical era. "Ventilators" weave or tie hair into a wig base; "mixers" create a desired shade of hair in a wig by blending strands of different colors. See Pete Martin, "Mister Wigs [Fred Frederick]," *Saturday Evening Post*, May 19, 1945, 28–29, 34–39, for discussion of the history of wigs in Hollywood films generally and at Max Factor's in particular; Factor's manufactured and rented or sold wigs to many of the studios.

37 Elizabeth Nielsen, "Handmaidens of the Glamour Culture: Costumers in the Hollywood Studio System," in *Fabrications: Costume and the Female Body*, ed. Jane Gaines and Charlotte Herzog (New York: AFI/Routledge, 1990), 175.

38 Clipping from *Lincoln [Nebraska] Journal-Star*, May 9, 1937, n.p., Perc Westmore papers, f. 14, Scrapbook #9, MHL.

39 Barrett C. Kiesling, *Talking Pictures: How They Are Made, How to Appreciate Them* (Richmond, VA: Johnson Publishing Company, 1937), 118. Margaret Farrand Thorp, in *America at the Movies* (New Haven, CT: Yale University Press, 1939), also discusses male stars' influence on fashion in the 1930s in chapter 4, "Cinema Fashions," esp. 116–117. On the Western Costume Company, see westerncostume.com/about-us/history.

40 Landis, *Dressed*, 245.

41 Irene Sharaff is not to be confused with Irene [Lentz; her married name at the time was Gibbons], who remained a couturière at Bullock's Wilshire in Los Angeles in the 1930s when she designed film costumes in the 1930s and 1940s; she followed Adrian as head designer at MGM from 1942 to 1949. On Irene see Frank Billecci and Lauranne B. Fisher, *Irene, a Designer from the Golden Age of Hollywood: The MGM Years 1942–1949* (Atglen, PA: Schiffer Publishing, 2013); on Irene Sharaff see her *Broadway and Hollywood: Costumes Designed by Irene Sharaff* (New York: Van Nostrand, 1976).

42 Landis, *Dressed*, 413.

43 See Annas, "The Photogenic Formula," 52–77; Martin, "Mister Wigs."

44 James Naremore, *Acting in the Cinema* (Berkeley: University of California Press, 1988), 96.

45 *Monster House* (2006) costume designer Ruth Myers found working on a digitally animated film "liberating": "As always, I started with the script and had talks with the director. I was given computerized models that were wearing homogeneous clothes and my job was to help turn these models into authentic characters—but I had no budget limitations! I could get whatever fabric in whatever color. There was no shopping, no cuttings, no fittings, and no staffing problems. My enthusiasm for this kind of costuming is endless." Quoted in Landis, *Dressed*, 479.

46 Kiesling, *Talking Pictures*, 116.

47 Jane Gaines, "Fabricating the Female Body," in Gaines and Herzog, *Fabrications*, 19.

48 Quoted in Michele Manelis, "Deborah Nadoolman Landis and the Art of the Hollywood Costume," an article about an exhibit in Los Angeles that ran from October 2, 2014, to March 2, 2015, www.goldenglobes.com/fashion/deborah-nadoolman-landis-and-art-hol-lywood-costume-25671. Landis has mounted several exhibitions of Hollywood costumes in addition to raising the status of the craft through her books.

49 Besides being a costume designer, she is married to the director John Landis. But it is true that many costume designers, in contrast to fashion designers, remain unknown, as was pointed out in a review of Landis's 2013 book *Hollywood Costume*—they "emerge only around Oscar time, even then making little impression on the culture at large. Almost two decades have passed since Lizzy Gardiner, one-half of the Australian team that outfitted 'The Adventures of Priscilla, Queen of the Desert,' accepted her [Oscar], jangling gently in a dress she'd made from 254 American Express gold cards. 'I'm broke,' she explained, 'and I didn't have anything to wear.'" Alexandra Jacobs, "Star Style," *New York Times*, December 6, 2013.

50 Deborah Nadoolman Landis, ed., *FilmCraft: Costume Design* (Boston: Focal Press, 2012), 8. The book is a collection of interviews mostly with working costume designers.

51 A particularly evocative description of a big studio's costume, makeup, and hair departments is Angela Cartwright's recollection of working at Twentieth Century–Fox as a child, in Angela Cartwright and Tom McLaren, *Styling the Stars: Lost Treasures from the Twentieth Century Fox Archive* (San Rafael, CA: Insight Editions, 2014), 16–17. The book's costume, makeup, and hair test photos are also illuminating, a practice now largely usurped by instant digital technologies.

52 Patrick Keating, quoting his own book *Hollywood Lighting from the Silent Era to Film Noir* (New York: Columbia University Press, 2009), in Patrick Keating, ed., *Cinematography* (New Brunswick, NJ: Rutgers University Press, 2014), 7.

53 All quotations here from Annas, "The Photogenic Formula," 56–59.

54 Ibid., 65.

55 Thorp, *America at the Movies*, 107. IMDb.com lists no credited or uncredited hairstylists or makeup artists for the film.

56 Ibid., 108.

57 Westmore and Davidson, *The Westmores of Hollywood*, 114. Four months after the completion of his work on *Gone with the Wind*, Mont Westmore died at the age of thirty-seven of a heart attack following a routine tonsillectomy; his physician related it to his "arduous work in charge of the makeup of the stars" of the film (130).

58 On specific anachronisms in Walter Plunkett's costumes for *Gone with the Wind* see Edward Maeder, "The Celluloid Image: Historical Dress in Film," in Maeder, *Hollywood and History*, 9.

59 Thorp, *America at the Movies*, 108.

60 Tamar Jeffers McDonald, *Hollywood Catwalk: Exploring Costume and Transformation in American Film* (London: I. B. Tauris, 2010), 135.

61 Ibid., 135–137.

62 Fred Stanley, "Hollywood Entertains," *New York Times*, May 13, 1945, X:1.

63 Peter Brunette and Gerald Peary, "James M. Cain" [interview], *Film Comment* 12 (May/June 1976): 50.

64 Leonard J. Leff and Jerold L. Simmons, *The Dame in the Kimono: Hollywood, Censorship, and the Production Code from the 1920s to the 1960s* (New York: Grove Weidenfeld, 1990), 132. The authors do not say where they got the press release.

65 All quotations here from Billecci and Fisher, *Irene*, 38–46.

66 Factor, "Make-up for the New Technicolor Process," 331.

67 On DeMille's own archives and the documentation of his films in the Herrick Library's Paramount Collection, see Mary Desjardins's chapter in this volume. For makeup and hair, the Perc Westmore Papers at the Herrick Library comprise forty-two scrapbooks covering the years 1925 to 1965, when the House of Westmore closed; while this collection is of enormous value for research into makeup and hair generally, and includes material on all the Westmores as well as some on Max Factor and other artists, there is no comparable collection for any other makeup and hair designer.

68 Billecci and Fisher, *Irene*, 122.

1 The Silent Screen, 1895-1927

1 All from Fenja Gunn, *The Artificial Face: A History of Cosmetics* (New York: Hippocrene Books, 1973), 127–139.

2 Anne Morey, "Geraldine Farrar: A Star from Another Medium," in *Flickers of Desire: Movie Stars of the 1910s*, ed. Jennifer Bean (New Brunswick, NJ: Rutgers University Press, 2011), 138.

3 *Courtesan* is a difficult social distinction to define today. Relationships with courtesans involved money for sex but on the grandest scale. These women were celebrities who "were the constant subject of columns printed in weekly journals, gossip about their romances, what they wore." Many owned massive properties and in some cases were artists themselves and/or supported artists. They "kicked their way past boundaries [and] had implicit and explicit androgyny . . . wit . . . luminescence . . . a capacity to fascinate and enchant." Some great actresses and other prominent women were in that circle. Bernhardt's mother had been a courtesan and Bernhardt began her career as one, as did Chanel. Costume designer Howard Greer worshipped Cécile Sorel, the French stage star (known for her part as a "coquette"), who ran a famed salon as a courtesan, in part, because of her name's stature. Susan Griffin, *The Book of the Courtesans: A Catalogue of their Virtues* (New York: Broadway Books, 2001), 2–4.

4 See Richard deCordova, *Picture Personalities: The Emergence of the Star System in America* (Urbana: University of Illinois Press, 1990), for an account of the development of the star system.

5 James Gardiner, *Gaby Deslys: A Fatal Attraction* (London: Sidgwick and Jackson, 1986), 79.

6 Cecil Beaton, *The Glass of Fashion* (1954; rpt. New York: Rizzoli Ex Libris, 2014), 69, 71.

7 Hillary A. Hallet, *Go West Young Women! The Rise of Early Hollywood* (Berkeley: University of California Press, 2013), 120.

8 Valerie D. Mendes and Amy de la Haye, *Lucile Ltd: London, Paris, New York and Chicago 1890s–1930s* (London: V&A Publishing, 2009), 184.

9 In 1918, Pearl White led a major trend for young working women by wearing a black velvet suit, white blouse, ribbon tie, and beret designed by director Louis Gasnier in *The Mysteries of New York* (1914).

10 Deborah Nadoolman Landis, *Dressed: A Century of Hollywood Costume Design* (New York: HarperCollins, 2007), 16.

11 Michelle Tolini Finamore, *Hollywood before Glamour: Fashion in American Silent Film* (Houndsmill: Palgrave Macmillan, 2013), 112.

12 Ibid., 1.

13 Landis, *Dressed*, 6.

14 The AFI catalogue gives Leisen sole costume design credit; David Chierichetti, *Mitchell Leisen: Hollywood Director* (Los Angeles: Photoventures, 1995), accords him one sequence (the Babylonian), as does William J. Mann, *Behind the Screen: How Gays and Lesbians Shaped Hollywood 1910-1969* (New York: Penguin, 2002), 6. W. Robert La Vine, *In a Glamorous Fashion: The Fabulous Years of Hollywood Costume Design* (London: Allen and Unwin, 1981), cites Iribe as dressing Swanson on *Male and Female* and West clothing the cast (16); Landis, *Dressed*, cites Iribe, Leisen, and West as collaborators (6). Madeleine Delpierre, Marianne de Fleury, and Dominique Lebrun, in *French Elegance in the Cinema* (Paris: Musée de la mode et du costume, 1988), state that Iribe was sole costume designer (44).

15 In David Bordwell, Janet Staiger, and Kristin Thompson, *The Classical Hollywood Cinema: Film Style and Mode of Production to 1960* (New York: Columbia University Press, 1985), 149.

16 Finamore, *Hollywood before Glamour*, 114. "Mother," not necessarily meant as familial, was a common name in that era for respected, intrepid women leaders such as political activists Mother Jones and Mother Shavelson, among many others.

17 Ibid., 112, and Elizabeth Leese, *Costume Design in the Movies: An Illustrated Guide to the Work of 157 Great Designers* (New York: Dover, 1991), 36. IMDb.com lists Coulter's MGM dates as 1927–1931.

18 Finamore, *Hollywood before Glamour*, 114.

19 Ibid., 113–114.

20 Landis, *Dressed*, 5.

21 *Motion Picture*, March 1925, cited in Susan Perez Prichard, *Film Costume: An Annotated Bibliography* (Metuchen, NJ: Scarecrow Press, 1981), 109 (#824).

22 Mann, *Behind the Screen*, 27.

23 Ibid., 120.

24 Landis, *Dressed*, 30.

25 Leese, *Costume Design in the Movies*, 35.

26 Ibid., 4, 121.

27 Ibid., 115.

28 Shelley Stamp, in the documentary film *The Thanhouser Studio and the Birth of American Cinema* (Ned Thanhouser, 2014).

29 "How the 'Movie' Derives Its Power to Influence Garment Sales," *Dry Goods Economist*, October 12, 1920, Ethel P. Chaffin interview.

30 Caroline Reynolds Milbank, *New York Fashion* (New York: Abrams, 1996).

31 Emily Burbank, *Woman as Decoration* (New York: Dodd, Mead, 1917), www.gutenberg.org/files/18901/18901-h/18901-h.htm.

32 Finamore, *Hollywood before Glamour*, 182.

33 Ibid.; see chapter 5, "Peggy Hamilton: Queen of Filmland Fashion," 141–167.

34 For information on West see Prichard, *Film Costume*, 247 (#1835a) (West's name is variously spelled Clair, Clare, or Claire. Prichard stresses that "Clare" is correct); Lisle Foote, *Buster Keaton's Crew: The Team behind His Silent Films* (Jefferson, NC: McFarland, 2014), 218; Landis, *Dressed*, 15; Finamore, *Hollywood before Glamour*, 118.

35 See www.westerncostume.com/about-us/history.

36 West's research for *The Ten Commandments* (1923), a feature costing close to two million dollars, was so thorough that her files were used for DeMille's 1950s remake.

37 Cited in Satch LaValley, "Hollywood and Seventh Avenue: The Impact of Period Films on Fashion," in *Hollywood and History: Costume Design in Film*, ed. Edward Maeder (Los Angeles: Thames and Hudson/Los Angeles County Museum of Art, 1987), 86.

38 As West was listed in the Famous Players–Lasky Corporation Studio Directory, May 1923. The quotation is in Finamore, *Hollywood before Glamour*, 124.

39 Finamore, *Hollywood before Glamour*, 151–152. Through the late teens, many designers, like Peggy Hamilton and Alpharetta Hoffman, drew their ideas from Europe.

40 Barry Paris, *Louise Brooks: A Biography* (Minneapolis: University of Minnesota Press, 2000), 121.

41 Finamore, *Hollywood before Glamour*, 139.

42 Landis, *Dressed*, 40.

43 Christopher Finch and Linda Rosencranz, *Gone Hollywood* (New York: Doubleday, 1979), 70.

44 David Chierichetti, *Hollywood Costume Design* (New York: Harmony Books, 1976), 47.

45 Mann, *Behind the Screen*, 42; Leese, *Costume Design in the Movies*, 75.

46 Landis, *Dressed*, 31.

47 David Chierichetti, *Edith Head: The Life and Times of Hollywood's Celebrated Costume Designer* (New York: HarperCollins, 2003), 20.

48 Dancer Ted Kosloff, Rambova's lover, took credit for these DeMille designs.

49 Landis, *Dressed*, 32.

50 La Vine, *In a Glamorous Fashion*, 12.

51 Delpierre, de Fleury, and Lebrun, *French Elegance in the Cinema*, cite René Hubert as sole costume designer (95).

52 Landis, *Dressed*, 31.

53 La Vine, *In a Glamorous Fashion*, 162.

54 Aileen Ribeiro, *Facing Beauty: Painted Women and Cosmetic Art* (New Haven, CT: Yale University Press, 2011), 298.

55 The use of blackface by Bert Williams (1874–1922) and Sophie Tucker (1884–1966) has bearing on what it represented. Williams, a Bahamanian international superstar comedian and singer, wore deliberately obvious blackface from 1893 (in his successful acts with African American George Walker) through 1910, after entering the Ziegfeld Follies, where he was the only black performer. Louis Chude-Sokei argues this blackface was a "subversion," where Williams's sense of self was "not banished, obfuscated, or erased; instead it multiplie[d], and its self consciousness [was] rendered prismatic" (*The Last "Darky": Bert Williams, Black-on-Black Minstrelsy, and the African Diaspora* [Durham, NC: Duke University Press, 2006], 23, 25). Torch singer Sophie Tucker, a white Russian Jewish immigrant, started her career in 1908 in blackface because she was told she was "too big and too ugly" to sustain an audience and was required (as women were often forced to do by managers) to black up to "hide" her defects. Sophie Tucker, *Some of These Days: The Autobiography of Sophie Tucker* (New York: Doubleday, Doran, 1945), 37; Marlis Schweitzer, *When Broadway Was the Runway: Theater, Fashion and American Culture* (Philadelphia: University of Pennsylvania Press, 2009), 110.

Starting as a "Coon Shouter at the Bijou" in "blackface for the ten afternoon shows, and whiteface for the ten night shows"—her blackface, according to Tucker, so convincing that she got a "gasp" and "laughter" when it was revealed—Tucker went to one-reel slapstick comedy (Tucker, *Some of These Days*, 41–46). Both Williams and Tucker were categorized by prejudice—Tucker as an immigrant, Jewish, ugly woman and Williams as an immigrant black man—yet both seemed to defend against bigotry by burying a self in this caricature and enacting the "unacceptable." These extreme uses of blackface masquerade as a bargain for social acceptance arguably reveal blackface as significant to American identity itself.

56 Anna Everett, *Returning the Gaze: A Genealogy of Black Film Criticism, 1909–1949* (Durham, NC: Duke University Press, 2001), 13.

57 Schweitzer, *When Broadway Was the Runway*, 117. Darkening or lightening skin or even remaining natural could be dangerous for black performers. Schweitzer cites the example in 1909 of vaudevillian Carita Day, a light-skinned African American, who refused to black up; when she and her dark-complexioned partner, Ernest Hogan, danced together some white viewers assumed they were a white woman/black man team, a combination that often incurred violent reactions. In one instance, her agent wrote to a newspaper to underscore that Day, like Hogan, was black.

58 Gunn, *The Artificial Face*, 109.

59 Richard Corson, *Fashions in Make Up from Ancient to Modern Times* (London: Peter Owen, 1972), 187.

60 Gunn, *The Artificial Face*, 137; Corson, *Fashions in Make Up*, 291 (in 1806, "Even the Empress Josephine, who devoted considerable time to her make up, was somewhat secretive about the cosmetics she used").

61 Leonard R. Berlanstein, "Dangerous and Influential Women: Actresses in Nineteenth-Century French Culture," in *Staging Fashion, 1880–1920: Jane Harding, Lily Elsie, Billie Burke*, ed. Michelle Majer (New Haven, CT: Yale University Press, 2012), 52.

62 Gunn, *The Artificial Face*, 143–145.

63 Ibid., 145.

64 David B. Green, "This Day in Jewish History: Makeup Mogul Max Factor Dies," www.haaretz.com/israel-news/this-day-in-jewish-history/.premium-1.544435, August 30, 2013. Other names that appear as Factor's original name are Firestone and Faktor.

65 Steven Zdatny, ed., *Hairstyles and Fashion: A Hairdresser's History of Paris, 1910–1920* (Oxford: Berg, 1999), 6. Fred E. Basten, in his *Max Factor: The Man Who Changed the Faces of the World* (New York: Arcade Publishing, 2008), states the second barber is "Anton of Berlin" but all indications are that he was the Pole who became Antoine of Paris.

66 Basten, *Max Factor*, 22–24.

67 Fred E. Basten and Paul A Kaufman, *Max Factor's Hollywood: Glamour, Movies, Makeup* (Santa Monica, CA: W. Quay Hayes, 1995), 41.

68 Alicia Annas, "The Photogenic Formula: Hairstyles and Makeup in Historical Films," in Maeder, *Hollywood and History*, 52–53.

69 Basten, *Max Factor*, 26–27.

70 Annas, "The Photogenic Formula," 52–53.

71 Ribeiro, *Facing Beauty*, 303.

72 Joshua Zeitz, *Flapper: A Madcap Story of Sex, Style, Celebrity and the Women Who Made America Modern* (New York: Three Rivers Press, 2006), 205.

73 Patrick Keating, ed., *Cinematography* (New Brunswick, NJ: Rutgers University Press, 2014), 25.

74 Basten, *Max Factor*, 62.

75 Gunn, *The Artificial Face*, 149, quoting Rita Strauss, *Book of Beauty*, 1924.

76 Ribeiro, *Facing Beauty*, 319, quoting Kate de Castelbajac, *The Face of the Century*, 65.

77 Teresa Riordan, *Inventing Beauty* (New York: Broadway Books, 2004), 6.

78 In Basten and Kaufman, *Max Factor's Hollywood*, 53.

79 Frank Westmore and Muriel Davidson, *The Westmores of Hollywood* (Philadelphia: J. B. Lippincott, 1976). Westmore's six sons fathered another generation of makeup artists, followed by another.

80 Emily Leider, *Dark Lover: The Life and Death of Rudolph Valentino* (New York: Farrar, Strauss and Giroux, 2003), 159.

81 Basten and Kaufman, *Max Factor's Hollywood*, 37.

82 Leese, *Costume Design in the Movies*, 75.

83 Westmore and Davidson, *The Westmores of Hollywood*, 51.

84 Jeanine Basinger, *Silent Stars* (New York: Knopf, 1999), 22.

85 Cecil Holland, *The Art of Make-Up for Stage and Screen* (Hollywood, CA: Cinematex Publishing, 1927). See also Helena Chalmers, *The Art of Make-Up: For the Stage, the Screen, and Social Use* (New York: D. Appleton and Co., 1925).

86 Gunn, *The Artificial Face*, 151.

87 Artists such as Anna Coleman Ladd and Francis Derwett Wood, as part of a project of the Third London General Hospital's "Masks for Facial Disfigurement Department," matched the original features with masks in galvanized copper painted to appear lifelike; www.industrialanatomy.wordpress.com/2010/07/17/608.

88 Quoted in Landis, *Dressed*, 54.

89 Ibid., 121.

90 Zdatny, *Hairstyles and Fashion*, 55. As Emile Long declared in "Paris Novelties: The 'Mysterious' Chignon," *Hairdresser's Weekly Journal*, February 4, 1911, "Only 3 or 4 years ago, it required more than an hour to wave, separate the puffy portions. Frizz and arrange them. Then there were garlands and bunches of curls, which had to be previously dressed with the fingers; afterwards a ribbon was interlaced in coiffure, a net was placed, the whole shape of headdress was adjusted, combs were inserted, together with a barrette for the neck, and, finally some fancy pins."

91 Ibid., 47.

92 James Stevens Cox, *An Illustrated Dictionary of Hairdressing and Wigmaking* (1966; London: B. T. Batsford, 1989), 276, plate 315.

93 Joanna Richardson, *The Courtesans: The Demi-Monde in 19th Century France* (New York: World Publishing, 1967), 221. See Cox, *Illustrated Dictionary*, 280, plates 34–51.

94 Basinger, *Silent Stars*, 34.

95 Richard Corson, *Fashions in Hair: The First Thousand Years* (London: Peter Owen, 1965, reprinted 1980), 164.

96 Albert Bermel, *Farce: From Aristophanes to Woody Allen* (New York: Simon and Schuster, 1982), 161.

97 Victoria Sherrow, *Encyclopedia of Hair: A Cultural History* (Westport, CT: Greenwood Press, 2006), 156.

98 Harlow died in 1937 from kidney problems but rumors persist that her death came from hair dye poisoning.

99 Landis, *Dressed*, 21.

100 The creator of the Swanson cut in 1924 is unknown.

101 Zeitz, *Flapper*, 245–246; Paris, *Louise Brooks*, 119, 122–123.

102 Paris, *Louise Brooks*, 180, plate 1.

103 Photos of Brooks show her in the cut since she was "five" (Paris, *Louise Brooks*, 123) or "nine or ten" (Zeitz, *Flapper*, 254); Wanger said he inaugurated Brooks's look (Paris, *Louise Brooks*, 96) and Banton claimed he did, by costuming Brooks in a helmet-like brimless cloche; the cut became known as the "black helmet" (Chierichetti, *Hollywood Costume Design*, 50).

104 Paris, *Louise Brooks*, 119–121. Antoine of Paris weighed in on the three "unrefined" and "American" cuts when he set up a salon in New York in 1927—Moore's was "vulgar," Bow's "heavy," but Brooks's "flattering."

105 Judith Mackrell, *Flappers: Six Women of a Dangerous Generation* (New York: Farrar, Strauss and Giroux, 2013), 326; Zeitz, *Flapper*, 246.

106 Daniela Turdich, *Art Deco Hair: Hair Styles from the Twenties and the Thirties* (Chicago: Streamline Press, 2013), 21.

107 See Neal Gabler, *An Empire of Their Own: How the Jews Invented Hollywood* (New York: Crown, 1988), 105; the quotation is from Burbank, *Woman as Decoration*, 1.

2 Classical Hollywood, 1928-1946

1 Memo, Cecil B. DeMille to Fred Leahy, February 15, 1935, Paramount Production Records, f.5, *The Crusades*, Special Collections, Margaret Herrick Library (hereafter MHL), Academy of Motion Picture Arts and Sciences Douglas Fairbanks Study Center, Beverly Hills, California. Robert S. Birchard, for his *Cecil B. DeMille's Hollywood* (Lexington: University Press of Kentucky, 2004), accessed the Cecil B. DeMille Collection at Brigham Young University for sources regarding the production of *The Crusades*, but finds (or uses) fewer documents about costumes from it than I was able to access from the Paramount Production Records at MHL.

2 Memo, Frank Richardson to Cecil B. DeMille, February 2, 1935, Paramount Production Records, f. 5, *The Crusades*, MHL.

3 Margaret J. Bailey, *Those Glorious Glamour Years: Classic Hollywood Costume Design of the 1930s* (Secaucus, NJ: Citadel Press, 1982), 330.

4 Out of economic necessity, some studios, such as Republic and Universal, had lead costume designers also function as head of wardrobe; other studios, such as RKO and Twentieth Century–Fox, went through shorter transitional periods in the 1930s with individuals working under combined titles of wardrobe head and lead or supervisory designer. See David Chierichetti, *Hollywood Costume Design* (New York: Harmony Books, 1976).

5 See Frank Taylor, "Jack Pierce: Forgotten Make-up Genius," *American Cinematographer* (January 1985): 33–41, for details on Pierce's process.

6 "The Hairdress of Women and Children Nanking 1906–34," William Tuttle Collection, f. 23, *The Good Earth*, MHL. Contextual information in the file suggests the photos were taken in China and that Tuttle and Dawn used additional photo booklets (presumably those documenting Chinese men's hair). For makeup and facial template charts, see Tuttle Collection, f. 54, *Marie Antoinette*, MHL. I attribute the makeup work done in these two films to both Dawn (the credited artist) and Tuttle because the primary source materials are in Tuttle's collection, and he worked closely under Dawn's supervision throughout the 1930s, eventually replacing him as head makeup artist at MGM. See also Tuttle Collection, f. 356; William Tuttle interviewed by Ann Burk, August 12, 1976 (SMU Oral History Project no. 106).

7 James Cagney, *Cagney by Cagney* (New York: Pocket Books, 1977), 73.

8 Vincent Sherman interview with John Kobal, *People Will Talk* (New York: Knopf, 1985), 562–563; Ed Sikov, *Dark Victory: The Life of Bette Davis* (New York: Henry Holt, 2007), 235–237.

9 Perc Westmore papers, f. 10, *Mr. Skeffington*, Special Collections, MHL.

10 A considerable amount of the publicity for Muni revolved around the makeup angle in his career. See, for example, "Deft Make-up Artist Changes Muni's Identity," *Toronto Star*, November 2, 1935; Douglas Churchill, "Actors Play Small Part in the Illusion of the Cinema," *San Francisco Chronicle*, April 15, 1937; Harold Heffernan, "Muni Again Wears Beard in New Film," *Hartford Courant*, July 27, 1937; "Story behind Making of 'Zola' Is Interesting Tale in Itself," *Washington Post*, August 29, 1937; "Problems of Makeup Never Bothered Muni," *Hartford Courant*, November 15, 1942; Gladys Hall, "The Muni behind the Makeup," *Motion Picture* (June 1939).

11 "Deft Make-up Artist Changes Muni's Identity."

12 Jack Warner quoted in Sikov, *Dark Victory*, 148.

13 Frank Westmore and Muriel Davidson, *The Westmores of Hollywood* (Philadelphia: J. B. Lippincott, 1976), 25.

14 Mary Astor, *A Life on Film* (New York: Delacorte Press, 1967), 175–178. Ronald Davis also quotes this passage in his *The Glamour Factory: Inside Hollywood's Big Studio System* (Dallas: Southern Methodist University Press, 1993), but incorrectly identifies Astor's remarks as describing Irene Sharaff's costumes. Astor also compliments the work of Sharaff, who designed Astor's costumes for *Meet Me in St. Louis* (1944), but in the passage quoted here is definitely speaking about Irene Lentz, who costumed Astor in multiple MGM films in the 1940s. It is not difficult to confuse the two (and more than one historian has), as they overlapped at MGM and Irene's supervisory position meant that she sometimes got screen credit for films for which Irene Sharaff and others did designing. For a complete listing of Irene's films and a discussion of the costume and design labor divisions within MGM, see Frank Billecci and Lauranne B. Fisher, *Irene, a Designer from the Golden Age of Hollywood: The MGM Years 1942–1949* (Atglen, PA: Schiffer Publishing, 2013).

15 Edith Head and Paddy Calistro, *Edith Head's Hollywood* (Santa Monica, CA: Angel City Press, 2008), 36–38. Maria Riva, in *Marlene Dietrich* (New York: Knopf, 1993), supports Head's claims, although both reminiscences perhaps exaggerate Dietrich's stamina.

16 Adele Balkan, interviewed by Barbara Hall, "Oral History with Adele Balkan," Academy of Motion Picture Arts and Sciences, MHL, 1999.

17 Accounts vary as to whether the first set of costumes, which Colbert apparently rejected in total, were designed by Paramount designer Banton (and sketched by assistant artists, such as Balkan), or by an unnamed designer who came to Paramount with DeMille's unit. Accounts do agree that Banton designed the costumes for Colbert that he is credited for in the final film and that Colbert was difficult regarding costumes and fittings, causing delays during the film's production.

18 Memos, R. L. Johnston to Fred Leahy, October 8, 1938, and Fred Leahy to Mr. Blumenthal, October 11, 1938, Paramount Production files, f. 3, *Midnight*, MHL; David Chierichetti, *Edith Head: The Life and Times of Hollywood's Celebrated Costume Designer* (New York: HarperCollins, 2003), 50–53.

19 Perc Westmore's scrapbooks at MHL contain clippings of many newspaper reports on the strike, especially events related to the vandalism of the Westmore salon.

20 See Murray Ross, *Stars and Strikes: Unionization of Hollywood* (New York: Columbia University Press, 1941); Ida Jeter, "The Collapse of the Federated Motion Picture Crafts: A Case Study of Class Collaboration in the Motion Picture Industry," *Journal of the University Film and Video Association* 31, no. 2 (1979): 37–45; and Elizabeth Nielsen, "Handmaidens of the Glamour Culture: Costumers in the Hollywood Studio System," in *Fabrications: Costume and the Female Body*, ed. Jane Gaines and Charlotte Herzog (New York: AFI/Routledge, 1990), 160–179.

21 Memo, Cecil B. DeMille to Fred Leahy, February 13, 1935; memo, Leahy to DeMille, February 14, 1935; memo, DeMille to Leahy, February 14, 1935; memo, DeMille to Leahy,

February 18, 1935; memo, Frank Richardson to Frank Leahy, March 8, 1935; memo, DeMille to Leahy, April 9, 1935; n.a., memo re Ralph Jester's contract, May 9, 1935. All memos are from Paramount Production files, f. 5, *The Crusades*, MHL.

22 Memo regarding Travis Banton's work on *The Crusades*, author unknown, n.d., Paramount Production files, f. 5, *The Crusades*, MHL. The memo refers to an event that took place on January 27, 1935, so it was probably written in early February 1935. The memo documents that Banton had designed only eight out of twelve costumes needed for DeMille and Young even though shooting had already commenced.

23 Alicia Annas, "The Photogenic Formula: Hairstyles and Makeup in Historical Films," in *Hollywood and History: Costume Design in Film*, ed. Edward Maeder (Los Angeles: Los Angeles County Museum of Art, 1987), 52–57, discusses this issue of anachronistic details in Hollywood period films.

24 Jane Gaines, "Costume and Narrative: How Dress Tells the Woman's Story," in Gaines and Herzog, *Fabrications*, 182.

25 As Jane Gaines argues, the tension between costume and character, or the "rightness" of a costume for a character, is naturalized when, "at some point, we see a character merely wearing clothes." Ibid., 192.

26 Sarah Street, *Costume and Cinema: Dress Codes in Popular Film* (London: Wallflower Press, 2001), 2.

27 See David Chierichetti, *Edith Head*, 78–83, and his *Mitchell Leisen: Hollywood Director* (1973; rpt., Los Angeles: Photoventures Press, 1995), 174–191, for discussions of who designed which costume in the film. As was characteristic of work done in the Paramount wardrobe department during the 1930s and early 1940s, rivalries and disorder during production laid the groundwork for subsequent conflicting stories about design credits.

28 Rosalind Russell with Chris Chase, *Life Is a Banquet* (New York: Ace Books, 1977), 112–113.

29 Yiman Wang, "The Art of Screen Passing: Anna May Wong's Yellow Yellowface Performance in the Art Deco Era," *camera obscura* 60 (2005): 159–191.

30 Jewel Smith, "Loretta Goes Chinese," *Screen Book* (March 1932): 49, 65. See also "Loretta Goes Oriental," *Photoplay* (March 1932): 71, and a one-page pictorial of Young before and after makeup in *Movie Mirror* (March 1932).

31 Betty Willis, "Famous Oriental Stars Return to the Screen," *Motion Picture* (October 1931): 44–45, 90; Audrey Rivers, "Anna May Wong Sorry She Cannot Be Kissed," *Movie Classic* (November 1931); Muriel Babcock, "She Doesn't Dare Love," *Movie Mirror* (January 1932): 62–63, 112; Robert McIlwaine, "Third Beginning," *Modern Screen* (December 1937): 41, 80; Louise Leung, "East Meets West," *Hollywood* (January 1938): 40, 55. See also Wang, "The Art of Screen Passing," for how Wong registered resistance to racist film practices by performing an ironic distance, or "yellow yellow-face," in films.

32 Sarah Berry, *Screen Style: Fashion and Femininity in 1930s Hollywood* (Minneapolis: University of Minnesota Press, 2000), 141.

33 "Modern Maidens, Medieval Modes," *Movie Classic* (September 1935): 48–49.

34 I take this expression from Charles Eckert, "The Carole Lombard in Macy's Window," in Gaines and Herzog, *Fabrications*, 109.

35 Jack Jamison, "How Clothes 'Made' Garbo," *Hollywood* (July 1931): 15–16, 61; Louise Walker, "Dressing Glamorous Garbo," *Movie Mirror* (January 1932); Dena Reed, "Gowns by Adrian," *Picture Play* (January 1935): 36, 73; "Adrian Answers 20 Questions on Garbo," *Photoplay* (September 1935): 36–37, 76. See also Howard Gutner, *Gowns by Adrian: The MGM Years 1928-1941* (New York: Abrams, 2001).

36 I have not been able to find much about this contest; my information derives from an eBay purchase of photos of some of the winning designs that still had intact the "snipes" (captions) on the back that the MGM publicity department had provided for press use.

37 In this Lombard was aided by her renegotiated contract with Paramount: she was no longer exclusively tied to the studio, and for her films elsewhere it was usually possible for Banton to follow her.

38 Sonia Lee, "Portrait of a Self-Made Woman," *Movie Classic* (December 1935): 32. See also "How Carole Lombard's Clothes Match Her Moods," *Movie Classic* (September 1935).

3 Postwar Hollywood, 1947-1967

1 Motion Picture Costumers Records (MPCR), program from the Eighth Annual Costumers Ball, September 29, 1956, cited in Elizabeth Nielsen, "Handmaidens of the Glamour Culture: Costumers in the Hollywood Studio System," in *Fabrications: Costume and the Female Body*, ed. Jane Gaines and Charlotte Herzog (London: AFI/Routledge, 1990), 170.

2 All five were awarded the Oscar for Best Costume Design (color) in 1956.

3 James C. Udel, *The Film Crew of Hollywood: Profiles of Grips, Cinematographers, Designers, a Stuntman, and a Makeup Artist* (Jefferson, NC: McFarland, 2013), 6.

4 Peter Lev, *The Fifties: Transforming the Screen, 1950–1959* (Berkeley: University of California Press, 2003), 168.

5 Paul Monaco, *The Sixties: 1960–1969* (Berkeley: University of California Press, 2001), 14. See also Thomas Schatz, "The New Hollywood," in *Film Theory Goes to the Movies*, ed. Jim Collins, Hilary Radner, and Ava Preacher Collins (New York: Routledge, 1993), 10. The market too was changing. In 1961, half of the $1.5 billion earnings of the Hollywood majors was generated by markets outside the United States.

6 Figures for production are provided by Monaco, *The Sixties* (143 films for 1964). Tim Dirks provides figures for release (121 feature releases in 1963). For 1964, Dirks gives the figures of 361 foreign releases in the United States against 141 U.S. releases. Tim Dirks, "The History of Film: The 1960s," *AMC Filmsite, Part 1*, www.filmsite.org/60sintro.html.

7 Monaco, *The Sixties*, 46.

8 Lev, *The Fifties*, 8; Monaco, *The Sixties*, 46.

9 Lev, *The Fifties*, 10. By 1960, all the majors were essentially out of the business of owning movie theaters in the United States. One consequence for those working behind the scenes was a reduction in the number of B-films being made because of the demise of the double bill. Subsequently, the focus was on the production of A-films only. Although individual studios responded differently to the changing environment, across the board the studio system dissolved throughout the 1950s and into the 1960s. RKO was hit hardest and folded in 1958.

10 Monaco, *The Sixties*, 41.

11 As Tim Dirks notes in "The History of Film: The 1960s," "Architectural wonders, such as the Paramount Theater in Times Square (New York), projected its last scheduled film in 1964. The RKO (Hill Street) Theatre in Los Angeles was destined to become a parking garage soon after. And the RKO Orpheum Theatre in downtown San Diego, built in 1924, was demolished to make room for a bank."

12 Lev, *The Fifties*, 9.

13 Ibid.

14 Samuel Goldwyn, "Hollywood in the Television Age," *Hollywood Quarterly* 4, no. 2 (1949): 145. Despite the genuine threat that television posed for the production of new Hollywood films, from 1955 studios responded by producing television series and ensuring that their back catalogues would fill television airtime. For a more detailed analysis, see Janet Wasko, "Hollywood and Television in the 1950s: The Roots of Diversification," in Lev, *The Fifties*, 127–146.

15 Deborah Nadoolman Landis, *Dressed: A Century of Hollywood Costume Design* (New York: HarperCollins, 2007), 140.

16 Ibid.

17 David Chierichetti, *Hollywood Costume Design* (London: Cassell & Collier Macmillan, 1976), 10.

18 Nielsen, "Handmaidens of the Glamour Culture," 172.

19 Ibid.

20 Ibid., 172–173. Membership was a prerequisite to working in the classifications of finished wardrobe or manufacture, and unemployed members waited by the phone for a call from the union hall or a key costumer. Established contacts were important and, not surprisingly, it was those costume workers with good connections or specifically requested by star actors that found the most secure employment. During this time, television production provided alternative employment in the field. See www.motionpicturecostumers.org/about-us/.

21 MPCR, *Costumers News* (June 1953), cited in Nielsen, "Handmaidens of the Glamour Culture," 162.

22 Linda Harris Mehr, "Dressing the Part," *Performing Arts Resource* 27 (2010): 69–81.

23 See www.westerncostume.com/about-us/history.

24 Monaco, *The Sixties*, 12–13.

25 Ibid., 12. This period was also characterized by a trend to pay more attention to the marketing of films, often at the expense of production.

26 Nielsen, "Handmaidens of the Glamour Culture," 178.

27 Maureen Turim, "Designing Women: The Emergence of the New Sweetheart Line," in Gaines and Herzog, *Fabrications*, 217.

28 Deborah Nadoolman Landis, "Setting the Scene: A Short History of Hollywood Costume Design 1912–2012," in *Hollywood Costume*, ed. Deborah Nadoolman Landis (London: V&A Publishing, 2012), 27, 30.

29 This system continued until 1967 when the number of black-and-white films had dwindled to the extent that a separate category was no longer necessary. In 1953, the 25th Academy Awards was the first to be televised. Both nationally and abroad, the broadcasting of the ceremony helped propagate and maintain the allure of Hollywood glamour.

30 As Bronwyn Cosgrove documents, in the postwar period many costume designers continued the tradition of designing the gowns worn by stars to the Academy Awards. See Bronwyn Cosgrove, *Made for Each Other: Fashion and the Academy Awards* (London: Bloomsbury, 2007).

31 Turim, "Designing Women," 217.

32 Members included Bill Hargate, Michael Woulf, Howard Shoup, Burton Miller, Erté, and Edith Head. See costumedesignersguild.com/about-cdg/overview-history/. The CDG Local 892 of the International Alliance of Theatrical and Stage Employees (IATSE) was established in 1953.

33 Nielsen, "Handmaidens of the Glamour Culture," 177.

34 See costumedesignersguild.com/about-cdg/overview-history/.

35 Landis, "Setting the Scene," 30; Chierichetti, *Hollywood Costume Design*, 165.

36 Landis, "Setting the Scene," 30. For example, Dorothy Jeakins, unlike Head, was never on the payroll of a major studio for more than one movie at a time; see Lawrence Van Gelder, "Dorothy Jeakins Dies at 81; Designed Costume for Films," *New York Times*, November 30, 1995.

37 Joy Spanabel Emery, "Dress Like a Star: Hollywood and the Pattern Industry," *Dress* 28, no. 1 (2001): 97.

38 W. Robert La Vine, *In a Glamorous Fashion* (London: Allen and Unwin, 1981), 124. Lastex is a formerly U.S. registered trademark of a type of yarn that was used in stretch fabrics. It consists of a latex core wound with cotton, rayon, and nylon or silk threads.

39 Landis, *Dressed*, 140.

40 La Vine, *In a Glamorous Fashion*, 216.

41 Nancy Friedland, "Costume Design and Film: From Magical Realism to Authentic Attire in Everyday Wear," *Performing Arts Resource* 27 (2010): 49–62. One designer from this period known more for her work in fashion than film is Bonnie Cashin, who designed over sixty films at Fox with Charles LeMaire, before leaving in 1949 to set up her own design business, ultimately becoming one of the pioneers of American sportswear. Turim, "Designing Women," 227.

42 Lev, *The Fifties*, 4, 34.

43 Ibid., 108.

44 Ibid., 109–115.

45 Caroline Young, *Classic Hollywood Style* (London: Frances Lincoln, 2012), 167.

46 See Jackie Byars, *All That Hollywood Allows: Re-reading Gender in 1950s Melodrama* (Chapel Hill: University of North Carolina Press, 1991), 128.

47 Young, *Classic Hollywood Style*, 168.

48 Lev, *The Fifties*, 240.

49 Half a decade later, Todd Haynes would pick up on Sirk's use of extreme artifice in *Far from Heaven* (2002), a film that had the production team painting autumn leaves to enhance their tones and costume designer Sandy Powell designing costumes from a table of swatches and Pantone charts. David Schwartz, "Heaven Sent: Todd Haynes, Mark Friedberg, and Sandy Powell on the Aesthetics of Melodrama," www.movingimagesource.us/articles/heaven-sent-20120727.

50 Young, *Classic Hollywood Style*, 199.

51 Chierichetti, *Hollywood Costume Design*, 128.

52 Ibid., 9.

53 Ibid., 128. Earlier in her career, Monroe wore a classic "New Look" gown to present the Academy Award for Best Sound in 1951. It is striking to compare her appearance here to the far more familiar image she learned to cultivate.

54 Many have noted that the New Look existed in various forms before the war in both fashion and film. See, for example, Colin McDowell, *The Forties Fashion and the New Look* (London: Bloomsbury, 1997), and Turim, "Designing Women."

55 Edith Head and Paddy Calistro, *Edith Head's Hollywood* (Los Angeles: Angel City Press: 2008), 69–70. Cited in Stella Bruzzi, "'It Will Be a Magnificent Obsession': Femininity, Desire, and the New Look in 1950s Hollywood Melodrama," in *Fashion in Film*, ed. Adrienne Munich (Bloomington: Indiana University Press, 2011), 163.

56 Head and Calistro, *Edith Head's Hollywood*, cited in Young, *Classic Hollywood Style*, 122.

57 Frank DeCaro, "Edith Head, the Costume Drama," *New York Times*, April 26, 1998. See also Turim, "Designing Women," 222, and Jay Jorgensen, *Edith Head: The Fifty-Year Career of Hollywood's Greatest Costume Designer* (Philadelphia: Running Press, 2010).

58 Stella Bruzzi, *Undressing Cinema: Clothing and Identity in the Movies* (London: Routledge, 1997), 64.

59 Bruzzi, "'It Will Be a Magnificent Obsession,'" 164.

60 Cited in Landis, *Dressed*, 175.

61 La Vine, *In a Glamorous Fashion*, 112. Jeakins replaced Karinska after she departed from the film.

62   Duane Valentry, "Famed Hand-Weaving Specialist Busy Spinning Success Story," *St. Peters-burg [FL] Independent*, May 28, 1958, 4B.

63   Christopher Frayling, "Blades," in Landis, *Hollywood Costume*, 243.

64   Landis, "Setting the Scene," 32.

65   Cited in Monaco, *The Sixties*, 127.

66   Lloyd Llewellyn-Jones, "'An Almost All Greek Thing': Cleopatra VII and Hollywood Imag-ination," in *Ancient Greek Women in Film* (Oxford: Oxford University Press, 2013), 326.

67   *Photoplay* (April 1962): 30, quoted in Llewellyn-Jones, "'An Almost All Greek Thing,'" 328.

68   Derek Granger, "Obituary: Stanley Hall," *The Independent*, June 5, 2014.

69   Wanger and Hyams, cited in Llewellyn-Jones, "'An Almost All Greek Thing,'" 327.

70   Suzanne Osmond, "'Her Infinite Variety': Representations of Shakespeare's Cleopatra in Fashion, Film, and Theatre," *Film, Fashion & Consumption* 1, no. 1 (2012): 55–80. Osmond writes: "More recently, fashion designers John Galliano and Alexander McQueen are amongst those who have celebrated and subverted the visual tropes of Ancient Egypt and the iconic figure of Cleopatra within the contemporary theatrical space of the catwalk. This influence is most evident in John Galliano's Autumn-Winter 1997 'Suzy Sphinx' Collection and his Spring 2004 Collection for Christian Dior, and Alexander McQueen's Fall/Winter 2007 'In Memory of Elizabeth Howe, Salem, 1692' Collection, as well as his subsequent range for Mac Cosmetics, which all referenced Cleopatran styling" (72).

71   Alicia Annas, "The Photographic Formulas: Hairstyles and Makeup in Historical Films," cited in Llewellyn-Jones, "'An Almost All Greek Thing,'" 327.

72   The ideology of the Cold War seeped into films that explored both sides of the political divide. Westerns, science fiction, and film noir, especially, were infused with themes of sus-picion and distrust. On the other hand, a film such as *Shane* supported the individualist approach and was a guarded critique of the HUAC/McCarthy witchhunts and the blacklist-ing of Hollywood writers and directors.

73   Kate de Castelbajac, *The Face of the Century: 100 Years of Makeup and Style* (London: Thames & Hudson, 1995), 98.

74   Ibid., 105.

75   Ibid., 106, 117.

76   Ibid., 101, 125.

77   Geoffrey Jones, *Beauty Imagined: A History of the Global Beauty Industry* (Oxford: Oxford University Press, 2010), 186.

78   Udel, *The Film Crew of Hollywood*, 6. See also Frank Taylor, "Jack Pierce: Forgotten Make-up Genius," *American Cinematographer* (January 1985): 41.

79   Udel, *The Film Crew of Hollywood*, 7.

80   Ibid., 8.

81   Ibid. Striepeke took over from Ben Nye at Twentieth Century–Fox at the end of 1967, when he started working on *Planet of the Apes*.

82   Nicholas Drake, *The Fifties in Vogue* (New York: Henry Holt, 1987), 98.

83   Apparently one retailer reported a 375 percent increase in the sale of men's T-shirts. See Young, *Classic Hollywood Style*, 131. For a discussion of the male body as object of display, see Steven Cohan and Ina Rae Hark, eds., *Screening the Male: Exploring Masculinities in Hollywood Cinema* (London: Routledge, 1993).

84   Monaco, *The Sixties*, 59.

85   The Code was revised many times. For example in 1956 there were new guidelines for the portrayal of drug addiction, the kidnapping of children, and brutality, and the removal of the explicit prohibition against miscegenation.

86 Landis, "Setting the Scene," 30.

87 Sharaff, cited in ibid.

88 Lev, *The Fifties*, 167.

89 Mehr, "Dressing the Part," 69–81.

90 Travilla made copies of the dress for his own fashion line in the 1980s. The original sold for $4.6 million at auction in 2011. Young, *Classic Hollywood Style*, 160.

91 Chierichetti, *Hollywood Costume Design*, 128.

92 In Gillian Armstrong's documentary-biopic about Orry-Kelly, *Women He's Undressed* (2015), these dresses are much discussed, most notably by Jane Fonda, who can barely contain herself when describing the impact on audiences of the vision of Monroe's tantalizing bust.

93 Michael Cathcart interview with Gillian Armstrong, "Orry Kelly, The Secrets Behind the Man Who Dressed the Stars," *Books and Arts Daily*, May 15, 2013, www.abc.net.au/radionational/programs/booksandartsdaily/orry-kelly2c-the-secrets-behind-the-man-who-dressed-the-stars/4688572.

94 Not surprisingly, the film provoked a fierce reaction from the Legion of Decency, which boycotted exhibiting cinemas and resulted in limiting its release. Lev, *The Fifties*, 82.

95 Friedland, "Costume Design and Film," 49–62.

96 No one moved across genres like Doris Day, who was originally contracted to MGM for seven years in 1948. In the sophisticated sex comedy *Pillow Talk* (Michael Gordon, 1959), Day had been convinced to move out of her comfort zone and, as successful career girl Jan Morrow, was dressed by Jean Louis in a "sensational wardrobe" with "wonderful makeup" and "a great hairdo," all with the intention to "chic" her up. Quoted in Jane Clarke and Dianna Simmonds, *Move Over Misconception: Doris Day Reappraised* (New York: William Morrow, 1980), 60. But despite appearing in a suggestive split-screen scene with Rock Hudson, both naked in their respective baths, she remained typecast as the girl-next-door. She was ranked the number one moneymaker in Hollywood in 1960, the only actress to achieve this ranking in the period 1950 to 1960, and continued to make films until 1968.

97 Quote from MPAA PCA files in Mehr, "Dressing the Part," 69–81.

98 Mark Cousins, *Scene by Scene* (London: Laurence King Publishing, 2002), 65.

99 Chierichetti, *Hollywood Costume Design*, 128.

100 Ibid., 71.

101 Jane Gaines, "Costume and Narrative: How Dress Tells the Woman's Story," in Gaines and Herzog, *Fabrications*, 192.

102 Chierichetti, *Hollywood Costume Design*, 133. Marjorie Best was the costume designer.

103 Ibid., 126. At the Academy Award ceremony in 1951, Dietrich presented the Honorary Foreign Language Film Award wearing a black Christian Dior gown, a fact announced by the host. She had specifically asked from which side she would enter the stage so that the split of her skirt would show her famous legs to the best advantage. Winthrop Sargeant, "Dietrich and Her Magic Myth," *Life*, August 18, 1952, 86.

104 Gaylyn Studlar, "'Chi Chi Cinderella': Audrey Hepburn as Couture Countermodel," in *Hollywood Goes Shopping*, ed. Garth Jowett and David Dresser (Minneapolis: University of Minnesota Press, 2000), 160.

105 Drake, *The Fifties in Vogue*, 6.

106 Hardy Amies introduced a line of menswear in 1961 and, in 1968, designed the costumes for Stanley Kubrick's *2001: A Space Odyssey*.

107 *Designing 007: Fifty Years of Bond Style* exhibition, Barbican Centre, London and EON Productions, 2012.

108 Ed Buscombe, "Cary Grant," in *Fashion Cultures: Theories, Explorations and Analysis*, ed. Stella Bruzzi and Pamela Church Gibson (London: Routledge, 2000), 203.

109 Young, *Classic Hollywood Style*, 151. It was written into his contract that Grant could keep the clothes.

110 Monaco, *The Sixties*, 45.

111 Thomas Lisanti, *Hollywood Surf and Beach Movies: The First Wave, 1959–1969* (Jefferson, NC: McFarland, 2005), 7.

112 Ibid., 184.

113 Ibid., 103.

114 Ibid., 339.

115 Betty Best, "Australian's Triumph in 'Camelot' Film," *Australian Women's Weekly*, June 28, 1967, 24–26. Much of this extravagance was created by illusion; with little money to work with, at least one "ordinary" costume was made to look more spectacular by being backlit with hundreds of candles.

116 Monaco, *The Sixties*, 44.

117 Young, *Classic Hollywood Style*, 202.

118 Ibid.

119 Lester D. Friedman, *Bonnie and Clyde* (London: BFI, 2000), 41.

120 Theadora Van Runkle, DVD commentary, *Bonnie and Clyde*, Two-Disc Special Edition, directed by Arthur Penn (1967; Warner Bros., 2008).

121 Friedman, *Bonnie and Clyde*, 39.

122 Ibid., 40–41.

123 David A. Cook, "Ballistic Balletics: Styles of Violent Representation in *The Wild Bunch* and After," in *Sam Peckinpah's "The Wild Bunch*," ed. Steven Prince (Cambridge: Cambridge University Press, 1999), 142.

124 Monaco, *The Sixties*, 167.

125 Schatz, "The New Hollywood," 14.

126 Monaco, *The Sixties*, 10.

127 Ibid., 15. See also Tino Balio, ed., *The American Film Industry* (Madison: University of Wisconsin Press, 1976), 329.

128 Deborah Nadoolman Landis, "The Exhibition Odyssey," in Landis, *Hollywood Costume*, 181.

129 Ibid.

130 Larry McQueen, "A Collector's Tale," in Landis, *Hollywood Costume*, 223.

131 Steven Morris, "Elizabeth Taylor's Cleopatra Wig Up for Sale," December 13, 2011, www.theguardian.com/film/2011/dec/12/elizabeth-taylor-cleopatra-wig-sale. The wig later sold at auction through Heritage Auctions, Dallas, Texas, for $20,315. Marice Richter, "Cape Worn by Elizabeth Taylor in 'Cleopatra' Sold," March 31, 2012, www.reuters.com/article/entertainment-us-taylor-elizabeth-cape-idUSBRE82U0F020120331.

132 "Auction Frenzy over Hepburn Dress," *BBC News*, December 5, 2006, news.bbc.co.uk/2/hi/entertainment/6209658.stm.

133 Young, *Classic Hollywood Style*, 160.

134 Peter Biskind, *Easy Riders, Raging Bulls: How the Sex-Drugs-and-Rock 'n' Roll Generation Saved Hollywood* (New York: Simon & Schuster, 1998), 74. Monaco quotes a figure of just under $300,000 (Monaco, *The Sixties*, 187). Either way, without taking into account inflation, one Monroe dress could finance numerous *Easy Riders*.

4 The Auteur Renaissance, 1968–1980

1 Qtd. in David Cook, *Lost Illusions: American Cinema in the Shadow of Watergate and Vietnam, 1970–1979* (Berkeley: University of California Press, 2002), 68–69.

2 In Deborah Nadoolman Landis, "Setting the Scene: A Short History of Hollywood Costume Design, 1912–2012," in *Hollywood Costume*, ed. Deborah Nadoolman Landis (New York: Abrams, 2013), 32.

3 Deborah Nadoolman Landis, *Dressed: A Century of Hollywood Costume Design* (New York: HarperCollins, 2007), 307.

4 Ibid., 317.

5 Beth Ann Krier, "Costume Design Revolution," *Los Angeles Times*, March 18, 1971, cited in "Costume Design and Film: From Magical Realism to Authentic Attire in Everyday Wear," *Documenting: Costume Design*, ed. Nancy E. Friedland (New York: Theatre Library Association, 2010), 58.

6 In fact, Head won the last of her record eight Oscars in the 1970s, for the period costumes in *The Sting* (1973).

7 Digital effects were not yet in competition with the traditional modes of costume, makeup, and hair during the 1970s, nor would they be for several more decades. See Richard Rickitt, *Special Effects: The History and Technique* (New York: Billboard Books, 2007), chapter 6, esp. 302–303, and Castonguay in this volume.

8 Landis, "Setting the Scene," 36.

9 Landis, *Hollywood Costume*; Deborah Nadoolman Landis, ed., *FilmCraft: Costume Design* (Boston: Focal Press, 2012). See also the catalogue published by the Academy of Motion Picture Arts and Sciences for a 2004 costume exhibition, with a foreword and interviews conducted by Landis, *Fifty Designers/Fifty Costumes: Concept to Character* (Beverly Hills, CA: Academy of Motion Picture Arts and Sciences, 2004).

10 Peter Biskind, "Ann Roth in Conversation," in Landis, *Hollywood Costume*, 169–173.

11 John Calhoun, "The Talented Ann Roth," livedesignonline.com/mag/talented-ann-roth; Biskind, "Ann Roth in Conversation," 171.

12 Biskind, "Ann Roth in Conversation," 173.

13 Carrie Seidman, "A Lifetime of Creating Characters," *Sarasota [FL] Herald-Tribune*, October 30, 2011, n.p.

14 Biskind, "Ann Roth in Conversation," 173.

15 Ibid.

16 Ibid., 169, 172.

17 In Landis, *Hollywood Costume*, 94. Roth suggests in the Biskind interview that although she talks with actors early in the process in a collaborative mode, she often has already planned and designed costumes and works to influence the actors.

18 Biskind, "Ann Roth in Conversation," 172.

19 Adrienne Munich describes the film *Mahogany* (1975), with costumes designed by the film's star, Diana Ross, as another example of a film that rejects fashion as the retrograde tool of capitalism and patriarchy within the context of feminism. Adrienne Munich, ed., *Fashion in Film* (Bloomington: Indiana University Press, 2011), 272–273.

20 Landis, *Dressed*, 324.

21 Ibid., 338.

22 Landis, *FilmCraft: Costume Design*, 149–251, and Kip Pullman, "Put Your Clothes On: Conversation with *American Graffiti*'s Costume Designer, Aggie Guerard Rodgers," kipsamericangraffiti.blogspot.gr/2010/11/aggie-guerard-rodgers.html.

23 Christopher Laverty, "*The Conversation*: Gene Hackman's Raincoat," *Clothes on Film*, clothesonfilm.com/the-conversation-gene-hackman-raincoat/23428/. Rodgers notes that many of the people working on the film were not qualified to do so, and that Coppola was a true mentor. She tells the story of Coppola's patience in reshooting when she caused a continuity error in relation to a nametag on Harry's suit.

24 See John Cawelti, "*Chinatown* and Generic Transformation in Recent American Films," in *Film Theory and Criticism*, ed. Gerald Mast and Marshall Cohen, 3rd ed. (New York: Oxford University Press, 1985), 503–520.

25 Robert La Vine, *In a Glamorous Fashion: The Fabulous Years of Hollyood Costume Design* (London: Allen and Unwin, 1981), 49, and Elizabeth Leese, *Costume Design in the Movies: An Illustrated Guide to the Work of 157 Great Designers* (New York: Dover, 1991), 17.

26 Landis, *FilmCraft: Costume Design*, 10.

27 Landis, *Dressed*, xxi.

28 Ibid., xx, 334.

29 In the DVD interview with the director, Polanski says that he based the makeup that both women wear, with the thin, drawn eyebrows and cupid's-bow lips, on his mother. *Chinatown*, Paramount Home Entertainment Video, 2006.

30 Jane Gaines, "Fabricating the Female Body," in *Fabrications: Costume and the Female Body*, ed. Jane Gaines and Charlotte Herzog (New York: AFI/Routledge, 1990), 208.

31 See Michael Gross, "Milena Canonero: Fashion On and Off the Big Screen," *New York Times*, February 11, 1986.

32 See Aileen Ribeiro, "Moving Pictures, Silent Movies and the Art of William Hogarth," in Landis, *Hollywood Costume*, 58.

33 Elizabeth Wilson, "All the Rage," in *Fabrications*, ed. Gaines and Herzog, 32.

34 See Charles Eckert, "The Carole Lombard in Macy's Window," in *Quarterly Review of Film Studies* 3, no. 1 (Winter 1978): 6, and Robin Blaetz, *Visions of the Maid: Joan of Arc in American Film and Culture* (Charlottesville: University of Virginia Press, 2001), 131–134.

35 Biskind, "Ann Roth in Conversation," 172.

36 Clive Barnes, "Theater: 'Hair'—It's Fresh and Frank," *New York Times*, April 30, 1968, 40.

37 Gene Siskel, "Movies: Robert Towne—Script, Scalpel, Action, Oscar," *Chicago Tribune*, May 9, 1976, sec. 6, p. 6. Another character from this period, Joe Buck (Jon Voigt) in *Midnight Cowboy*, who obliviously wears feminized cowboy clothes, could be said to function in a similar way.

38 Alex Simon, "Forget It Bob, It's Chinatown," *The Hollywood Interview* blogspot, thehollywoodinterview.blogspot.com/2009/10/robert-towne-hollywood-interview.html.

39 Rickitt, *Special Effects*, 280.

40 William Yardley, "Dick Smith Dies at 92; Makeup Artist of Vast Reach," *New York Times*, August 1, 2014, A17.

41 For more on the increased use of prosthetic makeup during the era, see Rickitt, *Special Effects*, 271–281.

42 Kate de Castelbajac, *The Face of the Century: 100 Years of Makeup and Style* (New York: Rizzoli, 1995), 148–158. See also Way Bandy, *An Illustrated Guide to Designing Your Face* (New York: Random House, 1977).

43 Alex Simon, "Forget It Bob, It's Chinatown." Without putting too fine a point on it, the many women costume designers in the industry, like Ginger Rogers doing everything that Fred Astaire did backward and in high heels, performed their work at the periphery of the process and with less pay.

44 Landis, *Dressed*, 348. The New York Public Library's collection (archives.nypl.org/the/21829) covers Morley's work in film, theater, opera, and television. The Margaret Herrick Library at

the Academy of Motion Picture Arts and Sciences (collections.oscars.org/link/papers/1321) contains 11.6 linear feet of material spanning the years 1958 to 1990, with drawings, scripts, contracts, correspondences, notes, and clippings. For this period, *Kramer vs. Kramer* (Robert Benton, 1979) is well documented but only clippings of interviews from the period exist for *Annie Hall* (Woody Allen, 1977).

45 Years later, when De Niro realized that this costume and others that had been so crucial to his work were showing up as decoration in Hard Rock Cafes, reused in other films, or discarded, he began to donate what he wore in his movies to the Henry Ransom Center at the University of Texas in Austin for study purposes. Deborah Nadoolman Landis, "Transformations: An Interview with Robert De Niro," in Landis, *Hollywood Costume*, 158–161.

46 Landis, *FilmCraft: Costume Design*, 145, taken from an interview in the *New York Daily News*, April 3, 1978. Nancy Friedland, in "Costume Design and Film," writes that Morley was told by Allen to let Keaton "do her own thing," which is the sort of comment that caused Morley's costume design to disappear from film history (62n28).

47 *New Yorker*, December 24, 1979, 81, qtd. in Friedland, "Costume Design in Film," 60.

48 In Friedland, "Costume Design in Film," 62n28.

49 Ibid.

50 In March 1974, the first copy of *People* magazine appeared with Mia Farrow in *The Great Gatsby* on the cover, costumed by Theoni V. Aldredge and with makeup by Gary Liddiard and Charles Parker and hair by Ramon Gow.

51 Landis, *Dressed*, 310. Nolan Miller, who designed the costumes for *Charlie's Angels*, is another designer who gained fame at this time by concentrating on glamour over substance.

52 Landis, *Dressed*, 311.

53 Elois Jenssen, "Visions of the Future: Costume in Science-Fiction Films," in *Hollywood and History: Costume Design in Film*, ed. Edward Maeder (Los Angeles: Thames and Hudson/ Los Angeles County Museum of Art, 1987), 97–112.

54 Peter Rinzler, *The Making of "Star Wars": The Definitive Story* (New York: Penguin Random House/LucasBooks, 2007), 129; John Mollo, "StarWarsHelmets.com Interview," www .starwarshelmets.com/john-mollo-interview.htm.

55 See Landis, "Setting the Scene," 36.

56 Rinzler, *The Making of "Star Wars,"* 111–112.

57 Landis, *Hollywood Costume*, 105.

58 Christopher Laverty, "*Alien* Anthology: A Revolution in Sci-Fi Costume Design," *Clothes on Film*, clothesonfilm.com/alien-anthology-a-revolution-in-sci-fi-costume-design/15672/.

5 The New Hollywood, 1981-1999

1 Richard Rickitt, *Special Effects: The History and Technique* (New York: Billboard Books, 2007), 302–303.

2 While licensed replicas of "'The Heart of the Ocean" were sold so that other women could possess an artifact tying them to the romance of Jack and Rose, clothing and accessories company J. Peterman went one step further, offering both facsimile clothing and film originals for sale in its 1998 winter catalogue. A copy of Rose's red outfit from the scene where she meets Jack would have cost the assiduous fan nearly $2,500 (including "Life Affirming Boots"), but the actual dress worn by Kate Winslet in the film was also available—with a Certificate of Authenticity from the executive director of Twentieth Century–Fox Archives—for $35,000. See Kristi Petersen Schoonover, "A Look Back at J. Peterman's Titanic Collection," April 15, 2012, kristipetersenschoonover.files.wordpress.com/2012/04/ ta87.jpg.

3 Self-reflexivity in U.S. cinema is not new, but earlier films had tended to parody their own past, albeit affectionately; see the 1952 musical comedy *Singin' in the Rain*, set in Hollywood during the transition to sound, featuring beautiful 1920s fashions—credited to costume designer Walter Plunkett, hair stylist Sydney Guilaroff, and makeup creator William Tuttle—that tread the line between exaggeration and anachronism.

4 See, for example, William S. McKegg, "Debunking the Cinderella Myth," *Picture Play* (July 1928): 18. Some sixty years later, Rita Kempley in her review of *When Harry Met Sally* praised the heroine of that film: "Neither naïf nor vamp, she's a woman from the pen of a woman, not some Cinderella of a 'Working Girl'"; *Washington Post*, July 12, 1989.

5 See Tamar Jeffers McDonald, *Hollywood Catwalk: Reading Costume and Transformation in American Film* (London: I. B. Tauris, 2010), particularly the idea of the "true self."

6 Tamar Jeffers McDonald, "Against Male Elegance," in *Seam & Star: Male Elegance*, ed. Dirk Lauwaert (Antwerp: MoMu–Fashion Museum, Province of Antwerp, 2011), 67–88.

7 Paul McDonald, *Hollywood Stardom* (Chichester, Sussex: Wiley-Blackwell, 2013), 186–187.

8 Jeffers McDonald, *Hollywood Catwalk*, 102.

9 Bettijane Levine, "Men Bullish on Wardrobe Worn by Actor in Wall St.," *Toronto Star*, January 14, 1988, K6.

10 Ibid.

11 This is true of Velma in *Murder My Sweet/Farewell My Lovely* (1944), Phyllis in *Double Indemnity* (1944), Cora in *The Postman Always Rings Twice* (1946), and Kathie in *Out of the Past* (1947).

12 Sharon Stone has worked to maintain this awareness through continually wearing dresses like it, either in design or color or both. This is also a way to keep current her personal celebrity. Cast as the mother in 2013's *Lovelace*, and costumed in drab conservative outfits with curled brunette hair, Stone cannily worked against the lack of glamour caused by her onscreen appearance by recalling her more famous *Basic Instinct* look, wearing white dresses at the New York *Lovelace* premiere and events during Cannes fortnight.

13 Since 1980, only six films set in contemporary times have been nominated for the Academy Award for Best Costume: *Toys* (1992), *The Adventures of Priscilla, Queen of the Desert* (1994), *102 Dalmatians* (2000), *Harry Potter and the Sorcerer's Stone* (2001), *The Devil Wears Prada* (2006), and *I Am Love* (2010). Of these, only *Prada* and *I Am Love* are not fantasies. *Priscilla* was the only one of these nominations to win.

14 For more on the way Smith created the aging faces in *Amadeus* and other films, see Rickitt, *Special Effects*, 280–281.

15 Pavel Cejka, "Mozart's Tailor: The Czech Costume Designer Who Won the Oscar and Lost His Country," *Vice*, April 19, 2012, www.vice.com/en_uk/read/mozarts-tailor-0000-v19n4.

16 Nina Hyde, "Composing 'Amadeus' Costumes: Theodor Pistek, the Oscar Winner Who Would Rather Paint," *Washington Post*, April 21, 1985, H6.

17 Ibid.

18 We see Crane without his black coat on several occasions, just in his waistcoat and white shirtsleeves, and occasionally in just his shirt, as in the scenes when he is in bed.

19 Catherine Spooner, "Costuming the Outsider in Tim Burton's Cinema, or, Why a Corset Is Like a Codfish," in *The Works of Tim Burton: Margins to Mainstream*, ed. Jeffery Weinstock (New York: Palgrave Macmillan, 2013), 57.

20 Ibid., 60.

21 See www.moma.org/interactives/exhibitions/2009/timburton/index.php.

22 Ula Lukszo, "Noir Fashion and Noir as Fashion," in *Fashion in Film*, ed. Adrienne Munich (Bloomington: Indiana University Press, 2011), 73.

23 Ibid., 74.

24 Lukszo cites Jans B. Wager, *Dames in the Driver's Seat* (Austin: University of Texas Press, 2005), 84; James Naremore, *More Than Night: Film Noir in Its Contexts* (Berkeley: University of California Press, 1998), 275.

25 See *Life*, December 21, 1951, 22–23, and December 22, 1952, 38–39.

26 "Veronica Lake's Hair: It Is a Cinema Property of World Influence," *Life*, November 24, 1941, 59; "Veronica Lake," *Life*, March 8, 1943, 39.

27 *U.S. News Review*, Bulletin No. 5 (1943). The bulletin is in the public domain and can be viewed via archive.org.

28 See "The Visual Style of *L.A. Confidential*," filmed interview by Gary Leva, with Ruth Myers's contribution beginning at 00:19, vimeo.com/46783170.

29 *Life*, November 10, 1941.

30 "Here Are the Not-So-Simple Cutting and Setting Directions . . . ," *Woman's Day*, May 5, 1977, 34.

31 See Christopher Laverty, *Clothes on Film*, "Boogie Nights Costume: Dirty Time," clothesonfilm. com/mark-wahlberg-julianne-moore-in-boogie-nights-dirty-70s/22318/. Here Laverty interviews Mark Bridges, the designer: "Virtually all costumes were sourced in Hollywood."

32 Ibid. The denim tuxedo suit "was inspired by a 1976 *GQ* magazine research photo of a denim double breasted business suit."

33 Reynolds was the number-one box-office star from 1978 to 1982 according to Quigley's annual poll, and in fact featured in the top ten for twelve consecutive years, one of the longest unbroken spans in this regard. See qpmedia.com/app.php?&view=stats&v= 5&refID=1934&chapter=The-Year%20-%202014&section=Quigley-Poll:-Top-Ten-Money-Making-Stars&category=Polls&subsection=QP-Money-Making-Stars—All-Years&sortby=year&sortorder=DESC&ispoll=yes.

6   The Modern Entertainment Marketplace, 2000-Present

I am grateful to makeup artist Tegan Taylor and costume designers Salvador Perez and Lisa Tomczeszyn for providing helpful information for this essay.

1 Tinsley continues, "There's no replacement for getting it right on set. But that requires time and patience, which don't seem to exist anymore." In John Young, "The Curious Case of Old-Age Makeup," *Entertainment Weekly*, November 11, 2011, 56–57.

2 In "Reaching Consumers in a Fragmented Entertainment Marketplace," *Yahoo! Advertising*, April 8, 2014, advertising.yahoo.com/Blog/ENTERTAINMENT-SUMMIT-RECAP.html.

3 In addition to traditional product placement, "digital dubs" have enabled Hollywood films to replace virtually anything in the mise-en-scène with something else, and have taken on increased importance through the selling of international as well as domestic placement rights. See "Dubbing In Product Plugs: How *Spider-Man 2* Made Dr. Pepper a Star in the U.S. and Mirinda a Star Overseas," *Wall Street Journal*, December 6, 2004.

4 See Eli M. Noam, *Who Owns the World's Media? Media Concentration and Ownership around the World* (New York: Oxford University Press, 2015). Beginning in the 1990s the cosmetics industry experienced a similar period of "consolidation through various mergers and divestitures [that] accelerated the move toward globalization." See *U.S. Industrial Outlook, 1994: An Almanac of Industry, Technology and Services* (Washington, DC: U.S. Department of Commerce, 1994), 33.

5   Brooks Barnes, "Disney's Third-Quarter Profits Soar, on Marvel's Back," *New York Times*,
    August 5, 2014. Disney and Marvel also announced that they were producing four live-ac-
    tion series for Netflix to be launched in 2015. See David Lieberman and Nellie Andreeva,
    "Netflix Picks Up Four Marvel Live-Action Series & a Mini Featuring Daredevil, Jessica
    Jones, Iron Fist, Luke Cage for 2015 Launch," *Deadline Hollywood*, November 7, 2013, dead-
    line.com/2013/11/disney-netflix-marvel-series-629696.

6   There are many versions of this story online; for one example, see stockmarket-today.com/
    disneys-frozen-will-become-the-biggest-franchise-ever/.

7   See "Gowns Fit for a Fairytale Wedding," *Daily Mail*, May 29, 2015; "Disney Fairytale
    Bridal," www.alfredangelo.com/Collections/Disney-Fairy-Tale-Bridal. For information
    about cosplay gowns, see also "Disney Previews Elsa Wedding Gown," *License! Global*, Sep-
    tember 18, 2014: "More than 3 million Elsa and Anna role-play dresses have been sold in
    North America. Elsa and Anna are leading costume sales at all Disney Store locations, [and]
    . . . the film was the top Halloween brand . . . with an estimated 2.6 million children dressing
    up as one of *Frozen*'s characters." See also "Disney's *Frozen* Continues to Reign," November
    5, 2014, www.licensemag.com. The marketing of *Frozen* wedding gowns, especially, works
    against what some critics have identified as the film's alternative model of empowerment
    that rejects heterosexual romance as the key to women's happiness.

8   See Henry Jenkins, *Fans, Bloggers, and Gamers: Exploring Participatory Culture* (New York:
    New York University Press, 2006).

9   These numbers do not include the social media presence of Marvel's parent company Disney
    or any of the specific Marvel franchises, which would make the numbers significantly higher.

10 See Christine Cover Ferro, "Comic-Con 2014," *Costume Designer* 10, no. 3 (Summer 2014): 29.

11 See Robin S. Rosenberg and Andrea M. Letamendi, "Expressions of Fandom: Findings
    from a Psychological Survey of Cosplay and Costume Wear," *Intensities: The Journal of Cult
    Media* 5 (Spring/Summer 2013), intensitiescultmedia.com.

12 "Men Buy, Women Shop: The Sexes Have Different Priorities When Walking Down the
    Aisles" (Philadelphia: Wharton School, University of Pennsylvania, 2007), knowledge.
    wharton.upenn.edu/article.cfm?articleid=1848.

13 Courtney Stoker, "'Oh, You Sexy Geek!': 'Geek Girls' and the Problem of Self-Objectifica-
    tion," Geek Feminism Blog, April 19, 2012, geekfeminism.org.

14 Derek Johnson, "'MAY THE FORCE BE WITH KATIE': Pink Media Franchising and the
    Postfeminist Politics of *Her Universe*," *Feminist Media Studies* 14, no. 6 (2014): 895. In addi-
    tion to attempts to increase the female fan base for the science fiction genre, the comics
    industry has identified women ages 17–33 as the fastest growing demographic for comic
    retailers.

15 Deborah Nadoolman Landis, quoted in Suzy Menkes, "Hollywood's Finest on Display,"
    New York Times, November 19, 2012.

16 Deborah Nadoolman Landis, ed., *FilmCraft: Costume Design* (Burlington, MA: Focal Press,
    2012), 8.

17 Ibid.

18 Peter Coogan, "The Definition of a Superhero," in *A Comics Studies Reader*, ed. Jeet Heer
    and Kent Worcester (Jackson: University Press of Mississippi, 2008), 80.

19 Anthony Lane, "The Current Cinema: Small Victories [*Ant-Man* and *The Look of Silence*],"
    New Yorker, July 27, 2015, 74.

20 Mark Harris, "Up Clothes and Personal: How This Year's Film and TV Style Reflected
    Larger Pop Culture Trends," *Entertainment Weekly*, December 20, 2013, 24–25. Superman's
    new look was number 10; number 1 was "Cate Blanchett's Pit Stains" in Woody Allen's *Blue
    Jasmine*, costumes designed by Suzy Benzinger: "This wasn't costuming as a substitute for
    characterization but as a reflection of it—an ugly, beautiful choice" (25).

21 Lisa Tomczeszyn, email message to author, November 3, 2014.

22 It is telling in this context that when Landis was asked in 2014 what her biggest challenge as a designer has been technically and artistically, she replied that she "would love to have the challenge of designing a superhero," because her costume design colleagues "are working with incredible teams of fabric and 3D printers, which fascinate [her]." But she then goes on to discuss separately her biggest *artistic* challenge, thus reinforcing the distinction between the technology-driven work of the superhero genre and the artistic costume design of others. See interviewly.com/i/deborah-nadoolman-landis-sep-2014-reddit.

23 For a history see Richard Rickitt, *Special Effects: The History and Technique* (New York: Billboard Books, 2007), 271–281, 302–303.

24 Rachel Abramowitz, "*Avatar*'s Animated Acting," *Los Angeles Times*, February 18, 2010.

25 See Peter Sciretta, "[Director] Matt Reeves Defends Andy Serkis' 'Digital Make-up' Comments," *Slash Film*, July 11, 2014. Serkis was quoted in a March 28, 2014, interview as saying "what [motion capture animators] are doing is painting digital makeup onto actors' performances." See Meredith Woerner, "Andy Serkis Built a New World for *Dawn of the Planet of the Apes*," March 28, 2014, io9.gizmodo.com/andy-serkis-reveals-the-new-ape-world-in-dawn-of-the-pl-1553706020.

26 See the "Andy Serkis Animation Reference," by Weta Digital, in the "Special Extended DVD Edition" of *Lord of the Rings: The Two Towers* (New Line Home Entertainment, 2002): "For the sequence where Sméagol confronts Gollum, Peter Jackson instructed his team of animators to follow closely the on-set footage of Andy Serkis. Andy's performance of these two alternate personalities became the live-action reference that helped the Animators bring this scene to life."

27 All quotations are from Steve Pond, "How *Planet of the Apes* Took Monkey Business to a New Level," *The Wrap*, July 9, 2014.

28 Stephen Prince, *Digital Visual Effects in Cinema: The Seduction of Reality* (New Brunswick, NJ: Rutgers University Press, 2011), 142.

29 Ibid., 26, 143. Many action films, like those in the *Hunger Games* franchise, list fifty or sixty costume, makeup, and hair personnel in their credits, in addition to the hundreds in the art department and the special and visual effects categories.

30 Mandalit del Barco, "Visual-Effects Firms Having Trouble Seeing Green," *Planet Money*, March 19, 2013, www.npr.org/2013/03/19/174703202/visual-effects-firms-miss-out-on-a-films-success.

31 Susan Cabral-Ebert, "From the President," *The Artisan* (Summer 2014): 4. Makeup and hairdressing were finally combined into a single so-named Academy Award category in 2012. Never before had hairdressing been given even an honorary Oscar except as a presumed subcategory of makeup.

32 As can be seen, one guild uses "makeup," the other "make-up." Todd Kleitsch, "Message from The President," 2014, www.798makeupandhair.net.

33 Susan Cabral-Ebert, "Makeup & CGI: The Future of Makeup Artistry," Study of Makeup YouTube Channel, September 16, 2011, youtu.be/TYNbeAa54hw.

34 Tegan Taylor, email message to author, November 30, 2014.

35 Tegan Taylor, email message to author, October 31, 2014.

36 Fred E. Basten, *Max Factor: The Man Who Changed the Faces of the World* (New York: Arcade Publishing, 2012).

37 Tegan Taylor, email message to author, October 31, 2014.

38 Tegan Taylor, email message to author, November 30, 2014. See also the MoCapFX website: www.mocapfx.com.

39 Prince, *Digital Visual Effects*, 227.

40 Abramowitz, *"Avatar's* Animated Acting."

41 See also Young, "The Curious Case of Old-Age Makeup."

42 See Deborah Nadoolman Landis, *Dressed: A Century of Hollywood Costume Design* (New York: HarperCollins, 2007), 479–481. Although Landis is describing costume design primarily, her points apply to makeup and hair designers as well; their "unique role in the process, and their contribution to character and story, cannot be automated or digitized" (481).

43 See "13 Old Beauty Products That Look Like Torture Devices," *HowStuffWorks.com*; and John Brownlee, "Max Factor's Beauty Capacitor," *Wired*, April 24, 2007.

44 "'Beauty Micrometer' Analyzes Facial Flaws for Makeup," *Modern Mechanix and Inventions* (January 1935): 66.

45 "New Anaface Facial Beauty Analysis Software Calculates Looks Instantly," *PRWeb*, May 13, 2009, www.prweb.com.

46 Ibid.

47 Kathy Peiss, *Hope in a Jar: The Making of America's Beauty Culture* (Philadelphia: University of Pennsylvania Press, 2011), 144. According to Sarah Berry, "The makeover epitomizes consumer marketing because it is a process that is simultaneously goal-oriented *and* its own reward—it offers the pleasure of potentiality." Sarah Berry, *Screen Style: Fashion and Femininity in 1930s Hollywood* (Minneapolis: University of Minnesota Press, 2000), 107.

48 Peiss, *Hope in a Jar*, 148.

49 Quoted in Berry, *Screen Style*, 125.

50 Peiss, *Hope in a Jar*, 149.

51 "Hitch Yourself to a Star," *New Movie* (February 1935): 30–31; this was the follow-up piece to "Which Type Are You" (January 1935): 30–31. Accessed through the Media History Digital Library's fan magazine collection at mediahistoryproject.org/fanmagazines.

52 In March 2015, shortly after Washington posted her *InStyle* magazine cover to her Instagram account, fans posted critical responses such as the following comment from a fan angered by the intentional lightening (or whitening) of Washington's skin: "This cover is a false representation of [Kerry Washington] and a clear indication that [*InStyle*] deems it necessary to alter the appearance of women of color." See Sophie Vokes-Dudgeon, "Kerry Washington's Skin Color on *InStyle* Cover Has Fans Up in Arms, Magazine Responds," *US Magazine*, February 6, 2015. Although *InStyle* has not to my knowledge received public criticism for encouraging women to digitally apply and remove different looks using its Hollywood Makeover tool, the criticisms of the whitening of Washington's skin were significant enough to require a public apology and explanation from the *InStyle* editors: "[Although] we did not digitally lighten Kerry's skin tone, . . . our cover lighting has likely contributed to this concern [and] resulted in disappointment and hurt. We are listening, and the feedback has been valuable. We are committed to ensuring that this experience has a positive influence on the ways in which we present all women going forward." See "A Note from *InStyle*: On Kerry Washington's Cover," *InStyle*, February 5, 2015.

53 Charles Eckert, "The Carole Lombard in Macy's Window" (1978), in *Movies and Mass Culture*, ed. John Belton (New Brunswick, NJ: Rutgers University Press, 1995), 104–105. See also Charlotte Herzog and Jane Gaines, "'Puffed Sleeves Before Tea-Time': Joan Crawford, Adrian, and Women Audiences," in *Stardom: Industry of Desire*, ed. Christine Gledhill (London: Routledge, 1991), 74–91; Satch LaValley, "Hollywood and Seventh Avenue: The Impact of Period Films on Fashion," in *Hollywood and History: Costume Design in Film*, ed. Edward Maeder (Los Angeles: Thames and Hudson/Los Angeles County Museum of Art, 1987), 78–96.

54 Kathy L. Peiss, "American Women and the Making of Modern Consumer Culture," *Journal of Multimedia History* 1, no. 1 (Fall 1998): www.albany.edu/jmmh/v011n01/peiss-text.html.

55 Kate Kelly and Stephanie Kang, "The Selling of a 'Geisha': To Promote Its Film, Sony Turns to Big Retail Partners," *Wall Street Journal*, October 21, 2005.

56 "Movie Tie-Ins for Grownups," *Advertising Age*, December 12, 2005.

57 Valli Herman, "'Geisha' Shoes? Only If They're Classy," *Los Angeles Times*, December 5, 2005.

58 Kelly and Kang, "The Selling of a 'Geisha.'"

59 Missy Schwartz, "The Stylish Marketing of *Memoirs of a Geisha*: We Look at How Columbia Is Luring Audiences to Its Asian Epic," *Entertainment Weekly*, December 2, 2005. For an extensive analysis of the global marketing campaign for *Memoirs of a Geisha*, see Ian London, "Hollywood Online: Movie Marketing Practices in the Dial-Up and Broadband-Eras of the Internet, 1994–2009" (Ph.D. diss., Royal Holloway/University of London, 2012), 229–255, pure.royalholloway.ac.uk/portal/files/10516199/201210ndoniphd.pdf.

60 Becky Ebenkamp and Todd Wasserman, "Beauty Brands Love Bridget," *Brandweek*, October 11, 2004, 8.

61 Ibid.

62 Benjamin A. Brabon, "Chuck Flick: A Genealogy of the Postfeminist Male Singleton," in *Postfeminism and Contemporary Hollywood Cinema*, ed. Joel Gwynn and Nadine Muller (New York: Palgrave Macmillan, 2013), 118.

63 Angela McRobbie, "Post-feminism and Popular Culture: Bridget Jones and the New Gender Regime," in *Media/Culture Studies: Critical Approaches*, ed. Rhonda Hammer and Douglas Kellner (New York: Peter Lang, 2009), 412.

64 Brian Morrisey, "Why Brands Love Mommy Bloggers," *Adweek*, March 30, 2009.

65 Maria Sipka, "How Open Conversation between Moms, Marketers Earns Influence," *Forbes*, May 17, 2013.

66 The "content marketing" for the collection included branded videos, a "meet the designer" section, images of artwork from the original costume and clothing design process, and a blog devoted to the collection. Brianne Manz, "Sunday Swoon: Annie for Target," *Stroller in the City*, October 12, 2014, strollerinthecity.com/sunday-swoon-annie-target/.

67 Unlike InStyle.com's intentionally public response to the negative fan reactions to its March 2014 *InStyle* magazine cover photo of Kerry Washington, CNN and Grio.com reported that Target would not be apologizing for its ad campaign, although the author of the petition, which received over 16,000 signatures, posted a letter of apology she received from Target's customer service department to the petition's web page. As the web page for the petition begins: "In the current stench of racism and division amongst Americans, why would Target singlehandedly disrespect Quvenzhané Wallis and add more pain to injury as it relates to race relations?" See Lasean Rinique Shelton, "Remove the TARGET Annie in-store ads if you cannot show better diversity in ALL of your stores!," www.change.org/p/target-remove-the-target-annie-in-store-ads-if-you-cannot-show-better-diversity-in-all-of-your-stores.

68 *U.S. Industrial Outlook, 1994: An Almanac of Industry, Technology and Services* (Washington, DC: U.S. Department of Commerce, 1994), 33.

69 Matthew Hall, *Metrosexual Masculinities* (New York: Palgrave Macmillan, 2015), 1.

70 Lauren Sherman, "Makeup for Men?" *Forbes*, April 11, 2007.

71 Colleen Mastony, "Real Men Wearing 'Guyliner,'" *Chicago Tribune*, June 20, 2007. Another sign of the mainstream acceptance of eyeliner for men was the addition of the word "guyliner" to the 2010 edition of the *Oxford Dictionary*.

72 Although celebrity musicians like Brandon Flowers (The Killers), Pete Wentz (Fall Out Boy), and Billie Joe Armstrong (Green Day) continued the tradition of their makeup-wearing male predecessors like David Bowie and Alice Cooper—as well as many of the 1980s new wave and glam heavy metal bands—the increased use and sponsorship of makeup by male movie stars and television celebrities represents a broader presence in the entertainment industry and mainstream marketplace than these earlier examples.

73 "Male Grooming Consumer Research," *Opinium Research*, September 24, 2010, ourinsight. opinium.co.uk/survey-results/male-grooming-consumer-research.

74 Barbara Booth, "Real Men Don't Cry—But They Are Exfoliating: Say Hello to 'Mampering,'" CNBC.com, December 6, 2014.

75 Mastony, "Real Men."

76 "Rob Lowe Launches Cosmetics Line for Men," *Toronto Sun*, May 26, 2015.

77 Peiss, *Hope in a Jar*, 166.

78 Drew Magary, "Will Male Makeup Ever Catch On?" *GQ* (April 2014), www.gq.com/style/grooming/201404/makeup-for-men-drew-magary. According to Magary, "Some women like to watch MMA. Some men like to get manicures. It's the twenty-first century—gender lines are blurry, and that's A-OK. But the next frontier might surprise you: lines of cosmetics, specially geared toward men." In response to an informal poll conducted in 2013, Askmen.com's lifestyle columnist Douglas Cooney had already declared, "It's official. Men are now wearing makeup" (Douglas Cooney, "Should Men Wear Makeup?" [July 2013], www.askmen.com/daily/austin_60/95_fashion_style.html). Similarly, in a 2013 column for *Slate* entitled "Men Should Wear Makeup," Farhad Manjoo implored "guys [to] pick up the airbrush already" (*Slate* [September 20, 2013], www.slate.com/articles/technology/technology/2013/09/men_should_wear_makeup_looking_younger_and_better_isn_t_just_for_women.html). See also "Boys in Bronzer: Makeup for Men Is on the Rise and No Longer a Taboo," *Daily Beast*, May 14, 2013, www.thedailybeast.com/articles/2013/05/14/makeup-for-men-is-on-the-rise-and-no-longer-a-taboo.html.

79 Michael English, "Some of the Best Movie Campaigns—From *Blair Witch* to *Hunger Games*: Technology and Social Media Give Hollywood Ads Real Star Power," *Adweek*, February 18, 2013.

80 See www.cafepress.com/+hungergamesmovie+gifts.

81 Erika Morphy, "*The Hunger Games* and Its Sleeper Fan Base of Men," *Forbes*, March 22, 2012.

82 Katy Waldman, "Why *Mockingjay* Is the 'End of Men' Movie of the Year," *Slate*, November 25, 2014, www.slate.com/blogs/browbeat/2014/11/25/mockingjay_and_feminism_the_new_hunger_games_movie_envisions_a_future_where.html.

83 Ibid.

84 Quoted in Drake Stutesman, "Costume Design, or, What Is Fashion in Film?," in *Fashion in Film*, ed. Adrienne Munich (Bloomington: Indiana University Press, 2011), 18.

85 Ibid.

86 Quoted in Michele Manelis, "Deborah Nadoolman Landis and the Art of the Hollywood Costume," an article about an exhibit in Los Angeles that ran from October 2, 2014, to March 2, 2015, www.goldenglobes.com/fashion/deborah-nadoolman-landis-and-art-hollywood-costume-25671.

87 Landis, *FilmCraft: Costume Design*, 11.

88 Ibid., 12.

89 Nicole Davis, "The Business of Fashion," August 1, 2014, www.licensemag.com/license-global/business-fashion.

90 See Solvej Schou, "Bond's Cool Stuff," *Entertainment Weekly*, October 26, 2012, 50.

91 Whitney Friedlander, "Pradux: For TV Fans Who Love Costumes with Character," *Variety*, January 16, 2015.

92 Salvador Perez, "President's Letter," *Costume Designer* 10, no. 3 (Summer 2014): 8.

93 Ibid.

94 Salvador Perez, email message to author, November 29, 2014.

95 Stutesman, "Costume Design," 19.

SELECTED BIBLIOGRAPHY

Archer, Mel. "The Make-Up Artist in Hollywood." *National Board of Review Magazine* (October 1939): 4–6.

Bailey, Margaret J. *Those Glorious Glamour Years: The Great Hollywood Costume Designs of the Nineteen Thirties.* Secaucus, NJ: Citadel Press, 1982.

Baird, John F. *Make-Up: A Manual for the Use of Actors, Amateur and Professional.* New York: Samuel French, 1930.

Balio, Tino. *Grand Design: Hollywood as a Modern Business Enterprise, 1930–1939.* Berkeley: University of California Press, 1995.

Barthes, Roland. "The Face of Garbo." *Mythologies.* Trans. Annette Lavers. New York: Hill and Wang, 1972. 56–57.

Basten, Fred E. *Max Factor: The Man Who Changed the Faces of the World.* New York: Arcade Publishing, 2008.

Basten, Fred E., Robert Salvatore, and Paul A. Kaufman. *Max Factor's Hollywood: Glamour, Movies, Make-Up.* Los Angeles: General Publishing Group, 1995.

Berry, Sarah. *Screen Style: Fashion and Femininity in 1930s Hollywood.* Minneapolis: University of Minnesota Press, 2000.

Billecci, Frank, and Lauranne B. Fisher. *Irene, a Designer from the Golden Age of Hollywood: The MGM Years 1942–1949.* Atglen, PA: Schiffer Publishing, 2013.

Bordwell, David, Janet Staiger, and Kristin Thompson. *The Classical Hollywood Cinema: Film Style and Mode of Production to 1960*. New York: Columbia University Press, 1985.

Bruzzi, Stella. *Undressing Cinema: Clothing and Identity in the Movies*. London: Routledge, 1997.

Cartwright, Angela, and Tom McLaren. *Styling the Stars: Lost Treasures from the Twentieth Century Fox Archive*. San Rafael, CA: Insight Editions, 2014.

Chalmers, Helena. *The Art of Make-Up: For the Stage, the Screen, and Social Use*. New York: D. Appleton and Co., 1925.

Chierichetti, David. *Edith Head: The Life and Times of Hollywood's Celebrated Costume Designer*. New York: HarperCollins, 2003.

———. *Hollywood Costume Design*. New York: Harmony Books, 1976.

———. *Mitchell Leisen: Hollywood Director*. Los Angeles: Photoventures, 1995.

Cohen, Meg, and Karen Kozlowski. *Read My Lips: A Cultural History of Lipstick*. New York: Chronicle Books, 1998.

Corson, Richard. *Fashions in Makeup: From Ancient to Modern Times*. Rev. ed. London: Peter Owen, 2003.

Cosgrove, Bronwyn. *Made for Each Other: Fashion and the Academy Awards*. London: Bloomsbury, 2007.

Cosio, Robin, and Cynthia Robins. *The Eyebrow*. New York: HarperCollins, 2000.

Davis, Gretchen, and Mindy Hall. *The Make-Up Artist Handbook*. Boston: Focal Press, 2008.

Davis, Ronald L. *The Glamour Factory: Inside Hollywood's Big Studio System*. Dallas: Southern Methodist University Press, 1993.

De Castelbajac, Kate. *The Face of the Century: 100 Years of Makeup and Style*. Ed. Nan Richardson and Catherine Chermayeff. New York: Rizzoli, 1995.

DeCordova, Richard. *Picture Personalities: The Emergence of the Star System in America*. Urbana: University of Illinois Press, 1990.

Desser, David, and Garth S. Jowett, eds. *Hollywood Goes Shopping*. Minneapolis: University of Minnesota Press, 2000.

Downing, Sarah Jane. *Beauty and Cosmetics, 1550–1950*. Oxford: Shire, 2012.

Dyer, Richard. *Stars*. Rev. ed. London: BFI, 1998.

Finamore, Michelle Tolini. *Hollywood before Glamour: Fashion in American Silent Film*. London: Palgrave Macmillan, 2013.

Fischer, Lucy. *Designing Women: Cinema, Art Deco, and the Female Form*. New York: Columbia University Press, 2003.

Friedland, Nancy E., ed. *Documenting: Costume Design*. New York: Theatre Library Association, 2010.

Gaines, Jane, and Charlotte Herzog, eds. *Fabrications: Costume and the Female Body*. New York: AFI/Routledge, 1990.

Greer, Howard. *Designing Male: A Nebraska Farm Boy's Adventures in Hollywood and with the International Set*. New York: G. P. Putnam's Sons, 1951.

Guilaroff, Sydney, as told to Cathy Griffin. *Crowning Glory: Reflections of Hollywood's Favorite Confidant*. Los Angeles: General Publishing Group, 1996.

Gunn, Fenja. *The Artificial Face: A History of Cosmetics*. Newton Abbot, UK: David and Charles, 1973.

Gutner, Howard. *Gowns by Adrian: The MGM Years, 1928–1941*. New York: Abrams, 2001.

Hall, S. G. "Make-Up for Color." *The Complete Photographer*, September 30, 1942, 2448–2453.

Hallet, Hillary A. *Go West Young Women!: The Rise of Early Hollywood*. Berkeley: University of California Press, 2013.

Head, Edith, and Jane Kesner Ardmore. *The Dress Doctor*. Boston: Little, Brown, 1959.

Head, Edith, and Paddy Calistro. *Edith Head's Hollywood*. 25th anniversary edition. Santa Monica, CA: Angel City Press, 2008.

Herzog, Charlotte, and Jane Gaines. "'Puffed Sleeves Before Tea-Time': Joan Crawford, Adrian, and Women Audiences" (1985). In *Stardom: Industry of Desire*, ed. Christine Gledhill, 74–91. London: Routledge, 1991.

Higgins, Scott. *Harnessing the Technicolor Rainbow: Color Design in the 1930s*. Austin: University of Texas Press, 2007.

Holland, Cecil. *The Art of Make-Up for Stage and Screen*. Hollywood, CA: Cinematex Publishing, 1927.

Kidwell, Claudia B., and Margaret C. Christman. *Suiting Everyone: The Democratization of Clothing in America*. Washington, DC: Smithsonian Institution Press, 1974.

Kiesling, Barrett C. *Talking Pictures: How They Are Made, How to Appreciate Them*. Richmond, VA: Johnson Publishing Company, 1937.

Klaprat, Kathy. "The Star as Market Strategy: Bette Davis in Another Light." In *The American Film Industry*, rev. ed., ed. Tino Balio, 351–376. Madison: University of Wisconsin Press, 1985.

Krützen, Michaela. *The Most Beautiful Woman on the Screen: The Fabrication of the Star Greta Garbo*. Frankfurt: Peter Lang, 1992.

Landis, Deborah Nadoolman. *Dressed: A Century of Hollywood Costume Design*. New York: HarperCollins, 2007.

———, ed. *Fifty Designers/Fifty Costumes: Concept to Character*. Beverly Hills, CA: Academy of Motion Picture Arts and Sciences, 2004.

———. *FilmCraft: Costume Design*. Waltham, MA: Focal Press, 2012.

———. *Hollywood Costume*. New York: Abrams, 2013.

Lauwaert, Dirk, ed. *Seam and Star: Male Elegance*. Antwerp: MoMu–Fashion Museum, Province of Antwerp, 2011.

La Vine, W. Robert. *In a Glamorous Fashion: The Fabulous Years of Hollywood Costume Design*. London: Allen and Unwin, 1981.

Lee, Sarah Tomerlin, ed. *American Fashion: The Life and Lines of Adrian, Mainbocher, McCardell, Norell, Trigère*. New York: Quadrangle/Fashion Institute of Technology, 1975.

Leese, Elizabeth. *Costume Design in the Movies: An Illustrated Guide to the Work of 157 Great Designers*. New York: Dover, 1991.

Maeder, Edward, ed. *Hollywood and History: Costume Design in Film*. Los Angeles, CA: Thames and Hudson/Los Angeles County Museum of Art, 1987.

Martin, Pete. "Make-Up Magician" [Perc Westmore]. *Saturday Evening Post*, March 11, 1944, 16–17, 62.

———. "Mister Wigs" [Fred Frederick, wig department at Max Factor's]. *Saturday Evening Post*, May 19, 1945, 28–29, 34–39.

McDonald, Tamar Jeffers. *Hollywood Catwalk: Exploring Costume and Transformation in American Film*. London: I. B. Tauris, 2010.

Moseley, Rachel. *Growing Up with Audrey Hepburn: Text, Audience, Resonance*. Manchester, UK: Manchester University Press, 2002.

———, ed. *Fashioning Film Stars: Dress, Culture, Identity*. London: BFI, 2005.

Munich, Adrienne, ed. *Fashion in Film*. Bloomington: Indiana University Press, 2011.

Naremore, James. *Acting in the Cinema*. Berkeley: University of California Press, 1988.

Peiss, Kathy. *Hope in a Jar: The Making of America's Beauty Culture*. New York: Henry Holt, 1998.

Prichard, Susan Perez, ed. *Film Costume: An Annotated Bibliography*. Metuchen, NJ: Scarecrow Press, 1981.

Prince, Stephen. *Digital Visual Effects in Cinema: The Seduction of Reality*. New Brunswick, NJ: Rutgers University Press, 2011.

Reese, Henry A. "Merlin of the Movies" [Maurice Seiderman, *Citizen Kane*]. *Saturday Evening Post*, February 28, 1942, 22–23, 37–38.

Ribeiro, Aileen. *Facing Beauty: Painted Women and Cosmetic Art*. New Haven, CT: Yale University Press, 2011.

Rickitt, Richard. *Special Effects: The History and Technique*. New York: Billboard Books, 2007.

Steen, Mike, ed. *Hollywood Speaks! An Oral History*. New York: G. P. Putnam's Sons, 1974.

Street, Sarah. *Costume and Cinema: Dress Codes in Popular Film*. London: Wallflower Press, 2001.

Strenkovsky, Serge. *The Art of Make-Up*. Ed. Elizabeth S. Taber. London: Frederick Muller, 1937.

Taylor, Frank. "Jack Pierce: Forgotten Make-up Genius." *American Cinematographer* (January 1985): 33–41.

Udel, James C. *The Film Crew of Hollywood: Profiles of Grips, Cinematographers, Designers, a Stuntman, and a Makeup Artist*. Jefferson, NC: McFarland, 2013.

Van Gelder, Linda. "Screen Savior" [William Tuttle]. *Allure* (March 1998): 176–179, 217–218.

Westmore, Frank, and Muriel Davidson. *The Westmores of Hollywood*. Philadelphia: J. B. Lippincott, 1976.

Westmore, Michael G. *The Art of Theatrical Makeup for Stage and Screen*. New York: McGraw-Hill, 1973.

Westmore, Perc. "Make-up for Black and White." *The Complete Photographer*, September 30, 1942, 2436–2448.

Westmore, Wally, and Pete Martin. "I Make Up Hollywood," Part I. *Saturday Evening Post*, August 4, 1956, 30, 83–86.

———. "I Make Up Hollywood," Part II. *Saturday Evening Post*, August 11, 1956, 17–19, 78–81.

Zolotow, Maurice. "Hairdresser to the Stars" [Sidney Guilaroff]. *Saturday Evening Post*, September 27, 1958, 32–33, 96–98.

NOTES ON CONTRIBUTORS

Prudence Black is an ARC-DECRA Fellow in the Department of Gender and Cultural Studies at the University of Sydney. She has taught courses on costume and dress and fashion and film at the University of Technology, Sydney, and the American University of Paris. A major theme of her publications is the analysis of the cultural and historical contingencies that surround iconic men and women in film and television. She is coauthor, with Catherine Driscoll, of "Strapped to the Drainpipe: Mrs. Peel and the Vinyl Catsuit," *Australasian Journal of Popular Culture*, and "Designed to Death: Tom Ford's *A Single Man*," for *Film, Fashion & Consumption* (both 2012). She has recently coedited, with Melissa Hardy, an issue of *Cultural Studies Review*, "On *Mad Men*" (2012). Her most recent book, *The Flight Attendant's Shoe* (2011), looks at the dress of flight attendants and the appearance of the profession in popular culture such as novels and films.

Robin Blaetz is a professor and the chair of the Film Studies Program at Mount Holyoke College. She edited *Women's Experimental Cinema: Critical Frameworks* (2007), in which her chapter on the films of Marjorie Keller appears. In addition to her work with avant-garde cinema, she has concentrated on issues of women and film in her book *Visions of the Maid: Women, War, and Joan of Arc in American Film and Culture* (2001) and in a chapter on Ingrid Bergman's work in Hollywood for *What Dreams Were Made Of: Movie Stars of the 1940s* (2011). She is currently writing an essay about the films of Joseph Cornell.

James Castonguay is a professor and the director of the School of Communication and Media Arts at Sacred Heart University. He has published articles in *American Quarterly, Cinema Journal, The Velvet Light Trap, Discourse, The Hitchcock Annual, Bad Subjects, Global-E*, and several anthologies, including *Glamour in a Golden Age: Movie Stars of the 1930s* (2011).

Karen de Perthuis teaches in the School of Humanities and Communication Arts at the University of Western Sydney. She has taught courses on fashion, film, and costume at the University of Technology, Sydney, and the Whitehouse Institute of Design, Australia, and writes on fashion and culture for *The Monthly*. Her many academic publications are in the areas of cinematic costume design, the fashionable ideal, fashion photography, fashion design, and material culture, and she also writes on fashion, style, and culture for a number of popular publications. In addition, she worked for many years as a costume designer and stylist for the film, television, music, and advertising industries.

Mary Desjardins is a professor of film and media studies at Dartmouth College, where she also teaches women's history and gender studies. She is the author of *Recycled Stars: Female Film Stardom in the Age of Television and Video* (2015) and *Father Knows Best* (2015), and coeditor of *Dietrich Icon* (2007). She has authored many essays on film and television history for numerous journals and book collections, including *Idols of Modernity: Film Stars of the 1920s* (2010).

Tamar Jeffers McDonald is a reader in film at the University of Kent. She is the author of *Romantic Comedy: Boy Meets Girl Meets Genre* (2007), *Hollywood Catwalk: Exploring Costume and Transformation in American Film* (2010), *Doris Day Confidential: Hollywood, Sex and Stardom* (2013), and a monograph for the British Film Institute on *When Harry Met Sally . . .* (2015). Her edited collection on representations of virginity in film, *Virgin Territory*, was published in 2010. Her research interests include film costume, romantic comedy, performance, and movie magazines.

Adrienne L. McLean is a professor of film studies at the University of Texas at Dallas, and the author of *Being Rita Hayworth: Labor, Identity, and Hollywood Stardom* (2004) and *Dying Swans and Madmen: Ballet, the Body, and Narrative Cinema* (2008). She is the editor of *Cinematic Canines: Dogs and Their Work in the Fiction Film* (2014) and the coeditor of *Headline Hollywood: A Century of Film Scandal* (2001) as well as of the ten-volume series *Star Decades: American Culture/American Cinema* (2006–2012). Her own entry in the series is *Glamour in a Golden Age: Movie Stars of the 1930s* (2011). She is currently working on a monograph on makeup and hair in the studio era. She has published articles in numerous film journals, and her work has been solicited for or reprinted in several anthologies.

Drake Stutesman teaches film costume design in the Cinema Studies Department at New York University and at the Pratt Institute, and is the editor of the cinema and media journal *Framework*. She has interviewed all honorees for New York Women in Film and Television's yearly costume/hair/makeup awards since 2000. She was the co-chair of the Women's Film Preservation Fund from 2006 to 2012 and organized panels and screenings annually at the Museum of Modern Art, the Film Society of Lincoln Center, the Tribeca Film Festival, and other venues. She is on the board of the New York/London "Fashion in Film" festival and the Critical Costume conference. She is writing a biography of milliner/couturier Mr. John, as well as a biography of silent era costume designer Clare West.

INDEX